W9-DBN-020

FLORIDA STATE
UNIVERSITY LIBRARIES

MAR 5 1999

TALLAHASSEE, FLORIDA

MOTHER'S TAXI

SUNY series on Sport, Culture, and Social Relations
Cheryl L. Cole and Michael A. Messner, Editors

MOTHER'S TAXI

Sport and Women's Labor

SHONA M. THOMPSON

STATE UNIVERSITY OF NEW YORK PRESS

GV
706.5
,T55
1999

Published by
State University of New York Press, Albany

© 1999 State University of New York

All rights reserved

Printed in the United States of America

No part of this book may be used or reproduced
in any manner whatsoever without written permission.
No part of this book may be stored in a retrieval system
or transmitted in any form or by any means including
electronic, electrostatic, magnetic tape, mechanical,
photocopying, recording, or otherwise without the
prior permission in writing of the publisher.

For information, address State University of New York
Press, State University Plaza, Albany, N.Y., 12246

Production by E. Moore
Marketing by Patrick Durocher

Library of Congress Cataloging-in-Publication Data

Thompson, Shona M., 1951–
    Mother's taxi : sport and women's labor /
Shona M. Thompson.
        p.   cm. — (SUNY series on sport, culture, and social
relations)
    Includes bibliographical references (p.   ) and index.
    ISBN 0-7914-4059-1 (hardcover : alk. paper). — ISBN 0-7914-4060-5
(pbk. : alk. paper)
    1. Sports—Social aspects—Western Australia. 2. Women—Western
Australia—Family relationships. 3. Women—Western Australia-
-Interviews. 4. Sex role—Western Australia. 5. Feminist theory.
I. Title. II. Series.
GV706.5.T55 1999
796.4'83—dc21   98-16743
                                                                                    CIP

10 9 8 7 6 5 4 3 2 1

Contents

ACKNOWLEDGMENTS

Many people contributed to this book, the most significant being the forty-six women who so generously and articulately told their stories. They cannot be named but they are nevertheless visible throughout, and most appreciated.

Others have helped considerably in the book's creation, offering comments, helpful criticism, and practical assistance. To the following people I am also grateful: Lynne Alice, Joan Eveline, Barbara Cox, Sandra Kirby, Jim Macbeth, Lorraine McCarty, Maxine Miller, Jill Roenfeldt, Susan Shaw, Lynne Star, Margaret Talbot, Bev Thiele, and Neroli Wood. Bob Marshall's assistance, especially, was way beyond the call of duty.

Much of the work involved was supported by Murdoch University and the University of Auckland, and assisted by a grant from the Australian Sports Commission National Sport Research Center.

I am indebted to Jim McKay for his continual encouragement, and for suggesting that this work might make a good book, and to Cheryl Cole and Michael Messner for agreeing with him.

Finally, I am grateful for the fine copyediting job done by Michele Lansing and the Production Editing done by Elizabeth Moore.

In this book I have included quotes from the women interviewed that have appeared in previous works, and I would like to thank the following publishers for permission to reprint them.

Presses de l'Université du Québec, for material from Shona Thompson, "Mum's Tennis Day: The Gendered Definition of Older Women's Leisure," *Loisir et Société*, 15(1) (1992): 271–89.

Addison Wesley Longman, for material from Shona Thompson, "Women and Leisure in Aotearoa/New Zealand and Australia," in *Time Out? Leisure, Recreation and Tourism in New Zealand and Australia*, edited by H. Perkins and G. Cushman (Auckland: Addison Wesley Longman, 1998).

ONE

INTRODUCTION

*There is a full range of social issues that get
tied up with sport.*

—*Jill*

Jill¹ is one of the forty-six women interviewed for this book. It is
about the work women do that enables others to play sport.
When I first met Jill she told me how surprised she had been to
receive my letter asking if she would agree to be interviewed.
Her initial reaction had been to think how ridiculous it was that
someone was doing university-based research about her role as the
mother of sports players. She said, "When I got your letter I
thought, oh for goodness sake! But then I had to pull myself in and
think, no, there is a full range of social issues that get tied up with
sport."

We were discussing how sport was frequently dismissed as
trivial, a frivolous part of people's lives not worthy of serious attention, and she explained how she had been "guilty" of thinking that
way herself. Then she added, "I mean, I should be one who should-
n't be guilty of that," recognizing how her life revolved around
sport, specifically the tennis played by her two youngest children
who, at the time, were members of a junior state representative
squad in Australia. During her interview, Jill said there were days
when the demands made by her children's sport left her so tired
that she felt she would fall asleep and never wake up. She talked
about juggling her paid work with their tennis, and said she considered this paid work to be her "leisure" because it seemed to be
the only time she had for herself. She explained that she worried
about how important her children's sporting successes had become

to their father, but how the huge increases she saw in her daughter's self-esteem made all of her efforts worthwhile. These were the kinds of social issues she had initially considered not worthy of serious attention.

The contradictions highlighted by Jill's comments are about society's perceptions of both sport and women's lives. On the one hand, despite its colossal global following, sport remains contextualized as separate from the "important" aspects of life, reflecting the nonserious, playful connotations that are popularly thought to characterize sporting behaviors. On the other hand, the work women do, which structures and gives meaning to their lives, is often unrecognized, undervalued, and mostly invisible. Combine these and it is easy to understand why Jill dismissed as unimportant one of the major features of her day-to-day existence.

In this book I focus on women's domestic labor, the work women do that facilitates and services the participation in sport of others, particularly the members of their immediate families. I hope to make visible the extent to which women are incorporated into the institution of sport through their domestic labor, the impact it has on their lives, and how this labor contributes to the maintenance and reproduction of sporting structures and practices.

Worldwide, the greater proportion of those who participate in sport are men and children, mostly male children. Even in countries where large numbers of women do actually play sport, the participation of boys and men is proportionally greater and men's sport invariably dominates. The relationship of adult women to sport, if they have one at all, is far more likely to be through their associations with others who play, such as their husbands, sons, and, less frequently, daughters.

In 1976, in order to explain why more men than women participated in sport and recreation, Ann Hall identified marriage and children as being a key constraint for women. She said,

> Married women with families simply do not have the same opportunities as men to participate in recreational activities because the institution of marriage as we know it today does not endorse completely shared roles. In general, husbands are the major breadwinners and wives are entrusted with the prime responsibility of childcare and housekeeping. (Hall 1976, 192)

This recognition of the familial relationships and responsibilities of women, influenced by second-wave feminism, represented a significant shift in the focus of theorizing women's lesser participation in sport from one that had previously been concerned with the socialization of girls into sporting roles and their attitudes toward physical activity. Over a decade later, with inequalities for women and girls in sport still a concern, Margaret Talbot wrote,

> Feminist insights from studies of the family have shown how women's relationship with sport is often merely to service it for others, either through their sexuality in glamorizing male sport, or through their labor (washing, preparing food, cleaning, acting as chauffeuse) in enabling other members of the family to take part in sport. (Talbot 1988a, 36)

These two insights draw together the background issues upon which the focus of this study was conceptualized. Women's responsibility for domestic labor and child care constrains their full participation in sport, while at the same time the labor they do in these realms facilitates the participation of others.

As Talbot pointed out, this understanding was not informed by or developed from critical analyses of sport. Rather, it came from feminist analyses of women's familial lives and the conditions by which these were lived. For the most part, the sociology of sport has conspicuously overlooked this particular and significant relationship between sport, leisure, and women's work.

That is not to say it has gone unnoticed. In contrast to the lack of academic attention, it has been well acknowledged in the popular press. The relationships of women to sportsmen is a relatively common focus in the media, driven mainly by the deemed importance and high profile of men's sport. Jim McKay (1991a), in his analysis of how the "sporting mediascope" is constructed, pointed out the selective ways in which women are portrayed as wives, mothers, and supporters of players rather than as players themselves, linking this to the construction of masculinity through sport. Rather than being problematized, these roles are highlighted to affirm a particular gendered experience of sport.

I became aware of this gendered experience, and its political and economic implications, during 1981 when a sport in my country (New Zealand) shifted from being apparently frivolous to blatantly political. The sport frequently described as New Zealand's "national" sport is rugby union. Until very recently, it was played almost exclusively by men and has long-standing significance to the construction of New Zealand male identity and nationalism (Crawford 1995; Phillips 1987).

In 1981, a men's rugby union team representing apartheid South Africa arrived in New Zealand at the invitation of the New Zealand Rugby Football Union to play a series of fifteen games. Although sanctioned by the government at the time, this tour contravened an international Heads of States agreement condemning sporting connections with South Africa.[2] Staging this sporting event in New Zealand resulted in massive and violent protests throughout the country and the continuation of the games was only made possible by government intervention and the deployment of the police force and army. The details of this conflict and their far-reaching impact have been well recorded (Barrowman 1981; Chapple 1984; Fougere 1981; Newnham 1981; Shears and Gidley 1981).

One significant feature of the protest action was the huge number of women involved. Women usually led the marches and took the greatest risks, especially Maori women. Feminist analyses showed a keen understanding of why we were there (Aitken and Noonan 1981; Dann 1982; Hall 1981; Star 1989; Thompson 1988; Waring 1985). We saw how we had been co-opted to support white supremist, male power and the current relations of capital, race, and gender that the sport of rugby had traditionally played a key role in maintaining. Against this display of amalgamated male power, the significance of decades of women's complicit labor that had traditionally facilitated and supported rugby became starkly obvious.

Even before this conflict, it was apparent that New Zealand women felt a simmering resentment toward rugby. Barrington and Gray recorded one woman married to a rugby player as saying,

> I dread the beginning of the rugby season. I hate it, every Saturday. I can't stand anything to do with it. I burnt all his gear once. I put it all out on the back lawn, put kerosene over it and burnt it, boots and all. I had had it. And I used to cut patches out of his rugby pants. I remember lying in the bath one Saturday night and he still wasn't home (he'd dropped off his gear earlier), and I thought, 'Well what can I do?' I thought, 'I'll go and cut a sleeve off his jersey.' So I did these childish things like cutting sleeves off or cutting big holes in his pants. . . . It's all I felt I could do. (Barrington and Gray 1981, 95)

Out of women's protest against The Tour in 1981 grew an organization called WAR, an acronym for Women Against Rugby. This organization called for women to stop doing the labor that serviced rugby for men and boys, such as laundering the clothing, providing food for visiting players, shopping for, driving or coaching young sons who played, discussing it at the dinner table, keeping children quiet while husbands watched it on television, and so on. Through these seemingly simple actions of resistance we came to realize how much women's work had contributed to men's sport. We realized also the extent to which this work had been co-opted and exploited by cultural ideology and "national interests." Thus the political ramifications of women's relationship as servicers of sport became very clear.

While many of the social conditions surrounding that event have since changed in New Zealand, and rugby has had to renegotiate its status of supremacy (Campbell 1985; Jackson 1995), globally the economic and political significance of sport appears to be continually increasing, having an impact at all levels of sporting practices. At the same time, capital relations that keep women on the economic margins have shifted only slightly and divisions of labor in which women do most of the child care and domestic work seem intransigent. The implications of this to women's lives remain salient. What does sport demand of women, and what does this labor mean, both to the women involved and to the sport?

Having been alerted to these questions by the "consciousness-raising" experience of 1981, it was several years before I had the opportunity to research the issue more fully. By that stage I had moved to Perth, Australia, and the only clear picture I had of the project on which I was about to embark was that it was based on a disquieting hunch that the institution of sport demanded and required the work of women for its maintenance and reproduction. Being unfamiliar with Australian society, I had doubts about whether or not my hunch would be applicable to the other side of the Tasman Sea. As it turned out, the process of settling in to a new place and meeting Australian women, particularly those with children, provided me with the best affirmation and encouragement I could have received.

In any gathering of new acquaintances I would inevitably be asked why I had come to Australia and what I was doing. Usually I said something self-consciously vague about research looking at the work women did that enabled others to play sport. Men would often shuffle in discomfort, but without exception women understood exactly what I was talking about and were often emphatic in exclaiming its underrecognized "universality." They would invariably engage me in further conversation to tell me about their own such experience, or that of women they knew.

It was in this context that Pamela told me about sitting in her car trying to do the required reading for a university assignment while waiting for her daughter who was playing netball, and feeling guilty about not being on the sideline to watch. It prompted Bonnie to show me a wardrobe full of costumes she had made for her daughter's figure skating competitions. I met a woman who told me that she and her husband had bought a van that quickly became the "bus" for transporting their sons' entire soccer teams, and Gayle, recently separated from her husband, explained with anger and sadness how he had spent so much time sailing that he had no time for her or their children.

These casual conversations confirmed for me that Australian women did have personal relationships with sport that far exceeded their experiences, or lack thereof, as players, and that these relationships had everyday consequences. Then two bumper stickers appeared for sale in my local news agency. One said simply, "Mum's Taxi." The other said, "If A Mother's Place Is In The Home, WHY AM I ALWAYS IN THE CAR?" Australian popular culture had affirmed my research—at least one aspect of it!

This study, therefore, investigated how women's labor serviced and reproduced the institution of sport and what this meant to the women involved. It was motivated by the astonishing paucity of information on, and recognition of, women's contribution to sport other than, and as well as, being players, and the dearth of attention paid to the impact on women's lives of having family members who play sport. It is founded on the hypothesis that sport is maintained and reproduced by women's work through unequal and usually exploitative gender relations. These relations have at their core divisions of labor by which women are disproportionately responsible for domestic work and child care. Such divisions of labor serve both to maintain and reproduce sport and are further reproduced by sporting structures and practices. For many women, the impact of this has considerable everyday and long-term consequences. This study offers a perspective on women's relationship to sport that has not been thoroughly investigated. While feminist theorists have been aware of women's caring and servicing labor, in the analyses and accounting of sport as a social institution it has remained invisible. Consequently, the contribution sport makes to the maintenance and reproduction of domestic and labor relations also has been ignored.

The research reported here is based on qualitative data derived from semistructured interviews with women in Western Australia. It focused on these women's various relationships to one sport—tennis. The women in this study are mothers of junior tennis players, domestic partners/wives of adult male tennis players, and women who are themselves long-term players of the sport. Collectively, they illustrate the multiple ways that women's labor contributed to the sport and show how this multiplicity can strengthen the ideological foundations upon which the contribution is made. Further details of the methodology and the women involved can be found in the Appendixes.

Tennis was chosen as the focus because it provided the opportunity for investigating these various possibilities. Large numbers of men, women, and children play tennis in Australia, mainly in volunteer-based community clubs. Further details of its cultural significance are presented in the Appendix, along with a description of how it is structured.

The study investigated the forms of labor demanded of women by the sport of their husbands and children, and through their own membership in volunteer-based tennis clubs. It examined the ways in which the sport was organized and the impact of these on the women's lives. It also looked at the implications of domestic work and child care to women's participation in sport. The analysis considers these issues in the context of the women's relationships to capital resources and gender relations, institutionalized through heterosexuality and marriage. It considers how these relations help maintain gendered divisions of labor and how they are reproduced within and by sport.

While it is inappropriate to generalize unconditionally beyond this group of women or this sport, I believe there are insights and implications that would apply, to a greater or lesser extent, to other sports and cultures. These insights are derived from an investigation that has as its core the analysis of women's work in Australia, a capitalist patriarchy where sport is considered to have great cultural importance. Throughout our world, there are many other similarly based societies where sports are closely or equally as significant, especially sports played by men.

There are aspects of this focus, however, which should be noted for their specificity. Tennis culture in Western Australia is conspicuously white and middle class. "Race" is an issue to the extent that the impact of colonization has largely excluded Australia's Aboriginal people from this aspect of social life. There were no identified Aboriginal women amongst the group interviewed, and only one non-Caucasian immigrant family.[3] On the other hand, amongst white Australians, both men and women, tennis has traditionally been played in very large numbers, making it a sport of mass popularity not commonly matched in other parts of the world. The majority of the women in this study were middle class, especially those interviewed as mothers. Most marriages represented were intact, and the majority of children were in two-parent, heterosexually-based families. In this respect, the research sample was a homogenous group, but not necessarily representative of Australian society.

I have approached the research as a feminist social scientist whose critical concern is for women's experiences of sport and leisure. I am not an Australian citizen, and my investigation was not done as an "insider" to tennis culture. The limitations of this position are explored in Appendix A. In reporting the findings, every attempt has been made to tell this as the story of the women who were interviewed and to have their voices speak loudly and clearly. The purpose is to make them visible within the institution of sport.

This book follows the three groups of women and their specific associations with tennis. It begins with the mothers of junior players, detailing what was demanded of them and highlighting, for example, the amount of driving required to support a child playing tennis at an elite level. It shows the extent to which these women's lives were constructed by their children's sporting schedules indicating how difficult, if not impossible, it would be for a child to succeed in the sport without the labor devoted by this parent. The anomaly of the term *parent* in this context is exposed to show how it can mask asymmetric contributions to children's sport from mothers and fathers and how it helps preserve male-serving associations between sport and men's contribution to child care. The ways in which mothers related to tennis administration show how they were marginalized within the culture and how their labor was undervalued and exploited.

The wives/domestic partners of adult male tennis players are introduced in chapter 3. Again, they highlight what this role demanded of them, showing in particular how their greater responsibility for child care created the space for their husbands' sport. Clear differences emerged between the experiences of the wives who were also tennis players and those who were not, which also tended to be the line differentiating the women who spoke positively about their husbands' tennis and those who did not. The women who played tennis alongside their husbands were more content and usually found themselves immersed in the sport that had become an all-engrossing, family-centered activity.

The focus then switches to women who were tennis players themselves, most of whom had played for decades. Their stories of having facilitating their own participation, often going to extraordinary lengths to do so, provide a stark contrast to the conditions experienced by the sports men highlighted in the previous chapter. Again, there were differences between the players whose husbands also played and those whose did not. The women in the latter group tended to keep their sport hidden from their families, not allowing it to detrimentally affect their ability to maintain their domestic responsibilities. The voluntary labor done by women players within their tennis clubs is also discussed. Predominantly an extension of gendered domestic roles, their work ensured the organization's continued viability and helped provide satisfactory experiences of tennis culture for other players. Meanwhile, their tennis was structurally and conceptually marginalized.

It is appropriate next for the women to talk about why they did all of this work. In chapter 5 they speak of the rationales that motivated their actions and the rewards they identified. These are necessarily framed according to differing expectations of each of the three groups interviewed. For example, motherhood encompassed the expectation of self-sacrifice, and rewards were expressed in relation to perceptions of their children's best interests. Wives, however, had reason to expect some reciprocity for their labor and presented rationales in terms of how it contributed to a marital partnership. For the women players, their participation in the sport was in itself a reward negotiated out of their expected domestic duties and appreciated for its contribution to their own satisfactory lifestyles.

In the final chapter, as a way of making sense of how and why these women service tennis in the manner described, I attempt to draw together my own analysis of the overriding structural and ideological factors that I see as shaping their lives. I discuss the economic relations and ideologies of normative motherhood, wifehood, and heterosexuality, which I think underpin the gender relations embedded in this sport. The women interviewed would probably not explain it in these terms. Their words are the lived response, not the cerebral theorizing. They would not necessarily conceptualize the sport to which they donated their labor as a patriarchal construction that exploits and denies them. Nevertheless, they deliver a clear message about what this means on a day-to-day basis and why it cannot be ignored.

TWO

BEING THE MOTHER OF A SPORTS PLAYER

You should just own a big car that you live in.
—Peggy

SERVICING LABOR

Sixteen mothers of junior State Squad tennis players were interviewed in Perth, Australia, focusing on what it meant to these women to have a child or children play the sport. During the interviews we discussed the labor required to support a child's tennis at this intense competitive level and what impact it had upon women's day-to-day lives. Overwhelmingly, the one demand that dominated all of these women's accounts of servicing their child's tennis was providing the necessary transport, driving the child to and from tennis engagements. All of these women held a driver's license and had more or less unrestricted access to a car. For thirteen of them, getting their child to and from tennis was their responsibility. The other three shared this labor with the child's father. In sum, all had been heavily involved in the provision of transport for their child's sport. It is difficult, if not impossible, to comprehend how these junior players could have been involved in tennis to the extent they were, or could have reached the level of competitive success they had, if their mothers had not been willing and able to provide the necessary transportation.

Doing this work, however, had an immense impact on the women's daily routines. For many of the mothers, it was the one single commitment around which all other activities revolved, thus it is where this discussion of the mothers' labor must begin.

'If a mother's place is in the home, why am I always in the car?'

FIGURE 2.1
CARTOON BY DONN RATANA.

Driving

The driving required to support a child's tennis in Western Australia was associated with three main aspects of a junior tennis player's program. First, transportation was needed during the week, getting the children to and from regular training and coaching sessions. This was considered the most onerous, particularly the transport required for "Squad training"—subsidized group coaching sessions sponsored by the fast food chain McDonalds and administered by the West Australian Lawn Tennis Association (WALTA).[1] These "squads," organized in groups mainly determined by age and gender, took place on weekdays between the time the children finished school mid afternoon and early evening (i.e., between approximately 3:30 P.M. and 7:30 P.M.). Younger children may have two of these sessions per week, while the older ones could have three, sometimes four.

The second major demand for transport was associated with junior tennis tournaments. In the Western Australian tennis calendar during the year that these interviews took place, there were thirty-nine possible tournaments for junior players. These involved twenty weekends, in addition to nine tournaments held over four or five consecutive days during school vacations. If junior players were receiving sponsored Squad training, they were expected by the tennis administration to compete in all major tournaments throughout the year, especially those that contributed to a national grading scheme of which there were thirteen listed.

The third and final demand for transport was for other commitments such as "pennants," the regular competition administered by WALTA and played in club teams during weekends. The summer competition for junior players is scheduled in two blocks of six continuous weekends. Older, more capable players may play in the senior competition, which could sometimes involve both days of the weekend and require extra practice sessions. Some children, especially those who were older, may be involved in other tennis commitments such as social tennis at their club, playing in a high school representative team, or helping with the coaching of other children. All of these added up to the sort of driving schedules that their mothers invariably described in the interview as being continuous and dominating. I shall attempt to convey the extent of this labor and its impact on the lives of the women who provided it in a manner that accurately portrays how they described its magnitude.

The biggest demand: "It's every day." When the mothers interviewed were asked to name the biggest demand that their child's tennis made of them, nine immediately specified driving, with replies such as Lyn's, "I suppose the driving. Yes, the driving," or Rosemary's, "I'd have to say the driving, being available to drive at all the different times." Five others said that their time was the main issue. For example, Beth said, "The biggest demand on me, personally? Probably just my time." Jill's answer was, "Time, just time." These time demands, however, were highly related to driving. There were several aspects to this. First, the actual amount of time that the women spent in the car getting to the tennis venue, perhaps waiting there until the child's tennis commitment was over and driving home again. Second, the time of day and how regularly this was required; and third, pressures created by other responsibilities and commitments that competed for her attention at those times.

For some women, particularly those with tennis-playing children in their mid teens or older, there was likely to be some driving required every day. For example, Sonia's son was fourteen years old, and she explained,

> It's just tennis all the time. It's not just tournaments, it's pennants, it's State squad training, it's State team training,

lessons with his own private coach and on the days he doesn't play you still arrange for his own hit-ups, to have a hit with someone, because he needs to play it every day. And of course he plays tennis for his school now. So it's *every* day!

The children of the mothers interviewed had been playing competitive tennis for an average of 4.5 years and the accumulation of this time over the period of a child's involvement can be appreciated. For two women, the amount of time they had spent providing their respective tennis-playing children with transport became clearest after they no longer had to do it. Yvonne's son, for example, was age seventeen. He had begun to play tennis competitively at age nine. The year prior to Yvonne being interviewed, her son had spent in residence at the Australian Institute of Sport in Canberra. She said about his being away from home, "Even though we missed him terribly, it was unbelievable, the difference in the lifestyle." She had driven him to tennis training almost every weekday afternoon for six years and afterwards, "I found those hours between 3:30 and 5:30 [P.M.] or whatever. It feels strange not doing something in that time. It's good."

Peggy's child was eighteen years old and had also been playing tennis since he was nine. Having reached the age of being legally permitted to drive, he had recently acquired a driver's license and now drove himself to tennis. Peggy observed,

> There was a terrible lot of running around, really terrible. I just can't believe the difference since he's been driving. I don't think I really realized. I was forever running, I couldn't stop. I'd come home, race home from somewhere, run in and do something quickly then quick, back in the car, we had to be such and such at such and such a time, and off I'd go.

She summed up her years of this routine with, "You should just own a big car that you live in!"

As a daily routine, driving continued in more or less the same intensity throughout the year. Although tennis is considered a seasonal sport and is most intense during the summer, in Perth it is actually played year round and children involved at this level train continuously. Kath explained that there was no time of the year she was not busy with her sixteen-year-old daughter's tennis, because there was not really a break, or "layoff," from the driving. She said,

We have a small layoff at the end of January although there are still tournaments on and she is hitting three of the five days through the week. We have still got to get her there, she has still got to hit, although there is no State training on at that time . . . but nonetheless she still has to be driven to practice and picked up. So if there is any layoff it is then up until Easter, perhaps. But she has still got tournament weekends during that time, though not all the time of course. And pennants, of course, on Saturdays, some Sundays when there's double headers. She has a pennant practice as well as her hitting. So really there is no layoff.

The accumulation of driving time could be further compounded if the women had several children involved in tennis. At the time of the interviews, four women had two children playing junior tennis, and another two had older children who had previously been involved. Although they mentioned advantages in having two children playing the same sport, a reduction of the driving required was rarely one of them. Liz described her life as becoming "doubly complicated" when her second child began playing the sport, saying, "Whereas before I only had to worry about one squad, one time in a tournament, . . . [now] everything I do is doubled."

A further effect of having two or more children involved in tennis (who in all cases were differing ages) was the overall accumulation of years providing transport as they each progressed through the junior tennis ranks. Selection for Squad training or into State representative teams began with children between nine to twelve years of age and, if they continued to play the sport, the transportation required was not likely to finish until they were eighteen, at minimum. Trish's youngest child had recently represented Western Australia in State Championships, where she had won a National age group title. They lived a three-hour drive from Perth but owned an apartment (a "unit") in the city to which they traveled for junior tennis tournaments. Trish gave details of her routine on these occasions.

If it's a weekend tournament, we've got to find out the draw before we head to Perth so that we know when Sandra's first match is. . . . Normally Sandra will be playing on a Saturday morning, at the commencement of the tournament, so that means she arrives home from school on the Friday at four o'clock, off the school bus, and she's rushed straight out onto the court for a quick hit and then into the shower and a bit of food. I've already got the car packed and then Sandra and I head off to Perth. Or maybe [husband] might come with us as well, it depends what's happening on the farm, and away we go. We arrive in Perth about eight o'clock perhaps and we pull up here and unravel everything from the car and eat tea[2] and the phone never stops ringing (laughs) and we pile into bed. . . . Then Sunday, if it's just a first weekend [of a two or three weekend tournament], well it's just business as usual and you play the last match of the day. It might be at 3 P.M., or she might not come off the court until 7 P.M. And then usually I like to come back to the unit and shower her and feed her and/or us and pack up and go. But if it's the finals of the tournament, presuming it's the final weekend. For example, she plays the finals that finished at, say, two o'clock and the presentation wasn't until five. Then I might leave her at the tournament and I'll zap back to the unit and pack everything up so that I'll go back to the club ready for the presentation and we can just take off straight away. Because I lose an hour, sometimes two hours, by coming back here to pack up. So that's how we manage that. It's a three-hour trip home so that makes it a late night.

When I asked Trish how often this routine would occur, she started to fetch her copy of the events calendar but stopped because she said, she knew it "off by heart." Her recital of it was a very descriptive portrayal of the tennis events in which all of the interviewed mothers would have been involved.

We start off in August with the Milo Little Masters, that's two weekends. Then there's the Metropolitan Hard Courts, two weekends. We have the State Hard Courts, which is in the country. I don't normally bother with that but I did last year because it was at [town] which is close to home. Then we have the State School Children's which runs for a week in the October holidays and then the Spring Tournament which runs for three weekends in a row after that, so that's up to five. Then we came to Perth for the Australian Titles, the Nationals, with the Margaret Court Cup, well that was a carry-on [for a week]. Then we were at the State Closed which was this weekend I've just told you about, and now we're here for this one. So that's eight [in eight months]. . . . There was a tournament on last week in Perth as well but I gave that one a miss because it gets to the stage that we're just here all the time and there are other things in life.

She continued to give details of the schedule for the remainder of the year, which included a tennis fixture every weekend in the town nearest where they lived and four other tournaments in the region. Trish was tired of this routine, explaining that she had been doing it for approximately eleven years, since the time her oldest child had begun playing tennis. In the meantime, a second child had taken up the sport. She said,

> I think there was one year that we were home for one weekend in the year! With all these tournaments! Both of them, you see, were in State teams.

Trish described herself as "due for retirement," but her third child was only twelve years old and had already demonstrated the most ability of all three. So, she said,

> I guess . . . [I'll] follow her until she passes through the junior ranks and then just retire. (sighs) And go fishing, do things that normal people do, you know, go to lunch on Sunday, have people over for weekends, have a social group in to play tennis, those sorts of things. (laughs)

Distances: "Eighty kilometers round trip." Adding to the overall amount of driving done by these women were the distances involved. Trish was one of four mothers interviewed who had lived in country areas outside of Perth and had regularly driven their children to tennis engagements held in the city. The distances usually precluded their children's involvement in Squad training held on weekdays, although both Trish and Beth had brought children to the city for training during weekends. Nevertheless, driving into the city for tournaments, as Trish illustrated, was a common practice. Rosemary and her family had moved to Perth from Kalgoorlie five years earlier. At that time, her oldest child was a State level junior player and they had regularly driven to Perth on Friday evenings for his tournaments, returning home on Sunday evening. This trip was eight hours each way, so, by comparison, she said the driving she now did within the city for her youngest child's tennis was "a breeze."

Beth was an interesting case. She, her husband, and her daughter had moved from a small rural town to the city especially to provide further opportunities for her daughter's tennis. This meant a job transfer for her husband, to a position with less seniority, and with both in their early fifties, they had for the first time in their lives taken on a mortgage to buy a home. Beth described this as "starting all over again" and being like "someone coming from another country." She said that driving in the city had been a "major thing" for her and, "for the first three months I was absolutely petrified."

She explained the series of events that led to this major decision, stemming from their first junior tournament in Perth in which her daughter Natalie had played. She recounted,

> We came down for a tournament when she was ten, because my son wanted to come down. He was older, he was a teenager. He wanted to play in this tournament so we thought we might as well enter Natalie too. Well he got knocked out first round. He got drawn against the top seed, and we had come all that way [260 km.]. Well, she got runner-up (laughs), and she was an afterthought in it. I think that spurred us on a bit. We thought, oh we'll come down and try again sometime. We came down once or twice a year for a couple of years and then she got invited to a country kids [training] squad. That is when it started. That's what it led to. We tried that for two weekends. We had to drive down on Saturday morning. She trained for two hours. But we thought it cost too much and it's too far to come, that's the end of it. We decided we weren't going to do that. We decided we'd just do one or two tournaments a year, just when we felt like it, and that's how we went, until she got the scholarship. . . . At the beginning of that year she won an Institute of Sport Scholarship, a country one, to help us take her to Perth. I think it was $800 she won. We used all that up on fuel just coming back and forwards to tournaments. We had a check on it that year, we used the whole lot in the year on fuel.

She explained that having received the money they then felt obligated to go to the tournaments in Perth. At the end of the year, however, they were told by a State level tennis coach that their daughter had to be in Perth if she wished to develop any further as a tennis player. Beth continued,

Even though we were spending that amount of money and that amount of time travelling, getting home half past ten at night after being down for the weekend. Sometimes you get three consecutive weekends, like the spring tournaments they play three consecutive weekends. . . . He said you are just wasting your time because the other [junior players] in the squads, who've been in them for years, are all training a few days a week after school and Natalie wasn't able to get there. But she was still beating them, a natural ability. So we said, what will we do? So we thought about it then. Up until then we were quite happy just to keep travelling, I guess.

Even living in the city, the distances these women were required to drive for their child's tennis were a concern to them. This was true for travel to tournaments as well as for regular week-day training.

The Perth metropolitan region covered an area of approximately 1,080 square kilometers, with suburban-based tennis clubs liberally spread throughout. Squad training took place at these clubs, designated by the tennis administration regardless of where the junior players lived or went to high school, which, in any one Squad group, could be a variety of places. Jill lived on the eastern edge of the city. At one stage, she had two children of different ages involved in Squad training on different days. She said,

It used to get pretty horrendous. We had the two girls and they were in two different squads, so it was every night of the week. It involved travelling from here to [club], the courts right on the river. I did clock it up one day, it was an 80 kilometers round trip, every night of the week.

Di similarly explained, "We used to live in [hill suburb], we shifted down here three years ago simply because we just seemed to be sleeping in the hills and travelling for tennis." She elaborated with an example of taking a child from there to a junior tournament at a frequently used venue in the far north of the city, a distance of about 45 kilometers one way. She compared this experience with where she now lived.

So you'd leave home at quarter to seven in the morning and you mightn't get back 'til eight o'clock at night because it was too far to go back again [between matches]. Here I can drop him anywhere, [naming several tennis clubs] and I can come home. I can say to him, I'm going home, I'll come back in two hours time, or ring me when you want to be picked up. But you do spend all your time in the car, dropping, picking up.

Both Virginia and Monica commented that they had made decisions on which tournaments their children would enter, based upon the distance between their home and the tournament venue. Monica explained that a "good" tournament was one held close enough to be able to drive home between matches and not have to stay there all day. However, not all of the mothers felt they had the flexibility to make that sort of decision. As a condition of accepting the sponsored Squad training package, their children were "required" to play in particular tournaments to receive ranking points and to be considered for State representative selection.

It was also not always a straightforward matter of getting a child to a tournament venue at the start of the day and home again at the end. To have access to the required number of courts, Junior tournaments would sometimes be held at several club venues concurrently, and a child's matches could be scheduled at either place. At one Junior tournament I observed, the two venues being used were a fifteen minute drive apart. No transport was provided, because it was assumed that "parents" would be available to shuttle the children back and forth. Sonia gave the following example of why she considered "chauffeuring," as she called it, to be the biggest demand of her child's tennis. She said,

> When they use different venues, like the 'North of the River' tournament . . . they used three venues. This is the thing. You have to be there at one o'clock for one match then you find yourself driving at three o'clock to another venue. It's the driving. It's time consuming.

The weather could also cause disruptions, as all Junior tournaments were played on outdoor courts. Virginia described the most recent tournament in which her daughter had played. Although it was held near her home, the games were interrupted by rain and were constantly being rescheduled. She explained how she had traveled back and forth to the tournament venue much more frequently than would have otherwise been necessary, and the tournament itself extended to an additional day.

Getting there: "You turn yourself inside out." The driving associated with Squad training was considered the most onerous because of its regularity, the distances, and the time of day it was demanded. These junior tennis players had to be at tennis venues at times specified by the tennis administration and determined by tennis structures. It was the responsibility of their caregivers to get them there at such times—late afternoon to early evening. The women interviewed described how this frequently required an enormous amount of organization and effort because of multiple and often conflicting demands made upon them at that particular time.

One of the possible conflicts with a child's Squad training time was a woman's employment in paid labor. Significantly, not one of this group of mothers was in full-time paid employment that could not accommodate having to drive a child to afternoon Squad training. Of the eleven mothers interviewed who had paid work, eight had no hours committed to this beyond midafternoon. In the total group of sixteen mothers, only three had paid work at times that could have possibly clashed with providing transport for their child's weekday afternoon tennis engagements, but because the work was part time and/or flexible, it did not always do so. This reflects typical patterns of paid work of women with children, it is so frequently organized to accommodate child care (Baxter et al. 1990, Baxter 1992). It also has huge implications to the sport, determining which children are likely to get the opportunities to excel. Nevertheless, the mothers interviewed who were in paid work spoke of the immense pressure of managing this as well as getting their children to weekday training. Yvonne said,

> The main thing that I found difficult, like, I didn't finish work until 3 [P.M.] every day and he was at [school], just picking him up and having to be at certain places for practice.

Jill worked three full days a week at a location in the central city business district. She explained how she had juggled her paid work to accommodate her daughters' transport requirements when the times conflicted.

JILL: Sometimes I used to leave work and collect them [from school] and then take them [to training].
Q.: Then go home?

JILL: No, go back to work and make up the time I'd taken off to collect them and then go back to get them. So we wouldn't get home sometimes until about 8 [P.M.].

Di's routine involved leaving work to go home to pick up her son (who had bicycled there from school), tooting the car horn to have him run out as she pulled into the driveway, and whisking him away to where his training was being held. She finished paid work at 3:30 P.M., it took her forty-five minutes to drive home (4:15 P.M.) and her son's training started at 4:30 P.M. at a venue normally ten minutes' drive along a freeway at a time of peak traffic. She said of this,

> You just turn yourself inside out, and then the tennis association will thank the parents once a year, [that] sort of thing, but I don't think they even realize what you go through.

During the interview, Di expressed considerable reservations about whether tennis had been, overall, a positive experience for her son, Matthew. She continued,

> Now we had an incident last year, I think that Matthew was [a] quarter of an hour late for a squad. . . . So I said to him, now Matthew you apologize for being late. You can say that I have just driven 30 kilometers, it was, to get home then to get you over here. . . . I don't know if he did [apologize] but anyhow this particular coach said to him, "Well, good *evening* Matthew" and Matthew said, "It really wasn't my fault, Mum was late getting home from work." "Oh, we're going to blame your mother are we?" Now little things like that get up your nose because I had turned myself inside out to get Matthew there, thinking that this is a commitment that we have all committed ourselves to. Because these squads are not just the child's commitment. The parents have to commit themselves, because he's got to get there somehow.

The mothers in paid employment spoke most frequently of the stress they experienced as a consequence of doing the driving for their children's tennis. Di summarized,

> I go mad with all the rushing. Look, we are just all exhausted by the time the term has finished. We've just had enough. You

keep going, you just keep rolling and you don't think about it. Because if you thought about it I think you would just burst into tears and say I can't do it any more. So therefore when Sunday comes we just totally do nothing.

Liz, responding to a question about what she thought she had contributed to her two children's tennis replied, "My sanity," referring to the pressures of meeting their scheduled tennis commitments. Yvonne spoke of the driving in these terms,

> I think I was always tired. I hate driving, I'm a nervous driver, and the driving was every afternoon, always having to be somewhere by a certain time. I really found it a strain, physically and mentally.

For those women who were not involved in paid work, time pressures still existed but were different. Sonia considered Junior tennis tournaments more stressful than weekday training commitments because,

> During the week, when Todd is at school, well that's great because I'm home from nine to three to do whatever I want to do. So I'm not behind in my household chores, I can do all those during the day. It's easier because I'm home during the day.

Even with available time during the day, however, the routine commitments associated with a child's tennis could still dominate and structure the way the women organized their time. Kath, for example, was talking about the activities in which she was involved during the week and said,

> Of course I'm always watching the clock because I have to pick Anna up from school at half past three and be at [the tennis club], by quarter past four, four nights a week.

She explained that she would take something for Anna to eat and have her tennis clothes ready for her to change into in the car on the way,

> She would strip off on the freeway! Well, not as bad as that but that is what she would have to do to be there. There is no such thing as being late, that wasn't on.

Lyn detailed what she considered was a "typical week," which illustrated the extent to which her day-to-day activities were constructed around her sixteen-year-old daughter's sport. This was perhaps more so than most of the interviewed mothers, because her daughter had arranged to use her high school physical education time for personal tennis coaching, and Lyn provided the transport necessary to facilitate that. She said,

> Monday I picked her up at school at 11:10 A.M. and took her to [club 1] to have her lesson with [tennis coach]. That was in her Phys. Ed. time. . . . [Afterward] we came on home here, [then] I took her back to school. I think I just did the washing and ironing to catch up that day. Then I had to go back for her at half past three and get her and bring her out to the local courts because she was having a hit with someone else. I helped them sweep the courts because they were a bit wet. Then I raced home and [other daughter] and I went out shopping and [someone else] brought her home, so I didn't have to go back for her. . . . Tuesday she was back on the court. I had to get back to school at 11:10 A.M. to get her to take her to [tennis coach] again but that was only an hour she had off, so I had to get her back to school by twelve o'clock. Then I went back for her at 3:30 and brought her back home. I had to feed her up fairly big because she wasn't going to get her tea 'til nine o'clock. . . . Then took off over to [club 2] for two hours, and that is pretty typical. Today [Wednesday] is a different day again because she has got to play [field] hockey for the school so she can't do any tennis. And she hasn't got any free periods so I won't pick her up now until, I'll actually go and watch the hockey at four o'clock and bring her home when that's finished. So Wednesday is going to have to be her day off [tennis] so that's going to be one of my quietest days. So tomorrow it is back to [club 3] but we have got to go straight from school because we haven't got time to get back here. I'll do shopping and do the house work tomorrow morning and pick her up at 3:30 and go straight to [club 3] and hang around for two hours. And then Friday it's [club 3] again but I'll just take her and then [husband] will go down for her when she's finished. So that's a typical week.

The women who were not in paid employment spoke less about the stresses they personally felt from servicing their children's tennis routines but tended to see themselves as being more available and duty bound to do so. For example, Rosemary said of the tennis-related labor she did for her son, "I don't even think about it. It doesn't bother me, it's just the job I do." Furthermore, the demands of their children's sport were cited as reasons that precluded their involvement in paid work. Trish talked about needing to be "at [her daughter's] disposal," Lyn explained that she could "not [get a job] now because I have to be available," and Beth said, "I'd hate to have a job or have to work. If I worked I wouldn't be able to help Natalie do all this."

The demands of Junior tennis tournaments were within different time frames. They presented different kinds of pressures, but most of the interviewed mothers considered them less difficult. First, the tournaments held during weekends were less likely to clash with women's paid work, and it was more likely that other drivers, such as the children's fathers, would be available to help. Weekday tournaments, however, which usually ran from Monday to Friday, were not so easy to accommodate if women were in paid employment. Liz's part-time work began at 4 P.M. She explained that tournaments meant constant, day-by-day management, which was her responsibility. For example,

> If I'm working, like, say today, I look at the draw. I think, Stephen is playing at three o'clock and I have to leave for work at half past three, how am I going to get him home? So the first thing I look at is, [another young player] who lives just up the road. If he's got a late-ish game then that's fine, they can come home together. If not I've got to say to [husband], Stephen plays at three and what time do you think you will be finished work? He'll say, I don't know, about half past four or five. Okay, so the next day I will ring him, if I can get hold of him, and say how are you going, are you busy? No, no problems I'll be there to pick him up. Then I say to Stephen, don't worry, your father will be there, give him ten to fifteen minutes, or if he is going to be late you might have to sit in the club and wait for three quarters of an hour or what ever. . . . It's so many notes left and phone calls.

Five of the women who were in paid employment with inflexible hours spoke of taking unpaid or annual leave during times their children were participating in tournaments held during school holidays. One of them, Monica, was a school teacher who therefore had those times available. However, she said, "These [past] holidays, both weeks there were tournaments but [sons] only played in one because it was my holiday too."

Junior tennis tournaments were described as being especially disruptive to the regular routines of the household. This was mainly because of the transportation necessary and the unpredictable nature of that demand. For example, the women rarely knew very far in advance at what times their children were drawn to play. During the interview with Trish, I was witness to the tedious process her older daughter was going through, late in the evening, trying repeatedly to telephone the tournament organizers to find out what time her younger sister's game was scheduled the following day. They spoke of this as being routine and typical. The efficient organization of a tennis tournament depends largely upon the skills and experience of the volunteer organizers, and such tasks are shared around the tennis clubs. While the mothers' accounts generally implied that the driving demands for the regular weekday training sessions were the more disruptive and difficult to accommodate, most said that their busiest times were during Junior tournaments. Peggy explained, "Everything else goes on hold on tournament weeks. You are completely involved with the tennis tournament. You sleep, eat, and drink it."

Conflicting Demands

The driving for regular training sessions was considered especially demanding because it was scheduled on weekday afternoons. For one thing, it coincided with rush-hour traffic, which according to Sonia meant a trip at that time of day took her thirty minutes when any other time it would only take ten. Lyn described this as her main dislike,

> I'm not mad on peak-hour traffic on the freeway, things like that. By quarter to four it's building up, and if I just drop her [at training] and come home, which I did on Friday, I'm stuck right in the middle of it and no, I'm not mad on that at all!

These were the sort of conditions that influenced how the women managed their time. For example, Di explained,

> I've dropped him and I've come home here to get tea ready, depending on the traffic, sometimes we have sat on the free-

way for thirty minutes, bumper to bumper. . . . I've had occasions where I've stayed there because I thought I'm not coming all the way home with that traffic. So I have sat there and we've bought fish and chips or something, because I'm not an organized person meal-wise, I do it day by day.

This account highlights another aspect of the demands of driving, such as how it conflicted with other responsibilities expected of the women at that particular time. The two they spoke of that caused the greatest concern were meeting the needs of their other children and preparing the evening meal for their families. The ways these were affected by the driving required for weekday training sessions will be discussed in turn.

Other children: "I felt they missed out a bit." Twelve of the women had other dependent, nontennis playing children living at home, and concerns for their needs were an additional stress. Yvonne had two daughters older than her tennis-playing son. She said in reference to the driving she did for him,

It was every day. Then you would have to go somewhere and it wasn't worth my while getting back and then I felt it affected the girls because I was always rushing around after him. Sometimes you wouldn't get home 'til 6:30 [or] 7:30 P.M. Then you'd have to get dinner, that sort of thing. I felt they missed out a bit.

Kath's nonplaying child was younger. She did not like to leave him at home on his own during his sister's training squad sessions, but she also did not consider it fair to take him with her. She said,

He'd come across and sit in the hall and do his homework. But of course it was pretty cold and unpleasant for him. I didn't think it was the right thing to do. . . . I didn't think it was fair. He gets car sick as well, suffers badly from car sickness. I felt it was pretty cruel to have him in the car for half an hour on an empty tummy after school.

Sibling order was frequently cited as the rationale for whether or not these mothers experienced conflict stemming from their responsibilities to other children. Overall, it appeared to be easier for the women to do the driving and other service work if the tennis-playing child was the youngest. It was understood that older siblings were better able to look after themselves and were more accepting of demands on their mother from younger children than were younger siblings. Both Peggy's and Beth's tennis-playing children were considerably younger than their siblings and the only one still living with their parents. Both Peggy and Beth explained that this was very significant, because they felt they would not have been able to devote that amount of time and energy to this one child's tennis if there had been others living in the same household.

Nine of the nineteen tennis-playing children whose mothers were interviewed were the youngest in their families. Four more came from families of two children who both played. Another two were the youngest children in a family of four. In total, only five of the sixteen mothers interviewed had children younger than those whose tennis they were servicing, and the youngest of these children was six years old. In other words, none were babies. Of these five, four of the tennis-playing children were sons.

These numbers are far too small to do anything but speculate about the relative importance that may be placed on sport for boys as compared to girls, allowing, for example, a boy's tennis to take precedence when there are younger sisters. There were cases, however, where the commitment required of mothers did impact upon opportunities available to younger siblings. One of these four sons was Sonia's. His tennis had meant that her younger child, a nine-year-old daughter, could not attend her chosen activity.

> At one stage she gave up her ballet. She was in classical ballet and she gave up three years ago because it was just so awkward, driving all the way from Sorrento, because most winter [tennis] tournaments were being played there when she was doing ballet. Then coming back to drop her off for an hour and then drive back to watch [son play tennis] and then back to pick her up and, ah, I just got a little bit lazy about driving up and down continuously and she got a little bit sick of it because I was coming late to pick her up and she didn't like it. So she gave up her ballet but she wasn't very happy about it.

She admitted that this child expressed her frustration and resistance, explaining that "the biggest battle" was to get this child out of bed and ready to go to her brother's tournaments early in the morning. "Well she used to complain before, she would say, 'always tennis, always tennis.'" She now no longer complained, however, because she had started to play tennis herself.

Tournaments, at which mothers might spend long periods of time, were a particular problem if there were younger siblings who had to be taken along. Louise referred to a Junior tournament that she and her three children had attended for its entire five-day duration. Her two oldest had been playing in the tournament and both had won trophies, so at the end of it she said she gave her youngest, a six year old, "his own trophy for being the best little boy who went along to the tennis and put up with it all. He thought it was wonderful." She commented on how much easier it became when her second child joined in the tournament alongside her oldest, because this gave the child her own reason to be there. She said, "It's usually, 'I'm hungry, I'm thirsty, I'm bored,' so it's good for her, it's one less [to worry about], like with [the youngest] now." Because of this it becomes easy to understand how several children in the same family became involved in tennis, which begs the question about whether or not the younger ones have much of an option.

Driving a child to her or his tennis engagements, with the amount of time and organization that that required, implied a particular priority and importance of that child, which the women would attempt to balance for their other children. This added to the demands made upon them, which did not necessarily ease if those children were adults and living elsewhere. In addition to having three daughters older than her tennis-playing son, Peggy had seven grandchildren. She explained,

> I felt guilty that I was putting so much time into him and not enough into my daughters and their families, and my mother and [husband's] mother. I really tried to push myself, trying to give too much to each one and then I found it really got the better of me. But [daughters] understood, it was just me feeling guilty. So they brought me down to earth. They said, "Hey Mum this isn't good enough, you can't do this," and they really understood, fortunately, so I was really lucky.

Jacqui's tennis-playing child was the oldest of three. She said,

> We try and equal it up. But I would say that is the most demanding thing about Nicholas's tennis, without a doubt. The physical demands don't worry me at all. It's trying to keep the other children as much an important part of the family as Nicholas is.

Another equity issue concerned the amount of money being spent on the child who played tennis. The women described various ways they would try to balance this for their other children, such as providing holidays, opportunities to travel, and buying special birthday presents and tennis equipment of the same caliber. For example, Kath explained,

> We try in different ways to make up to [younger son], or to make up for the time in which we spend with Anna. Holidays we have always tried very hard, . . . to make a point of getting him or taking him somewhere at holiday time, always have done because Anna is always off somewhere. . . . Even at birthday time or Christmas time Anna gets very little, and has done for a number of years because she knows she is having a lot of money spent on her and she has accepted it very well too. She never asks for anything, never has done. But of course as far as [son] is concerned we have always made up at Christmas or birthdays.

Yvonne had recently helped her nonplaying daughter buy a car. She said,

> My husband and I feel guilty sometimes, putting so much into one. I mean we make up to them in other ways but I've often thought about it. . . . Now if we sat down and added up what we spent on Peter, then what we spent on the other two, there would be quite a big difference.

Evening meals: "What to do first?" All sixteen of the mothers interviewed were responsible for preparing their family's meals. This task was the topic most frequently raised in the course of discussing the impact of the driving regime demanded by their children's tennis program. They spoke of how this affected their ability to adequately prepare meals, the time pressure under which they did so, and/or when the meal was eaten.

Once again, the details differ a little between regular weekday training schedules and tournament time, but the themes are similar. Beth was discussing the impact of her daughter's regular training sessions on running the household when she said,

> It becomes major when you have got to think about the tea on the days I'm out until nearly seven o'clock. That's fairly major

because you have to make sure you have something for them to come home to, otherwise it is bedlam coming into the house. It was worse last year. The squads went for three hours last year, four nights a week. And because my husband is a shift worker, often he wasn't home and you would get back home after seven o'clock at night, to a cold house, and we hadn't got a microwave or anything, so you would be trying to heat things up and organize tea. Natalie would be starving because she leaves home every morning at 7:30 and by the time you get home at 7:30 at night, that is a twelve hour day before she even has her tea and starts on homework. A very long day.

Nine of the women interviewed in this group spoke of recently having young players from other parts of Australia staying in their households for a National junior tournament. It was a special event that did not often take place in Western Australia. Three of the interviewed mothers had specifically taken leave from their paid employment during this event. Liz was one. In addition to her own son, she had two visiting teenage boys to prepare meals for that week. She recalled,

I'd come home at night and not know what to do first, do their washing or get them some dinner. Boys can only wait half an hour at the most for dinner, they'll eat everything else instead while they wait, all the cookies, all the apples, so I had the dinners all cooked already, and frozen. I could just take it out of the freezer the night before so it would be thawed, then I could just put it in the microwave and they'd be eating in half an hour. I took the week off work.

Tournaments were an all day commitment for several days in a row, coupled with late returns home in the evening. Women who were experienced at this ritual usually prepared in advance. For example, Rosemary explained,

You plan. When [a tournament's] coming along you plan for it, like the rest of the family want their dinner and so you prepare things a bit before, knowing that you'll be tied up with tennis. The [game] times don't always [work out], if they're meant to be playing at three o'clock they don't always play at three o'clock. So you can expect to be home at 4:30 but often it's six or seven at night.

For Trish, Junior tournaments in Perth meant leaving her husband at home in the country and staying the week in their city "unit," where her two older children, both tertiary students, were living. Meal preparation for her meant catering to two households.

> Yesterday I was up at six o'clock and I was flat out cooking for four hours. I was cooking things to leave at home for [husband] and cooking for things to bring to Perth. I mean, I'm mad, that's it. But it's so much easier. [Husband's] totally undomesticated. He can't even cook a piece of toast. Sure that's my fault and his mother's fault and everyone else but I just feel happier if I can leave him something. He's actually [learned] to use the microwave so I can leave him a couple of roast dinners or something and he can actually zap those and I feel sort of freer about leaving him. And the same thing here I feel easier, like tonight when we all pile in at half past six and I can just heat something up instead of thinking, oh what am I going to cook? It's easier. We're always tired and grumpy, at least the kids are and it's much easier to have something all ready. So it's better that I do that preparation at home.

Regular weekday training, such as the Squad sessions, put ongoing pressure on mealtimes. Driving tennis-playing children to and from these was made more stressful because it coincided with the time of day when evening meal preparation would most usually be done. Virginia said,

> I do not think there is any way of making it any easier, unless you prepare your meals before three o'clock or something, because you know you have to be racing around at that time, after school.

This was precisely what Kath did. She said,

> When I had to stay over [at the training venue] I'd have my dinner cooked before I'd leave here at half past three. I would prepare my evening meal before I went across to training so when I got home I could just throw it in the microwave or reheat it somehow. That would start at one o'clock so by three o'clock I was ready.

These three women were not in paid employment. While they had greater flexibility in terms of time to prepare meals, there seemed to be a greater expectation of them to provide the meals consistently, and meals of a higher quality. Kath certainly felt this, explaining,

> I have always, right from when I just got married, I've never worked and [husband] has said that he never wanted me to work, as long as I was here when he got home and I had a meal cooked of a night time and I've always done that. Okay, weekends now I don't go to any great trouble . . . Monday to Friday I've always got, in the winter mostly, three-course meals for them and I've always done that and always will because I'd feel extremely guilty if I didn't have a dinner cooked, through the week, with the kids doing what they are doing and [husband] working. It has always been important.

For those women who were in paid employment, meal preparation occurred under greater constraints, but compromises were more readily made. Monica, for example, explained,

> Well since I've been working, meals are anything that can be got quickly (laughs) . . . our meals aren't quite what they used to be. We don't buy takeaways, but it's got to be able to be ready in half an hour.

Concern for this duty, and the extent to which driving a child to tennis inhibited their ability to satisfactorily achieve it, was reflected in the following comments. An "ideal" day for Liz was

> [a] nice relaxed day, not having to have my tea cooked by one o'clock and actually cook my tea when the kids get home from school. That to me is just sheer heaven.

Peggy described the effect of her son getting his driver's license in terms of her meal preparation. She said,

> Once he got his license he was driving and I found, oh this is great, I can stay home and actually cook the tea now. He can take himself off, which meant we had meals at a decent time.

Their responsibility for the preparation of the family's evening meal, together with the care of other children, were the main means these women could transfer the tennis-related driving to someone else. Eight of the interviewed mothers spoke of how their husbands would, varying in frequency, pick their child up at the end of Squad training or a tournament because she had other domestic commitments at that time. Usually this would coincide with his travel home from paid work. Jacqui explained, "[Husband] always picked Nicholas up because I was at home getting the dinner and the homework with the kids, the other two." Older children provided assistance with driving at this time of day for three of the mothers.

Waiting: It's "a waste of time." The final driving-related issue about which the mothers frequently spoke was what they considered to be wasted time—time spent waiting. While providing transport for their children's tennis frequently created tight, often frantic schedules, it also created times when the women "did nothing." Peggy said,

> Then of course once you got there it was sitting waiting. It was always too far, it would probably be for an hour and a half or something and was too far to come back and go back again so you'd be sitting and just wait. So a lot of time was spent running around but a lot of time was spent waiting too.

According to Kath, having to wait was "a waste of time as far as I'm concerned."

The waiting was particularly frustrating during Squad training sessions and other weekday engagements, because the women felt pressured at that time by the other important commitments they were unable to do, such as attending to other children or the family meal, as just described. Whether or not they waited at the venue for the child to finish depended largely on the feasibility of driving home again, considering the distance, traffic, expense, the intensity of other demands, or the availability of another driver. Beth explained all of these.

> See I'm the one that's waiting, whereas people like [father of another child], . . . he knocks off work perhaps at six o'clock, probably, so he can be at tennis at 6:30 to pick them up. So he's working back an hour. They haven't got the waiting time.

She continued,

> I'm only doing it to save fuel because I could easily come home from [club]. But I sort of think well, I leave here, I go to

[school] to pick her up then drive along Canning Highway to [club]. It would only take me twenty minutes to get home, quarter of an hour, but it's the fuel all the time. So I think, well, make use of the time, go for a walk, do something, and that's what I do. But I could come home, but it is the financial cost of double tripping all the time. The fuel bill is big enough now without having to do that.

The expense associated with driving was another important issue. As Kath remarked,

We just keep putting petrol in the car and thinking nothing of it. Because you have to have petrol in the car you do it. So it is a full tank of petrol a week when she's training three or four nights.

If the women did not return home, they described the time-filling activities they would do. Aside from watching their child in training, which was most usual, they mentioned going for walks, shopping, reading, and visiting friends who lived nearby.

Driving their children to and from tennis, with all of the associated issues concerning conflicts, time management, and stress, was without a doubt the major demand made of the interviewed mothers. The organization of junior tennis in Western Australia was such that providing this transportation was necessary if a child was to be fully involved in the activities considered essential for playing the sport competitively. This administrative structure determined when the driving was required and how much, which in turn constructed the women's lives. To a large extent it also determined who did the driving. Only an adult who was not in full-time paid employment during what are understood as "normal" working hours could possibly have provided the transport requirements as outlined by the women interviewed. This meant it was done mainly by the children's mothers. Furthermore, there was a follow on effect. Doing the driving incorporated them further into their children's sport, so they picked up more of the other tasks demanded by their children's participation. Those that the interviewed women spoke of most frequently included the paperwork and management tasks associated with the sport and the extra demands of having other tennis-playing children billeted to stay in their homes. Jill summarized,

Time wise, it is not just the driving. It's all the other things, like sewing tennis gear for them, organizing sponsorships and scholarships, having other people to stay. Just all of those sorts of things.

Some of the Other Things

Being a "manager." Paperwork and meeting deadlines were examples of "those other sorts of things." Kath recalled,

> I manage all the forms to fill in, things to apply for, entries to get away, etcetera. I missed a sponsorship of $900 once, because I got the due date wrong. It was my fault. I didn't sleep well that night, I tell you.

Rosemary described herself jokingly as her son's "manager." Three women spoke of how their tennis-playing children sometimes did some tasks, such as filling in tournament entry forms, but as Beth said, "I'm the one who's got to put the money in. . . . She'll often fill the form in and I'll organize the money order or whatever and post it."

Rita was the one exception. She said she never did any of that because she "hated paperwork" and her husband did all the management of their child's tennis career. Rita considered the labor for her son's tennis equally shared between herself and the child's father, although the division of tasks was gendered. He did the "public" tasks; she described hers as "all the motherly things." She gave the following explanation:

> It's very equal, because he does all these letters and organization, registration for this tournament, that tournament, arranges billets and airlines. Things like that are his job. I am getting him ready, new undies, new socks, stringing rackets, dropping to coaching or squads. So we are really equal.

Generally, however, the paperwork was something the mothers usually did. If it was predominantly the women's responsibility to physically get their children to events such as tournaments, it made sense for them to keep track of these commitments. However, it was more than that. Peggy said of herself,

> Definitely a manager. We felt he needed a manager, a secretary, and a chauffeur. Because we were always on the phone.

You always had to keep up with the paperwork, because you are never notified there is a tournament coming up. You get the calendar at the start so you have always got to be checking that to make sure, if a tournament's coming up, you have got the entry form and that you have got it in on time and, if it was a tournament up the country somewhere, you had to make sure that you've booked ahead to get accommodation. If we couldn't go up we had to organize a lift for him and make sure, where he was staying that he could get from the house to the courts and what have you. Yes, we were never off the phone.

Having "billets." Many of the women had frequently hosted billets from other parts of Australia or other countries, especially those with children who had traveled outside Western Australia for tennis competition and been provided similarly with accommodation. In this undertaking there was a sense of obligation to reciprocate, and many did it reluctantly. During the interview, Di spoke for half an hour recalling an extremely difficult and demanding experience she had when a young tennis player from Europe stayed with her family for five weeks.

Jill said she usually enjoyed having extra teenagers in her house, but acknowledged the extra work. She described a day she spent preparing for the arrival of three young players from other parts of Australia.

It was the most unbelievable day in that I had to shift the boys out of their rooms into the girls' rooms and the girls up to the boys' rooms and then get in, I think it was five extra mattresses, because those that I initially borrowed were so thin. I needed two to bolster them up. And getting them on the floor, dragging them up the passage way, dusting out the boys' rooms, cause if you know anything about boys, they live in a perpetual pigsty. So that was a major exercise in itself, to clean out their rooms, to get these mattresses in, then making up all the beds, changing all the linen because I had had two billets the week before, that had just gone. Trying to get all the linen organized and then racing down to the airport. And the planes were late and so we were just sitting on the floor of the airport for an hour and a half waiting, meanwhile knowing I hadn't done any shopping and there was still washing piled up like this. Then I had to get Helen from one venue where she was playing a [tennis] final, over to [another] and then they all decided they'd go into town. So I came back and was finishing all of that off and then preparing the evening meal. Then getting them all settled into their rooms when they came home from town and racing to the airport to get the next one. . . . Just the physical effort and the constant running, trying to get the washing dry, vacuuming under the beds, getting the pillows out and trying to remember where extra blankets were. Making things homely for them. It was just a day when, by the time it was finished, I just wanted to go to bed and never wake up.

Behind this system of providing accommodation for visiting junior players lies the assumption that the work women do for their own children's tennis will be automatically extended to other tennis-playing children, and will be reciprocated. A lack of understanding about what that entails is frequently obvious. For example, Liz expressed her frustration concerning laundry.

[The two billets] only had one team shirt, that's all they were given. I had to wash them every night, spin dry them, roll them in towels, and hang them up inside and hope they'd be dry by the next morning. I don't have a dryer and it's too damp this time of year to hang them outside. Sometimes they were still damp in the morning and I'd have to iron them dry. I'd be there drinking my coffee and ironing these shirts dry, and yelling at the kids to get them out of the shower and organized to leave. If they'd been given two shirts it would have been so much easier, I could have left one drying each day.

Laundry. The mothers interviewed did not usually mention the laundry generated by their child's tennis unless they were specifically asked about it. Then the response would typically be like Yvonne's.

Yes, I never thought about that, to be honest, but now when you mention it, I only wash a couple of times a week now [that son is away]. I would've been washing every day [when he was here], of course.

In addition to her daughter, Virginia's older son and husband were tennis players. When asked if tennis clothes made a noticeable impression on the household laundry, she replied, "Yes!" with such an expression of surprise it was as if this was something she had only just realized. She went on to exclaim how amazed she was that her washing machine still continued to function.

When asked specifically, the interviewed mothers did describe the labor of laundry, mainly following themes concerning its volume and the management of specific clothing. It was generally described, however, as Lyn did, as "a very minor point" because on top of all the other demands made of these women by their children's tennis, laundry appeared insignificant. Yet laundry generated by those who play sport is not insignificant, as the wives of sportsmen will attest in the next chapter.

Where Were the Fathers?

The labor associated with children's sport was overwhelmingly done by mothers. This was true for several reasons. First, servicing children's sport was considered part of the responsibilities of child care, responsibilities that were undertaken by mothers more than fathers. Child care is predominantly women's work, thus servicing children's participation in sport slips fairly seamlessly into women's work. Second, this situation was rationalized by the relationship of these women to paid labor through marriage. When women are married to men who are in full-time paid work as the major wage earner, and they themselves are not, domestic work and child care are viewed as their side of the division of labor "bargain" and includes children's sport-related labor. Nonetheless, married women's own participation in paid employment did not necessarily break down this arrangement, partly because their paid work was more likely to be organized in such a way as to accommodate the demands of child care, including children's sport. When the structures of junior sport demand labor of children's caregivers, at times difficult for full-time paid workers but possible for those whose paid work is part time, flexible, or otherwise organized to accommodate such demands, it is those caregivers who do the work, and they are mostly mothers.

At the same time, this work can be undervalued and diminished. Because it is the care of children, it is considered menial and of no (capital) value (Waring 1988). It is also associated with domestic labor, which again, having no ascribed value, is hidden within the private realm of home and family life and thereby made invisible. The enormity and impact of the labor demands described by the mothers so far beg several questions, the most glaring of all being, where are the men? What did the fathers of these children contribute toward their children's sport?

Junior tennis is organized on the assumption that tennis-playing children live in two-parent, heterosexual families with each parent having the normative, gendered relationship to paid and unpaid work, as described earlier. This was obvious in the structural practices of the sport that demanded labor on the expectation that it could and would be provided at the designated times and in the necessary form. Junior tennis participation in Western Australia, especially at elite levels, relies on the provision of private transport, mainly during weekdays. Without this, it could not exist in its current form. However, while this means it is largely mothers who provide the necessary labor, there is also the popular assumption that fathers are at least equally involved in this junior sport, even though its structural organization is such that men are not normally available to do so. Nor are they generally as committed to or involved in child care (Koopman-Boyden and Abbott 1985; Mercer 1985; Wilson et al. 1990), which is what invites and justifies women's labor on behalf of their children. Nevertheless, the androcentricity of sport insists that male interests be profiled and protected, and the perceived significance of fathers' contributions to junior sport is one such interest. To illustrate this point, I will explain a large and rather elaborate example.

The Australian Sports Commission (ASC), is the federal statutory authority responsible for sport in Australia. My interaction with the ASC in connection with this research illustrates how androcentric assumptions and interests drive the practices of patriarchal sporting agencies and how women's experiences can be negated to maintain a patriarchal order and protect male interests.

A Survey of Parents

In the early stages of this research project, I applied to the Australian Sport Commission National Sports Research Center (ASC-NSRC) for funding to assist with some of the data processing costs. The proposed research project was presented as a sociological, feminist investigation into the impact of sport on women's lives. The proposal outlined the three groups of women who were the focus for the research, mothers of junior tennis players, wives of male senior tennis players, and older women players of tennis. A concern for women's accounts of their experiences of sport pertaining to those roles and the project's qualitative methodology was emphasized.

As is the usual practise of the ASCNSRC, the merits of research grant applications are appraised by a committee that consults two academic reviewers. In my case, the committee's decision was to grant financial assistance for the research project and, moreover, to allocate considerably more money to it than had been budgeted or requested. These funds, however, were offered with one proviso, which was that men's experiences were also to be included in the study. Apparently an investigation of the impact of sport on women's lives could not be based on women's accounts alone but required the validation of men's voices, and the ASCNSRC was prepared to pay more to ensure that this happened.

The requirement that men be included in the research had been conveyed as a specific recommendation from one of the reviewers. While it is not an uncommon procedure for the suggestions of reviewers to be made a condition of research grant awards, it was evident from analysis of the research projects previously funded by this agency that the necessity to include both men and women as subjects in the research was far from being a standard or even a usual policy. Indeed, most of the research funded by the ASCNSRC to that date had focused only on males, with no indication that this was problematic.[3] Furthermore, the condition placed on my research was specified by only one of the two reviewers, who was male. While his recommendation was considered important enough to warrant allocating extra funding to ensure it was done, those of the other female reviewer were ignored.[4]

Through negotiations with the director of the ASCNSRC, it became obvious that the only aspect of the research to which the committee insisted men be added was that which focused upon children's sport. In other words, the only men it considered important to include were the fathers of junior players. This required a shift in the focus of that aspect of the research, which was subsequently to be conceptualized as an investigation of "parental" support for junior sport, and for which a new project was designed.

I interpreted the requirement to shift the research focus from mothers to parents as an attempt to degenderize the labor implications of junior sport and deny the specificity of women's experiences. It stemmed from the androcentricity of an institution that insists that men's definitions and experiences represent reality, and any attempt to present an opposing view is evaluated as unacceptably biased. It is an example of sexist research practices such as those described by Eichler, who explained how efforts to conceptualize gender inclusive or neutral research can be androcentrically biased when it masks present asymmetrical social relations. Androcentric perspectives can result in "overgeneralizations concerning males and undergeneralizations concerning females" (Eichler 1983, 20), distorting the experiences of both. Such bias prevented members of the male-dominated ASCNSRC from finding merit in the research as proposed and provoked the need to reassert a male-centered perspective. It is significant, in my opinion, that the ASCNSRC's concerns were only for the bias as it pertained to fathers, which I shall elaborate on later.

The inability of the ASC to fully sanction research based on a critical analysis of sport in Australia, such as one based in feminism, is indicative of what McKay (1991a) has identified as the "scientism" of the sport academy. It legitimates technocratic and instrumentally rationalized research at the expense of the critical. Furthermore, it highlights tensions surrounding research concerning gender. Mine was not an isolated example. Within the same round of research grant applications McKay was also awarded funds from the ASCNSRC to investigate gender inequalities in sport administration in Australia (McKay 1992a). Ironically, our two projects were launched to a media audience in Canberra immediately prior to an "Equity for Women in Sport" seminar.[5] At that time, the ASC was under scrutiny for its own poor gender equity record, and it was undoubtedly politically expedient to profile the granting of funds to research projects that seemingly addressed gender equity issues in sport. The conditions placed on my research and the subsequent discrediting of McKay's final report illustrate how this political agenda became subverted (McKay 1993b, 1994, 1997). McKay has described in detail the ASC's extraordinary response to his findings in his book *Managing Gender* (1997), showing how state agencies maintain dominant masculine order. He continues,

> The Commission's attempt to discredit my findings and changes imposed on Thompson's research—especially when both studies were specifically targeted and funded by the Commission itself to investigate gender inequalities—are sober reminders of some men's formidable capacity to contain and resist women's experiences of gender oppression. (McKay 1997, 140)

While McKay's final research report was discredited, amidst much media attention and controversy, mine was ignored.[6]

Shifting my research from an analysis of women's experiences to that of parental support carried with it an expectation that the research would be theoretically informed by socialization theory,[7] thus giving it a more functionalist framework. White (1989,1) aptly pointed out that while the early socialization studies in sport provided useful information, "the theoretical models and methods used have precluded critical sociological analysis of the family at structural, ideological, and cultural levels." White's work was concerned with the participation in sport of teenagers in Britain, and she illustrated the strong reliance girls in particular had on their mothers for providing transport or accompanying them on public transport; participating with them; buying the necessary equipment, and not expecting help with domestic work at home. White began to answer questions of "how" cultural and ideological structures influenced participation, rather than the previous, more positivist questions of "who" did "what."

Deconstructing "parents." Research that attempts to understand the participation of children in sport through an investigation based upon the concept of "parental support" has the tendency to obscure such cultural and ideological structures as the gendered divisions of labor with regard to child care and domestic work, and assumes that the contributions of each parent are equal in form, quantity, and quality. The underlying rationale for the existence of the ASC, whether acknowledged or not, places importance on exploiting the conditions perceived as necessary for creating future sporting champions as key actors for its authentication and validation. It allows little space therefore for a critique of exploitative practices, especially as they pertain to gender, race, and class relations. The differentiated and unequal roles of mothers and fathers would seem irrelevant in the process of making champions. For example, Benjamin Bloom's edited book *Developing Talent in Young People* (1985) utilizes qualitative research as a way of discussing the optimum conditions surrounding the achievement of excellence in various sporting, academic, and artistic fields in the United States.[8] At no stage is a gender (or race or class) analysis applied, and the contribution of the parents as gendered individuals remains largely ignored. The direct quotes from the athletes themselves provide the only breakdown, for example, in statements such as, "It was Dad who set the direction and Mom who kept the ball rolling" (Bloom 1985, 197), or "My mom used to drive me around to all different tournaments . . . she was the patient mother waiting for us while we had our games, I guess" (230). When the undifferentiated and "neutral" term *parent* is used, any imbalances that may exist within the parental "unit" are obscured, allowing the labor of one parent who may provide the greater amount to be underrecognized, while at the same time inflating that which is credited to the other. Thus, by obfuscating the individual members who do the work described as "parental support," the dynamics of gender and their impact upon individual lives are denied and the specificity of women's labor is hidden.

Comparing Mothers' and Fathers' Labor. To meet the ASCN-SRC requirements, I undertook a separate survey of mothers and fathers of another group of twenty junior tennis players in Western Australia (Thompson 1995). Details of the methods and figures showing some key results are included in Appendix C. While numbers were small, the survey was helpful in providing data from which direct comparisons could be made, in the same context as the interview data, between the labor done for a child's tennis by mothers and that done by fathers. These have been useful for deconstructing the notion of a symmetrical parental unit and the assumption of equal or equivalent labor contributions.

The major conclusion drawn from the survey data was that overall, while the fathers surveyed spent almost the same amount of time on average as the mothers in away-from-home labor requirements servicing a child's tennis, the conditions of that time, how it was spent, and when it occurred varied considerably. Furthermore, there were differences in how voluntary this could be. Whereas it was possible for some of the surveyed fathers to spend no time at all servicing their children's tennis, it was apparently not possible for any of the mothers to do so.

The couples surveyed were asked to individually fill in a Time Usage Form for one week. These provided only a relatively crude measure of each person's time allocation, but the time spent involved with their children's tennis outside the home was clearly indicated. Comparisons between the mothers' and fathers' schedules showed that the mothers' time was often fragmented and more likely to be constructed by the tennis schedule, around which other labor was fitted. For example, one mother recorded in a four-hour block,

4 P.M. Came home [from work], prepare veges, do a load of washing.

5 P.M. Take [daughter] and [son] to tennis, come home, prepare tea.

6 P.M. Pick up [daughter], come home, have tea.

8 P.M. Pick up [son]. (Mother #13)

Another recorded between 7 A.M. and 2 P.M. during a junior tournament,

Took [son] to tennis, watched for a while. Went home, did some washing. Back to tennis at noon, watched for a while, games delayed by rain. Went home for lunch, cleaned house, more washing. [son] rang, tennis cancelled, went to pick him up. (Mother #20)

Fathers' time involved with their children's tennis was more usually arranged in conjunction with other commitments, being neither disruptive of them nor inconvenient. The following are examples:

Finish work, drive from city to [tennis club] to pick up [son]. (Father #12)

Played golf, drink after golf, watch [son's] tennis practice, drive [son] home. (Father #16)

The fathers' involvement was more frequently spent in larger blocks, such as continuous time at tournaments or junior competition, and these were concentrated during weekends. Furthermore, this commitment was generally not "instead of" the time spent by their wives but "as well as." The men who spent the most time involved in their children's tennis were married to women who also spent long hours at their children's tennis tournaments, and it was an activity done together.

The relationship of paid work to the time spent on children's tennis also differed between mothers and fathers. For the men there was an apparent correlation that was not so for the women. The three fathers surveyed who recorded the most time involved in their child's tennis were all, for one reason or another, not involved in their usual or previous (one was retired) paid employment that week. Two of these three fathers were surveyed during a week in which a junior tennis tournament was held on five consecutive days and at which they had spent considerable time.

In contrast, there were no similar patterns associated with the paid work of the mothers surveyed. The mother who had spent the second greatest time involved in away-from-home commitments related to her child's tennis had also spent forty-two and a half hours in paid employment that week. Conversely, of the two mothers who had spent the least time servicing their children's tennis, one had spent forty-five hours of the week in paid employment and the other had spent none. Unlike the fathers, there were no clear patterns that related the women's paid work to the amount of time they spent servicing junior tennis.

If we briefly consider the other group of mothers involved in this research, those who were interviewed, the same patterns are reflected. All of their male partners worked full time in paid employment, and the time committed to children's activities was fitted around and rationalized by this. None of these fathers was deliberately working in jobs that finished at times that coincided with when children finished school. In contrast, none of these interviewed mothers were in full-time paid employment with hours that could not accommodate their attention to child care after 3 P.M. For the fathers, living as they all were in heterosexual relationships with the greater responsibility for the care of their children being taken by their female partners, none would have needed to provide the rationale for choosing paid work during evenings as Liz did when she said,

> Somebody said why don't you work during the day. As I said, if I do that then I have trouble when tournaments come and school holidays. . . . If [the children] had a tournament and they played at ten o'clock and I started work at 9 A.M. or 8:30 A.M. then I can't get them there and I can't get them home. You can't do anything. Whereas [working] 4 P.M. to 9 P.M., sometimes I'm usually fairly lucky and I might only miss a set [of tennis] or a couple of times be a few minutes late for work. But it can usually be worked out by working in the evenings. It fits in better than a day job. I've thought of [working in a day job] many times but it just doesn't work as well. In one way it is good for when the squads are on because I think, well I will be home to take them, there will be no hassles. Then what do I do with them when it's [tennis] all day? I can't take them to the tournament at eight o'clock and say you have to stay there

until your father picks you up or I pick you up after work. I can't do that, I feel I'm neglecting them. [Son] probably, he would be fine because he's older but I couldn't do it with [younger daughter]. So the 4 P.M. to 9 P.M. does work in.

Jacqui's husband had recently changed his paid work and since then had done most of the driving of their child to and from squad training sessions. His ability to do this, however, had not been the motivation for his change of job, and he was not additionally doing the other domestic work and child care usually required at that time of day. While he drove, Jacqui was at home cooking dinner and overseeing their other children's homework.

Beth's husband was one who had compromised his paid work for the sake of his child's tennis. He had shifted location and transferred within the company to a position with less favorable work conditions so the child could pursue her sport in the city. This did not, however, alter the form of his contribution to his child's sport but had in fact made him less available to assist with such things as driving and further ennobled his paid labor. Beth said,

> It's probably more difficult for him because he's the one who's got to make the whole thing work, all the time, with just one wage coming in. It's more difficult for him. . . . You'd probably get a very different story if you talked to the Dads. It affects different people differently. He's the breadwinner. . . . Sometimes he says, "That's all I'm good for around here, just to pay the bills." They let the wives do what they want and they pay the bills.

Another aspect of the Parental Support Survey (Thompson 1995) was to determine which parent did what tasks out of a list of twenty-one duties associated with a child's tennis participation. These tasks had been identified from the earlier interviews as the major labor demands. One question asked each parent which of the tasks she or he had done during the past year. The responses showed eight tasks that all mothers reported having done and only one that all fathers reported. In total, there were seventeen tasks that more mothers than fathers reported having done. This question, however, gave no indication of how frequently these had occurred, and a better measure of the work load was indicated from responses to a question concerning who most often did each task.

The mothers' responses credited their husbands with doing

only two of the twenty-one tasks more often than themselves, and these were playing tennis casually with the child and actively coaching the child. Even so, the majority of mothers reported that these activities were more often done by someone else entirely, such as a professional coach. When these two tasks are compared to the list that the women said they most often did, the contrast is illuminating (See Appendix C, Figure 6)

There also was a range of tasks which, although a majority of the mothers surveyed identified as being usually done by themselves, many nevertheless considered their husbands did equally as often. These were all related to the actual playing of competitive tennis, being,

> driving the child to/from tournaments or competition
>
> watching/waiting for the child at tournaments or competition
>
> talking with the child about how to cope with disappointments (such as losing)
>
> talking with the child about appropriate on-court behavior
>
> talking with the child about tennis skills and technique

The majority of fathers considered these tasks equally shared, along with the two more routine tasks of driving the child to and from training and urging the child to get herself/himself organized.

The tendency for a mother to consider a task more frequently done by herself while a father tended to view the task as being equally shared between him and his wife was a phenomenon even more pronounced on the question of responsibility. This was included in the survey in an attempt to understand where the "buck stopped." In other words, who did the management necessary to make sure the task got done? Liz, for example, was previously quoted describing how she went about organizing her husband to pick up their son when he had a late game at a tournament and she was at paid work. While it was the child's father who carried out the task, she took responsibility for it and provided the management labor to ensure that it happened.

There was one task that was considered by the majority of the surveyed mothers to be either solely the father's responsibility or the equal responsibility of both parents. Playing tennis/hitting with the child scored highest as being the fathers' responsibility, but it was equally rated as being either shared by both parents or the responsibility of someone else, usually outside of the family. On the other hand, fathers, by majority, considered six tasks to be equally shared, and their responses on a further three were equally split between stating it was the mother's responsibility or it was shared between them. While fathers confirmed the view that not one of the twenty-one tasks was, by majority, their responsibility, there was a remarkable disparity between the fathers and the mothers concerning the degree to which the responsibility for them was shared.

It is entirely understandable that, between partners in one household, perceptions can differ on the type and amount of work required to maintain a household, care for children, and service a child's out-of-home activities such as sport. Some discrepancy in the responses of those surveyed is expected. However, this trend replicates Michael Bittman and Frances Lovejoy's large-scale survey on domestic labor in Australia which showed identical types of discrepancies between men and women in performing housework. They described the phenomenon as "pseudo-mutuality," "a false complementarity, where the emphasis is on the actor maintaining a sense of reciprocal fulfillment by denying or concealing evidence on nonmutuality" (Bittman and Lovejoy 1991, 1). Maintaining a perception of mutuality when it does not exist is a means of effectively hiding the actual labor done, contributing to its invisibility. It is women's labor that becomes hidden in this way.

Hidden labor and invisible time. The perception of women's and men's involvement and contribution to children's tennis in Western Australia may be further inflated for fathers and deflated for mothers by the different forms their respective contributions take. For example, the tasks done more by mothers were domestically related, based at home and part of the day-to-day labor associated with maintaining a household and caring for children. Because of this, women's work tended to remain invisible, being mainly within the privatized realm of home and family life. Furthermore, it mostly took place in "hidden" time, when the "public" world is in paid employment. Even though the tasks done specifically serviced and supported tennis, they were done under the guise of child care and were considered an extension of the responsibilities of motherhood. They were also tasks that were more frequent, routine, time consuming, and their schedule controlled by outside influences, such as the administration and structure of junior tennis.

By comparison, the tasks in which the fathers were more frequently involved were those that tended to be less frequently required. They were "special" rather than routine tasks, with the timing and degree of parental involvement more discretionary and under the control of the father, such as when he plays tennis with the child. Also, the tasks were more likely to take place in the public arena, where they were socially visible. To illustrate, one surveyed father reported having attended a television promotion associated with a Junior State team, for which he left his workplace for several hours. Over the surveyed week, this was the only activity he had done related to his child's tennis. In contrast, his wife, who did not attend the promotion, had spent an estimated six and a half hours transporting the child to, from, and waiting at Squad training.

Because the fathers' involvement usually had a more visible public profile, it contributed to an inflated perception of their contribution to junior sport. Janet, interviewed because her husband played tennis, offered an observation that came from a lifetime with tennis as one of its main foci. She said of tennis in Western Australia,

> The grass roots is women, that's for sure, yes, everything. Well they are basically the ones who do the running around with the children too. Maybe on the weekends the fathers go to the tournaments and that, but that is the nice bit at the end of it. It's the getting them to the squads, their training and all this, that the women do, because the men are at work. Plus coping with the children emotionally, I think. That's quite a thing. They need a lot of guidance, how to take winning and losing, not to get big heads and all this sort of thing. I think the mother probably plays a bigger role than the father. The father might be at the end, when the kid has won or lost but he hasn't been to the lead up.

Throughout the research, both men and women in tennis circles with whom I came into contact regularly referred to two particular fathers as "proof" that men and women were equally involved in servicing children's tennis. While they would acknowledge that these two men were sole parents, it would not be recognized that this perhaps gave them little option. One of these men in particular provides a contraexample for my thesis. He was separated from his wife, with whom his tennis-playing daughter lived for part of the year. He was retired from paid work and played a very visible role in her tennis career, which included attending all of her tennis engagements and regularly communicating with tennis administrators. The combination of his very high profile and the perception of him as a sole parent led to a conclusion within junior tennis circles that he negated any possible notion of fathers' lesser involvement in children's tennis. However, he did not drive, and his wife (who lived elsewhere and in addition, had other younger children to care for) provided virtually all of the necessary transport to and from tennis venues for both him and the tennis-playing child, labor that was discounted. The process by which this father was exemplified to "disprove" the rule was to reflect what he did at twice the size of that done as the norm by mothers.

The sport specificity of fathers' involvement. Throughout all of the survey questions, the tasks that were featured consistently as those fathers were likely to do were those that were strongly sport oriented and sport specific, such as playing tennis with the child, talking about techniques or appropriate sporting behavior, and coping with disappointments from losing in competition. The sport specificity of these, in comparison to such tasks as chauffeuring or ironing a tennis shirt, would suggest that fathers' efforts were concentrated on tasks more attuned to successfully creating a sports player than to the general provision of child care and support of a child's interests.

Support for this hypothesis may be provided by the answers to the survey question, which asked the parents what they considered to be the best thing about their child playing tennis. This could be considered a guide to what motivated the parents to provide their support. The most frequently cited answers from the mothers (by half of those surveyed) were concerned with the health, fitness, and physical welfare of the child. They made statements such as "keeps him fit" (Mother #7), "it gives her a healthy pastime" (Mother #9), "general fitness" (Mother #16), "keeps him occupied and healthy" (Mother #10), "a good form of exercise . . . it is not a violent or contact sport" (Mother #19). There were only two comments from fathers on this theme. Most frequently cited comments from the fathers were those concerned with the fundamental elements of sport or a general notion of what would be termed *sportsmanship*. There were nine of these such answers, which included "learning the importance of good sportsmanship" (Father #9), "love of sport" (Father #15), "ability and technique" (Father #1), "seeing the improvement over the years and seeing her win" (Father #3), "teaching him competition, seeing him grow as a sportsman" (Father #20).

The results of the survey showed that fathers do indeed contribute to the sporting activities of their children. However, when the gender neutrality of "parents" is not deconstructed, and the domestic labor for children's sport remains conceptualized as "parental support," the very real differences between the labor generally done by mothers and that done by fathers are masked. The assumption remains that the contribution by each is equal in form, amount, and impact. Contributing to this phenomenon is the type of labor done and its perceived value. When men are seen to be actively involved in the specifics of the sport, at more visible times and places, their contribution is attributed with greater relevance and attains a higher value than the sorts of tasks that are not so sport specific and are invisible, such as doing the day-to-day management. It is this sort of labor, however, which keeps the child playing. From the group of interviewed mothers, Jill talked about being involved in running a junior tournament at her local tennis club. Earlier she had explained how meaningful her children's tennis was to their father. Responding to a question about what might have been the outcome if she had not been prepared to do what she had done for their tennis, she said,

We probably would never have got started because [husband] still doesn't know much about the program, and when tournaments are on or when entry forms have to be in. So probably none of that would've happened, therefore they wouldn't have entered tournaments therefore they wouldn't have got caught up in the whirlpool of it all. It is interesting, at this tournament that we're running now, I had a call from a little boy. The entries closed on Friday at lunchtime. I had to get all of the entrant's names over to WALTA that afternoon for seeding and once the seeds are done then no further entries can be taken. And on Saturday morning I had a call from this little boy. He said, can I still enter the tournament, because the State coach has told me that if I don't play in it then I will be dropped from the Squad. I said, I'm sorry I can't accept any more entries. The whole process has been done. We can't just slot you in, and he said, well okay and hung up. Then his father rang back a couple of hours later and said, is there nothing you can do because the State coach has said he will drop him. I said, look, I'm sure the State coach won't drop him. It is just they want to try to get a bit tough to make sure the kids are doing the right thing. The father said, well the thing is I don't know anything about the tennis schedule and the boy has been staying with me for the last two weeks because his mother has been away on holidays. He gave me the impression that it was a split marriage and the child was now staying this particular fortnight with the father, and the father knew nothing about the whole managerial aspects of it, therefore had not put the form in. That is why the child wasn't in the tournament. And I thought then, you know, the fathers tend to sit back and things happen and it is generally the mothers who make sure it happens. And when there is a split marriage it does often reflect in what does happen with the children and I have noticed that over the years. The number of children who start off in tennis, the marriages that have broken up, not as a result of tennis, they just have, and you can see that child's performance or participation changes dramatically. There is no longer that organization aspect that the mothers seem to put in. Fathers have other concerns and don't really know what goes on.

It cannot be assumed that the ASC's insistence on including men in a study pertaining to children's sport was a deliberately calculated measure to diffuse the focus on women to undermine and deny the contribution mothers make. If so, the results have shown otherwise. Rather, I suspect ideologies surrounding hegemonic masculinity in Australia are so strongly associated with sport that, when they translate into fatherhood, sport is perceived as a major site for fathering to occur and for the development of men's relationships with their children. As popular logic would have it, sport is a male interest, therefore fathers must necessarily be involved in and contribe to their children's sport. To propose research that looks only at mothers, which I had originally done, would seem to be leaving out the greater part of the equation and would be evaluated as a seriously incomplete analysis of children's sport. Also, to focus upon mothers and thus to highlight the extent of women's contribution to junior sport begins to expose the limited nature of the contribution made by men, not just to child care but also to the institution of sport itself. When women and their labor as mothers are profiled as being essential to the process of sport reproduction, the significance of men's labor as fathers is thrown into question.

Mothers in the Patriarchy

As already mentioned, the survey results confirmed rather than contradicted the experiences related by the mothers interviewed. There was a high degree of consistency between the tennis-related labor done by the mothers in both groups. All were mainly responsible for domestic labor, including child care, meals, shopping, and laundry. All drove their tennis-playing children to routine training sessions as well as tournaments. Thirteen of the sixteen interviewed mothers said that the responsibility for meeting the demands of their child's tennis lay entirely with them. The remaining two said they shared it with the child's father.

Among the interviewed mothers, the explanations for why fathers were not as involved in tennis-related labor invariably had to do with his paid work. This was so even when his job was flexible enough that he could have been more involved. Di, for example, said,

> [Husband] does as much as he can. But his job doesn't allow, well it allows him in as much as, if we're stuck, I mean he can just come and go as he likes, he doesn't have to explain himself, but his job is such a high pressure job that he can't really afford the time. . . . I try and do as much as I can because I know he can't afford the time.

Even with flexible work time, the "importance" of his job excused him from this labor.

Similarly, the tennis-related labor done by these fathers, if it had substance, was likely to be in activities that were more directly and technically related to the sport. Those who were most highly involved were, or had been, professional tennis coaches, such as Yvonne's and Jacqui's husbands. Yvonne's had been their child's coach for most of his career to date. Jacqui's husband was doing most of the necessary driving and had taken on all of the management for their son's tennis career. She was the only one of the sixteen interviewed mothers who said this responsibility was the child's father's.

However, if a tennis-playing child's father was involved in tennis in this way, and had the ability and interest to coach or hit with the child, it did not necessarily mean less servicing work was required of the child's mother. Because Yvonne's husband coached professionally during weekends, she had provided the transport for their child's tennis at that time, as well as weekdays. Unlike some of the other mothers, she could not expect assistance with this from her husband during the weekend. Furthermore, he and their child would regularly go training at 6 A.M., and she would get up earlier than usual on those mornings to "get him organized."

Because fathers' labor was more tennis specific, it would likely be attributed with higher value. Mothers would frequently undervalue or dismiss the significance of their labor by comparison with the input from the child's father, elevating the significance of his contribution and diminishing their own. For example, Yvonne said,

> [Husband] did all the technical work with [son's] game, because, being a tennis coach, he spent *hours* on the court with him. Mine was purely getting him to and from where he had to go. That's all I did.

Later in the interview, she repeated this point about how much time her husband had spent coaching their child and said, "Really, he's the one that should do the interview."

Self-effacement was common in the responses of the women interviewed. They would regularly use words such as "only" and "just" when describing what they did for their child's tennis or its impact on them. Domestic tasks were especially dismissed, or simply taken for granted as being part of their providing child care.

However, contributions to technical tasks, such as hitting with or coaching the child, also could be dismissed by a mother if she assessed her husband's tennis skills as being "better" than hers. She would then likely consider herself less capable and place a higher value on what he did. Monica spoke of how her husband had taught their two young children "all the tennis they knew," and even though she played the sport herself, she said,

> I'm not as competitive, I'm not as good, I couldn't do it, I wouldn't have the ability to do it. [Husband's] fortunate enough to have that level of skill that he can hit with [the children].

Six of the nine interviewed mothers who spoke of their husbands playing tennis with their children also did so themselves, but would generally downplay their contribution. Louise, for example, when describing her husband's contribution to their two children's tennis, said, "He hits with them more than I do." Even so, she had organized junior pennant teams for them to play in so that they could play with their school friends and, on two afternoons a week, she coached all members of both of these teams. Jacqui, who had played internationally competitive tennis herself, gave a long explanation of how, when her son was age seven, she felt that the grip he had on his tennis racket needed adjusting because he was having difficulty hitting a backhand shot.

> So I'd get up at six o'clock in the morning, Nicholas would get up, he'd want to get up, and we used to go down to [tennis club] to train, and I changed his grip.

She explained that the child then started to have trouble executing other tennis strokes and her husband stepped in and said,

> Jacqui, just leave Nicholas's tennis to me, . . . [and] from then on I probably thought I will just stay in the background now, in terms of Nicholas's technique.

Although hitting or playing tennis with a child was the one activity in which fathers were seen to be making the greatest contribution, there was no reason to conclude that mothers did not make significant contributions in this area also, even though it was not likely to be something that they would highlight or necessarily value. The exception was Trish, who at the time of the interview was her child's sole tennis coach and methodically trained the child daily. She was the one mother who did not downplay her contribution to her child's technical ability, and she spoke also of deliberately talking to the child about technical aspects of a game she may be about to or had just played. She explained how the car journey to or from the match was frequently the most appropriate time for such discussions. Kath also described this opportune timing.

> I know a fair bit about tennis but never interfere too much as far as the coaching is concerned. But nonetheless, if she's doing something wrong I can pick it up. And we always have a chat when she finishes, whether she has won or lost, spoken about the game. If she has played well, why she won, why she lost, the right things and the wrongs things, so yes, I've probably been more support in that way than certainly [husband] has simply because of the fact he's seen her play very little.

Kath highlighted how mothers became involved in the technical aspects of their children's play simply because they were "there."

Beth spoke about this as being an important aspect of supporting her child's tennis. She was discussing, and ruling out, possible alternatives to her providing transport, and said of taxis,

> But taxis are not going to give them any support either. They're not going to be able to talk about the match and say, well what went wrong today or how do you feel about today's match.

Parents' contribution to their child's technical training in tennis is, to a large extent, dependant on how well the parent's ability and experience can match the playing level of the child. Eight of the mothers were tennis players themselves, and seven regularly hit with, and/or played competitively with their children. Seven of the ten tennis-playing fathers did this. However, any popular perception that a male tennis player is automatically "better" than a female player leads to valuing fathers' contribution in this area as being greater than mothers', especially if it was the only area in which he contributed. Nevertheless, in most of these cases, the technical training and coaching of these tennis-playing children were done by someone outside of the family, such as a professional coach. The labor most attributed to fathers could be bought elsewhere.

In whose interest? Women's labor, done to service and facilitate a child's tennis, does not simply follow some nebulous ideological commitment to the value of the sport to which all mothers in Western Australia are equally as likely to subscribe. On the contrary, there was evidence to suggest that much of the hegemonic persuasion is induced on a much less haphazard basis, following the interests of the children's fathers. The agenda for the work women did servicing children's sport may have in fact been largely set by the fathers of their children and generated by a commitment to their marriages, family relations, and the fostering of congenial relationships between men and their children.

The survey data presented results that suggested that fathers were interested in their children's tennis for reasons directly related to their beliefs about sport. The interview data strengthened this and further suggested that the fathers' commitment to sport, sometimes tennis specifically, set the agenda for the work the mothers did.

Ten of the male partners of the interviewed mothers were tennis players, of whom three were or had been professional tennis coaches. Five others had been involved in other sports. It could accurately be said of only one of the interviewed mothers that her child's father was disinterested in, or neutral about, sport generally and tennis specifically.

In most cases, therefore, the children were following an interest of their fathers. Beth phrased her explanation of why it was sport and not some other activity in which her family had become involved by saying "because my husband has always played sport, and so have I." When Monica explained that her sons' tennis was "pretty important" to their father, she added, "but it would be for any sport."

Three of the mothers interviewed, Trish, Jacqui and Kath, had been elite-level tennis players themselves, and their labor was generated as much, if not more, from their own interest in tennis as from their husbands'. There were six mothers, however, who were not participants in any sport. One of them, Peggy, said,

> [Husband] is a sportsman really, so he just loves all sports, the typical Aussie, I suppose you could call him. He just loves all sports and he was good at most sports and I think [son] has just followed him because I was never a sports person.

Rosemary explained what she considered a logical progression of being drawn into a man's sporting interests and having children follow.

> Sport is an interest to me now only because of the involvement I've had since I've had the children. And my husband, of course. When I met him he was deeply involved in cricket. That was much the same as tennis. You know, you'd go along and do the afternoon teas and watch the cricket and get involved there, in the social way, and we did that for many, many years. But before, I was never a great sportsperson.

By having sport participation become part of family life, and a focus for the relationships between family members, these women were ensuring their children did things to which their fathers could relate, fostering for him his relationships with his children. Jill commented of her husband,

> He was a very good sportsman, and comes from a very sporting family and it is just very important to him. And as you are probably well aware, girls tend to worry a lot more about pleasing parents than boys do.

For some women, their partners' focus on sport had further ramifications to the labor it generated. Yvonne, Monica, and Jill all talked about having to "manage" their husbands' approach to their children's tennis, which they assessed in various ways as being overly zealous. Jill, for example, explained how she deliberately "downplayed" its emphasis in her children's lives, saying,

> I think because my husband tends to be very much focused in on the tennis. He is not an ugly parent by any stretch of the imagination, he is very, very good, but he is very keen on sport. He is keen for the girls to do well and he is someone who never does things by halves, so he sometimes finds it a bit difficult if they don't put in the same sort of intensity that he feels it deserves. So I guess I try and be the balance of it, the counter for him.

Jill's husband's intense interest in sport meant she not only had to manage its impact upon her children but also its resulting impact upon him. Forecasting how her life might be when it was no longer dominated by her children's tennis, she said,

> What will life be like after tennis? I worry about it more for my husband's sake than for mine because I have a number of different interests but to him it has more or less become his life. I really do get concerned.

While fathers did less of the tennis-related labor, for many of the mothers this labor was generated by their husbands' interests, setting the agenda for what they did. This servicing work could be viewed as a form of social control, constructing their time and behavior, contributing to their containment in a lifestyle of financial dependency and keeping them invisible. Their interactions with tennis administration also kept them silenced.

Relationships with the administration. Servicing their children's sport prescribed women's lives in such a way as to determine who they were. This included who they were in relation to their children, their children's father, a wider social group such as their extended families and friends, the paid work force, and the administration of the institution. The definition of being a "Tennis Mum" in Western Australia is accompanied by a specific set of expected behaviors. It also may be a controlling definition—she can not behave any other way.

When children's sport is considered an important cultural experience, being responsible for the care of children necessitates making that experience available, facilitating it to provide "the best" child care as judged by cultural standards. When the work to do this is the responsibility of motherhood, it defines women's relationship to the institution of sport as one of service through children, but at the same time their labor is seen as being primarily of benefit to themselves because of what their children are considered to be individually gaining through participation. This was illustrated in the interviewed mother's responses to the question that asked who appreciated their labor. All of the mothers felt that their efforts were well appreciated by the children, but there was a sense that their efforts did not need to be appreciated by anyone else. For example, Jill was asked if the tennis administrators appreciated what she did. She replied,

> Oh I think so. Yes I think they do. Mind you I don't think they really need to appreciate what I do, I do it for the girls. That's for them to appreciate what I do and I don't do it for [the Association] to appreciate what I do. The Association could say, well look what her girls have got out of tennis, I should be appreciating what the Association (is) doing for my girls, which I do, rather than them appreciating what I do for the girls. I really feel that I would have more need to appreciate what they do, than they appreciate what I do.

The perception of rewards as being one way and privatized within child care denies mothers the right to question what the association asks of them, or to influence institutional practices.

Influence: Having no say at all. The practices of tennis administration not only placed demands on a woman's labor but could also define the sort of person she should be and how she should behave. Her behavior is monitored in such a way as to "train" her to be a particular kind of person appropriate as a "tennis mother." Within tennis culture, a mother is expected to be silent, acquiescent, and accepting, yet willing to provide whatever labor is necessary, whenever it is demanded, for the reward of her children acquiring what are believed to be the benefits of participation. When the mothers were asked if they felt they had any say in how junior tennis was administered, twelve of the interviewed mothers replied with an unconditional "no." This proved to be the one question to which the responses from all sixteen mothers' interviewed were most uniform and succinct, typified by the following three examples:

Oh no, you don't get any say at all. (Di)
No, I don't think you have any say at all. (Peggy)
No, I don't at all, nothing. (Jacqui)

Various issues were mentioned about which the mothers interviewed would liked to have had some influence, but there were two that seemed to create the most frustration and anger. The first concerned the Squad training schedules, such as their timing, frequency, and venues. Kath explained how "everyone" in her family was being required to "make sacrifices" for her daughter's tennis, and at one time they had decided they could not cope with the proposed Squad training schedule. Her daughter had written to the administration requesting to have her schedule reduced, but she had been asked to first "try" to cope. As a result, Kath explained, they had adapted the family's routines and coped, but with difficulty.

Di felt contempt for how the tennis administration seemed to show no consideration for the pressures faced by parents trying to get their children to Squad training. She described how it had been suggested that her son ride his bicycle which she explained was impossible given the time constraints and the dangerous route. She recalled how it had been suggested to Jill that if she could not manage to drive the required 80 kilometers to and from Squad training every weekday, she should hire a taxi.

After the interviews had taken place, I was talking with the State Head Coach of junior tennis who mentioned he had recently introduced Squad training sessions at 6 A.M. I asked how this new development had been received by the parents of the children involved. He replied that he had had a few "grizzles" from parents and gave one example of a mother who had phoned to say it would be difficult for her at that time of day because she "worked." He went on to explain quite contemptuously how she "should" be able to manage, "with all the money they have." He also explained that he was needing to drive several of these children to their schools afterward, being forced for the first time into the unusual situation of having to provide transport to retain junior players in training.

Although the mothers believed the tennis administration was unaware of the pressures on them and lacked an understanding of their concerns, they felt silenced by a perceived threat that their children would experience retribution if they complained too much. Liz explained this when she referred to a complaint she had wanted to make about the amount of money she was asked to pay when her daughter had been selected into a nontraveling State team.

> I was tempted to write and complain, but once you start writing letters it's the kids that suffer. Once you start complaining, you can guarantee next time the kids will get a bad draw or a bad seeding or something.

In order for their children to experience tennis as positively as possible, these mothers had to "behave."

An especially severe form of retribution for a child was missing out on selection into a State representative team, which was the second major issue to have caused many interviewed mothers a good deal of angst. At the time of her interview, Rita was extremely upset because her child had not been included in a recently named junior team due to travel to Europe, even though, she argued, his tennis results had merited selection. Rita suspected her child was being punished and explained that the tennis administration had said he did not have a good "attitude." She also suspected his exclusion was racially based, as he was, in her words, the only "colored boy" in the Squad. Her husband was considering legal action. She spoke about trying to get support from other parents but how they had not been successful. Her husband had written a letter of complaint to the tennis administration, and she explained,

> We asked parents to sign it. It's very hard to find people to sign it. [Another junior player's] parents did not want to sign it because they thought that would damage [their son's] future.

Di's son, the same age as Rita's, also had not been selected for the trip abroad, but he neither expected nor wanted to be. He had been playing in junior State teams for seven years, and Di explained how, over that time, because of the inconsistent and often negative ways he had been treated by tennis administrators, he had lost interest in the sport and she and her husband had become cynical because of his experience. She identified strongly with what Rita was going through, and the incident gave her the opportunity to express some of her own frustrations. She talked about finding an appropriate opportunity to tell someone in the junior tennis administration what she thought about it, and continued,

Now I wouldn't have said that twelve months ago. I would have been too frightened to because Matthew would get a circle around his name and he will be left out of something else. We have really been under a threat. "You tow the line"—you parents; "you get the results"—the child, "and you might be lucky enough, you'll get in a State team." Honestly, that's how it's been. They dangle the carrot and we have all, you can see the new parents coming into tennis now, they are bending over backwards to get their child [into a State team], and what an honor, what a glory (sarcastically). And we are all sitting back and thinking you don't know what you are getting involved in . . . but [husband] and I have made this decision that we are not going to be dictated. . . . We have been intimidated, you must do the right thing and if you do the right thing, everything will be all right, but it is not.

Trish had experienced the demands and disappointments associated with her older children's tennis and had made a decision with the youngest. "I'm keeping more control this time."

Three of the mothers had not been in conflict with tennis administrators and had had what Jacqui described as "a pretty good dream run." Yvonne had also and thought this was because her child had always been a top-ranked junior player. She described ways in which she felt he had been especially accommodated, saying, "We were very lucky." The fathers of all three of these children were tennis players, and two were professional coaches.

Jill talked about the advantages of being an "insider" to tennis organizations and how this had allowed her to have influence in an informal manner. She explained,

. . . through contacts. You meet people from WALTA and you click with them, chat away at tournaments with them, you can give them ideas, or your thoughts in an indirect way, and I'm sure that has had an influence. But as I say, not dramatically.

However, she said,

You have to be very careful because if you make too many waves and jump up and down, you can get a reputation as being a difficult parent. . . . If you get a label, they just seem to block off. So you have to ride that fine line between not being totally acquiescent but not being totally demanding either.

Her description of how to "ride that fine line" included her assessment that mothers were better at this behavior than fathers.

> Also too, you notice where some of the children's major parental involvement [with WALTA] is from the father, they don't have the same, what's the word, 'favor,' with the association and therefore opportunities opening up, as with the mothers. Fathers tend to be a bit more abrasive and demanding and they don't play the fine tune as well with the coaches and the association as the mothers do. . . . [Mothers are better at] the subtleties of keeping the balance, of getting their point across, but not making too many waves. Whereas the fathers are much more bombastic, demanding and agro, and that doesn't help, and I can sometimes see it in the way some of the children have gone.

Rita's husband had a reputation for being the kind of father Jill described. The "correct" behavior for parents, which more likely brought rewards for children from the tennis establishment, was being controlled, silent, and acquiescing. This behavior is also gender marked—the sort of behavior expected of women. Jill continued,

> I often smile to myself because you do have to play a lot of these subtlety games. You have to play them like a fiddle because a lot of them are older retired men, who occupy these positions in WALTA, and have grown up with an idea of women's role and place and are not comfortable with modern women and find it a little bit threatening and certainly have them typecast as being a 'stage mother,' not very bright, just tap them on the head and say, yes dear, and send them off and don't really listen to them. You get that patronizing feedback sometimes and you've really got to hold your tongue and maneuver.

"Ugly" parents. The "difficult" or "ugly" parent is a stereotypical construction that looms large in junior sporting culture, the ogre most despised and blamed for all "wrongs" in children's sport. Being somewhat disproportionately inflated, it was an effective controlling mechanism for keeping parents silenced. Again, it is a gender-neutral term that can obscure differing behaviors.

While "ugly parent" behavior was not a deliberate focus in the interviews, and was never directly asked, it was obviously highly topical within junior tennis circles, and invariably the interviewed mothers would raise the subject and give examples. They had all seen the ogre, but it was not them. Many described "ugly parents" they knew in junior tennis, or recalled specific incidents of behavior that fit this description, continually measuring their own behavior against it and being ever vigilant so as not to be described this way themselves.

The strength and pervasiveness of this construction of parental involvement in sport was evident in various other ways. For example, when I submitted an earlier, unsuccessful research grant application to the ASCNSRC, which focused only on mothers, an anonymous reviewer suggested the need for "observational and interactive" data, especially at major tennis tournaments. The accompanying comment suggested that the proposed research appeared to be "an attempt to 'bleed' the data to get mainstream sympathy." I interpreted that as meaning that the proposed research was perceived as having been conceptualized too sympathetically of mothers and that their "real" (read "ugly") behavior needed scope to appear. Second, the previously mentioned discussion with a Junior State Coach had come about when I visited the administration office and it was suggested that I speak with him. This discussion consisted almost exclusively of him telling me how "parents [were his] biggest problem." At one point he asked for my confirmation of his classification of them, saying, "I'll tell you which parents are sane. Well, no, you tell me, which ones have you found that are sane?" The third indication of institutionalized negative attitude toward parents in sport came in 1992, when the ASC published a draft National Junior Sport Policy for Australia. This twenty-four-page document contained a sole, thirteen-line reference to the role within sport of parents/guardians of junior players, portraying them by implication as discourteous, disruptive, dictatorial cheats. Five of the seven points listed included the following:

> . . . parents/guardians should:
>
> Be courteous in their communications with players, coaches, officials, and administrators;
>
> Not interfere with the conduct of any events;
>
> Encourage children to participate in sport, without forcing them to do so;

Encourage children to always participate according to the rules;

Provide a model of good sports behavior for children to copy. (National Sport Working Party 1992, 19)

The conclusion to be drawn is that parents within junior sports are perceived as being perversely negative, which is interesting considering the possibility in a sporting culture based on community volunteer labor that organizers and administrators of junior sport are most likely to also be parents. More important, however, it denies and diminishes the immense labor that they, mothers particularly, contribute to the institution. Alongside the assumption that it is parents who gain the greater rewards from junior sports, the space for them to have any say in the nature of their children's experience in sport is further restricted. Parents can therefore be, at best, ignored as inconsequential to the institution, or, at worst, considered so destructive as to necessitate control or exclusion.

The interviewed mothers devoted labor to this issue. They had internalised the assumption that children's poor behavior in tennis was in some way incited by the attitudes and behavior of their parents. With this in mind, the mothers carefully monitored their children's behavior and would explain at length their intolerance of what they considered bad on-court behavior. Six explained specific occasions where they had taken some action to modify a child's intolerable behavior at tennis, and four described themselves as being fortunate because their child did not behave badly. For example, Trish said the best thing about her child's tennis was the way she was admired for her on-court demeanor, and Jacqui said of hers, "Luckily, he has got a fantastic reputation" for never cheating. She explained that the one thing that would motivate her to withdraw her support of his tennis was if "he was being a little jerk . . . I would find that very, very demanding."

Once again, the collective term *parents* hides mothers and masks the specific impact on them of a constructed "ugly parent" ogre. During my aforementioned visit to the WALTA administration office, I was shown a very fat file of letters described to me as being from "complaining parents." On further questioning, it was revealed that all of the letters were in fact from fathers, mostly from only two. Every one of the mothers interviewed who spoke of "ugly" parental behavior they had witnessed in tennis gave examples describing fathers. In other words, the concept of "ugly parents" is perpetuated broadly to control the behavior of all parents, but hides the possibility of gender bias and asymmetry in how the behavior may be both displayed and managed.

SUMMARY

In the various ways described, the labor done by mothers of tennis-playing children has been diminished and denied within the androcentric institution of sport. Consequently, these women have been marginalized by an organization that exploited their work, controlled their behavior, and denied them the possibility of determining their own, and frequently their children's, experiences of the sport. Nevertheless, their contribution to junior tennis was enormous, proliferating from their responsibilities for child care, which included servicing children's interests beyond the home environment, such as their involvement in sport. The women interviewed illustrated a particular style of mothering that had not only incorporated a commitment to sport but that, more importantly, prioritized children's activities, allowing these activities to construct and define their lives. This style of mothering was made possible for these women by middle-class financial security, supported by ideological values by which it is regarded appropriate for mothers to establish all-serving relationships with their children and to transfer this relationship to hegemonic cultural practices such as sport.

Junior tennis in Western Australia needed this relationship. It depended upon the mothering practices demonstrated by the women interviewed. Not only is it difficult to imagine children being able to continue competitive participation in tennis in Australia without the support labor provided by mothers, but the sport in its current form could not exist without the mothers' continued service.

Andrews (1997) has illustrated how the promotion of soccer in the United States has identified the sport with the suburban middle class, particularly through media constructions of successful "Super Moms" serving this sport for their children to create happy, middle-class families. Serving sport becomes an ennobled way to "be" a mother, a form of mothering well glorified by both the Australian and New Zealand media, either as mothers of sports stars (Maddaford 1996; McFadden and Reid 1994; McGrath 1990a) or as mothers of sports stars' heirs (McFadden 1995a, 1995b). Janet

Chafetz's and Joseph Kotarba's (1995, 240–41) analysis of upper middle-class women in Texas servicing their sons Little League baseball described the ways in which these mothers "behaved like proverbial martyrs," treating their male children like "son gods" as a way to feel like "good mothers." Chafetz and Kotarba focus their analysis on the ways these women were "doing gender" in their performance as mothers.

Feminist analyses of motherhood have rarely mentioned children's sport and, if so, it is likely to be only with regard to sons. Early work by Judith Arcana showed this contrast. Her (1983) treatise of mother/son relationships included a discussion of sport in the process of "making men," but her earlier work about mother/daughter relationships (Arcana 1979) had very different concerns that did not include girls' sporting activities. "Making men" of sons was presented in terms of boys' sporting experiences, which were placed alongside a discussion of American male heroes as cultural icons, and violence. Arcana nevertheless indicated the tensions felt by the mothers she studied, and the inability of mothers to address them when she said,

> Obviously, mothers cannot be described as anti-sports. Mothers are not especially outspoken in the criticisms they do have; many appear to have accepted the athletic requirement on the list. As a group, the interview mothers do not seem to have made connections between the universal training of male children and youths in competitive sports and the behavior of 'most men.' Few of these women discussed violence, the team mentality, the overriding goal of winning, or even the exclusion of women, and none defined these as serious dangers at the core of the huge national and international athletic networks. Whether they appreciate the value of play and exercise to human health or consider the activity to be proof of their son's success in the world . . . most women want their sons to be active in sports. (Arcana 1983, 132)

The mothers interviewed in Western Australia may have expressed some reservations about details of their children's sporting experience, but they were equally committed to the sport of their sons and daughters, the case for their daughters obviously boosted by the traditional cultural acceptability of tennis for women. Why these mothers of junior tennis players did the immense servicing labor for their children is discussed in later chapters, first in terms they expressed, such as the rationales they gave and the rewards they identified. Then, in the final chapter, the gendered relations that construct this form of servicing labor as the responsibility of mothers are discussed. Next, however, I focus on women in sport as constructed by another family relationship—being the wife of a sports player.

THREE

BEING THE WIFE OF A SPORTS PLAYER

*I suppose, because now we are living to-
gether . . . he plays more tennis.*

—*Anthea*

Tennis is our life.

—*June*

SERVICING LABOR

Because the lifestyles of the interviewed mothers were so profoundly structured by the driving necessary for their children's tennis, it is not surprising that when they described their day-to-day
routines they seldom highlighted the domestic work required of
them at home. In comparison to the demands of providing transport, such tasks as laundry, for example, were less significant. For
the women married to men who played tennis, however, the home-
based labor generated by an adult male partner's participation in
tennis came into focus more clearly, with laundry being a specific
example. Lorelle was one of the fifteen women in Western Australia interviewed because they were married to tennis-playing
men. When asked what she considered the biggest demand her husband's tennis made of her, she replied, "I suppose, washing." I will
therefore begin this discussion of the labor done by wives of male
tennis players with the dirty laundry.

Laundry: "There are always tennis clothes in the wash."
There were two ways in which the women spoke of the labor associated with their husbands' tennis-related laundry. The first was
the sheer volume generated by a husband's regular training and
competitive play. Describing the amount of tennis her husband
played, Pauline said, "Well there are always tennis clothes in the

'Sport! this is it for me.'

FIGURE 3.1
CARTOON BY DONN RATANA.

wash, put it that way." Lorelle explained that when her husband
trained for tennis during a weekday, "he can go through three sets
or four sets of clothes in a day." But it was Anthea who spoke most
lucidly of the amount of laundry generated by a male tennis player.
This was a relatively new experience to her, having only been living with her partner for nine months, and she was still surprised by
the volume. She said,

> I do, and I'm not joking, three loads of washing a day. I have
> got so much ironing it is astronomical. Three loads of wash-
> ing! Okay, I have got quite a small machine, but still, three
> loads for two people a day! He changes his shirt about three or
> four times a day because of the sweat. It is a helluva lot of
> washing, a helluva lot. I can't believe it and, the neighbors
> always see a full thing of washing on the line, and it is just
> constant, absolutely constant. . . . I've already done two loads
> this morning [8:30 A.M.]. It's amazing, it's just amazing.

The second recurring theme concerned the organization
required to meet their husbands' specific tennis clothing needs. Deliberate management of the laundry was frequently necessary because of

the specialized nature of the clothing worn and the regularity of playing schedules. While the women interviewed could detail what this
required, such as the need to have a particular shirt washed and ironed
and ready for a particular day, generally they did not consider it difficult to manage because doing this laundry was seen as an integral part
of their domestic routine. As Pauline explained, "I don't really think
about it. I mean, it's in the wash on Monday so it's ready by [the next
weekend]." These men were financially able to own an extensive
wardrobe of tennis clothing, providing an adequate supply for several
ongoing occasions. When Karen was asked about the management of
specific tennis clothing, she replied,

> Because we've got enough [clothing to get by], I don't find that
> a problem at all. I end up doing a lot of the washing on a Sat-
> urday. If he plays five times a week, he's got enough there.

In this situation it only became "a problem," for example, if he had
a specific team uniform that had to be worn for a pennant competition two days in a row. Sally described this in the following way:

> The problem with State grade is sometimes they play Satur-
> days *and* Sundays, what they call doubleheaders, so that you
> had to be ready on Sunday to front up and do the same as you
> did on Saturday. You do that several times in the season.

Lorelle elaborated,

> The only time it becomes difficult, laundry wise, is if he does
> play the doubleheader, the Saturday and the Sunday, particu-
> larly if he stays at the tennis club afterwards [on Saturday] and
> has a drink and doesn't get back in until eight o'clock and you
> are rushing to go out. Then you have got to jump out of bed on
> Sunday morning and get it washed and dried before they can
> go off to pennants at one o'clock.

She added, "A drier is essential."
Sally's definition of tennis-related laundry was "sweaty,
smelly things that have to be organized and ready to be used again."
Her husband and two teenaged sons played tennis and she had,
until very recently, done all their laundry. Her comment highlighted the specific type of labor this demanded. Tennis clothing is
predominantly white. It gets stained by sweat, grass, blood, and the

red earth characteristic of Western Australia, to name just the common soil resulting from play. There are socks, shirts, and shorts, all of which are predominantly white. They may need to be soaked. They need to be washed separately to retain their whiteness. They are frequently made of cotton, which requires ironing. In summary, tennis clothing is labor-intensive laundry.

Ellen told a story she found amusing about her husband and son and how, during tournaments, they would develop superstitions regarding the clothing in which they played.

> Oh particularly if you had a good win in one particular color, you might have to wash that out the same night because we have got to wear it tomorrow. My god, yeah, that was the lucky shirt, you have got to wear that, yeah (laughs). Yes, you would have to do that.

Her use of "you" and "we" masks their identities and incorporates herself in the behavior, but she did not use "I" to indicate who actually did the "washing out." The example illustrates the extent to which her labor was at the whim of these men. The tone of her explanation denoted how silly she considered this behavior, which she nevertheless accommodated.

In ten of the fifteen cases it was the woman interviewed who did all of the household laundry. Sometimes they had assistance from other women. For example, June and Pauline mentioned their older daughters sometimes helped, and Lorelle explained how her mother "is always ringing and saying have you got a basket of ironing you would like to bring over, or something like that." Sally had paid help. Since recently returning to paid work, she employed a woman to help with housework once a week, and this woman did some laundry.

None of the husbands of these ten women did their own tennis laundry. Lorelle said of hers, "He wouldn't know how to turn the washing machine or the iron on, he just wouldn't know." Anthea explained that when she had complained about the ironing, the only aspect of all the housework she did that bothered her, her husband had suggested she "get an ironing lady." Sally described with great relief how, for the first time in many years, she had not gone away at Easter with her husband and sons to a tennis tournament in a country town where they usually camped. Her relief was due to the amount of domestic and organization labor she "got out of" by not going with them. But she said,

> When they come home, then you just start washing and iron-
> ing, I mean, they don't do any of that. They just put it on the
> laundry floor. So I still didn't get out of that aspect.

June's family of five tennis players (herself, her husband, and
their three children) regularly went with Sally's to this event. She
explained the laundry aspect in the following way:

JUNE: They will have up to six or seven tennis shirts, four or five
    pairs of shorts each, socks, a couple of pairs every day. All
    these white socks, shorts and shirts all have to be ready, and
    their rackets, hats, jumpers, track suits, and so on.
Q.: Who does that?
JUNE: Oh I do. And when it comes back from a country tournament
    it's putrid, I mean it's absolutely filthy. And it takes me, after a
    country tournament it'll take me two weeks to get all the gear
    actually through the process of being cleaned and washed. It's
    just loads and loads of washing. And I grizzle my head off but I
    still do it next time (laughs). Because it's a dirty little town. It's
    muddy and it's damp. Most mornings the courts are wet and
    there's a degree of red mud in between the grass and their socks
    just come home putrid and you have to soak them for days to
    try and get the mud out of them. And because they're sitting
    around on the ground the backs of their shorts will get filthy.
    And because they're very keen they'll dive at every ball and the
    sleeves of their shirts will be muddy and horrible.

Although two of her three children were daughters, her closing
examples refer to the shorts and diving behavior of her son and husband.

Both Tania and Marie were resistant to and angry about their
husbands' tennis. The intensity of this anger and its origins will
become clearer as I speak more of these two women in following
sections. For both of them, laundry had become a site where they
expressed this anger, although in differing ways.

Tania explained how she no longer did her husband's tennis-
related laundry. She said,

> I insist he does that himself now. He went off his face when I
> did it wrong. I didn't put enough softener in or something, or
> I got marks on something by washing it with something else.
> So I made him do it himself after that.

The conflict over the laundry his tennis generated had been resolved by her resistance, forcing him to take on this labor. Although she later described how the "marks" had come about because he left the wet clothing in a sports bag that had leached color, this highlights the issue that a certain standard of laundry care is necessary for tennis clothing and it is socially recognized. Marie used this to her advantage as a way of expressing her considerable and long-accumulated anger. In comparison to Tania, whose marriage was six years old, Marie had been married for thirty-eight years and her husband, a butcher by trade, had played tennis throughout. Her treatment of his tennis clothing was a visible form of rebellion against its labor demands. She told this anecdote with much retrospective humor, which belied the original emotions behind its motivation.

MARIE: Poor old codger. There was a joke down at the tennis club apparently. They used to say to [husband], "whose mum's got a Whirlpool?" You wouldn't know that joke. There used to be this ad on TV. Whirlpool was a brand of washing machine and the line was 'whose mum's got a Whirlpool?' Well they used to say that to [husband] because his tennis gear looked as if it had been washed with the floor mats.

Q.: Had it?

MARIE: Yes. (laughs) Well there was just so much washing and ironing, with all his butcher's aprons and the children, his tennis clothes used to just get thrown in.

Along with Tania's, four more of these women's husbands' usually did their own tennis laundry. The domestic labor in Kerry's and Sarah's households had been renegotiated later in their marriages to a more equitable division since both had taken on paid employment and most of their children had left home. Kerry described how she and her husband shared the laundry, but added that she ironed the more difficult items. Bronwyn and Rebecca also were in paid employment. Both described domestic labor as being shared equitably between themselves and their husbands, and they did not consider that their husbands' tennis added significantly to the laundry. Their husbands were playing tennis usually twice a week at most and "managed" their own clothing needs.

Child care: "I've brought up the children by myself." As has just been illustrated, laundry labor and its management was affected by the amount of tennis the husbands played and when it was scheduled. An important point to remember is that virtually all the tennis these men played took place outside the hours of regular paid work. All of the husbands were in full-time paid employment and their tennis was played as a leisure-time pursuit, during weekends, and late afternoon/early evening on weekdays. All thirteen of the wives who had children took primary responsibility for their care, including when their husbands' played tennis. Men's tennis took place at times when these women could expect some assistance with child care from the children's fathers, but because of their tennis this assistance was not usually forthcoming. Their playing meant that they were not available to undertake child care. The situation, however, has a double logic. Because the women did the child care, the men were released from the necessity to do so, which enabled them to play tennis. From whichever side this is viewed, these men's participation in sport and their lack of involvement in child care were directly related. The social construction of women's role as being primarily responsible for child care, which determines that mothers service the tennis of their children as detailed in the previous chapter, also operates to allow men the freedom from this responsibility so that they too can play tennis.

Although all thirteen women had performed the greater proportion of child care, only four of the wives interviewed stated that this situation was the most demanding aspect of having a tennis-playing husband. This is related to there being eight wives who were involved in tennis themselves. However, the intensity with which such statements were made show the depth of its impact. For two women, both of whom were not tennis players themselves, it had caused immense resentment. They will be highlighted first.

Marie had six children, the oldest of whom was thirty-eight. She described this child as being intellectually handicapped and the child still lived with her. She consistently referred to them as "my children," which she said she did deliberately because she had raised them on her own as their father was always playing tennis. When asked what she considered her contribution had been to his tennis, she replied emphatically, "Everything! Look, I've brought up the children by myself!"

Throughout the interview, she made reference to the labor of raising her children unaided, to illustrate the devastating impact she thought her husband's tennis playing had had on their marriage. She recalled,

When the children were little, I'd go off my brain. I was *very* angry. He was a butcher and I'd have buckets of bloody aprons soaking, one for every day, and they had those tapes around them that had to be starched and ironed, and I'd have buckets of nappies soaking and piles and piles of laundry and six kids and I'd say *please* don't go [to tennis] this afternoon, but he'd go. He was ruthless.

She continued,

He would pick me up from the hospital with a newborn baby, drop me off at home, and go to tennis. He'd say, you'll be okay. I say now that I used to be standing out the front with a baby on my hip and another wrapped around my knees screaming at him not to go to tennis. It's funny, but it's not far from the truth. I was just so full of anger. It was so easy for him to just come and go, to do what he pleased.

These examples illustrate the ways in which this man prioritized his sport, above any responsibility to his children beyond earning money to support them, or to any notion of partnership with his wife in their children's upbringing. They also show how he was able to use his sport to avoid engagement in the family and the labor of child care.

Marie's was not an isolated case. Tania had one child age three and another only nine months old. She explained that since the youngest had been born, she had been able to get her husband to reduce his tennis playing from five to three times a week and that he no longer went away to weekend-long tournaments out of town. This change had come about after she had left him for a short period of time. However, his tennis was still the source of serious conflict between them, mainly because she felt as though she was raising their children on her own. She said, "Nothing changed for him when they came along." She explained how they "never saw" their father, and that as a result he had no relationship with them. In reply to the question about what the greatest demand his tennis made of her, she said,

Him expecting me to have patience through this, and having to be the main parent. I'm bringing [the children] up single-handedly. [Daughter] screams every time he picks her up, . . . she doesn't know him, so it's me having to do everything.

Pauline also said that the greatest demand her husband's tennis made of her was "more responsibility for the kids," and said about his tennis, "I suppose I used to get resentful of it, I guess when the kids were younger and I was stuck at home."

In the earlier years of Pauline's marriage she had tried to play more tennis herself because she thought it was something she and her husband could "do together" and involve their children. But, she explained, it took so much more organization to get herself and their young children to tennis and they would get bored and want to go home. She did not find it necessary to say, until asked, that it was she who took them home.

The following chapter, which focuses on women tennis players, explains in more detail the dynamics of child care when both parents play tennis. To some extent, this situation resulted in fathers being more involved in the care of their children, or at least not walking out of the house leaving their wives with the children. Karen explained how her husband had always encouraged her to play tennis. She continued,

> So I suppose from that point of view it is not quite fair to say he's gone out and said you stay at home and look after the kids. He always wanted the kids to come and me to be playing as well.

This, however, was not always easy and a mother's tennis was much more expendable. Karen explained how she felt about his tennis when their children were babies and she was not playing the sport herself.

> Sometimes we have had enormous rows about it. I'd feel he has been gone all Saturday and Sunday and for some reason I haven't been at tennis and I've felt that I have had more of the load with the kids. In fact, I suppose you forget so quickly, but I can remember being really fed up sometimes when he, not so much that he had been at tennis, but that he stayed afterwards at tennis and got home at eight o'clock or something while I had these two littlies, this size, that have been driving me nuts. So I suppose then, although as I say you forget so quickly, I say now there has been no problems, but I can remember feeling very fed up and wanting to say, you stay at home with the kids and I'll go and play tennis.

Karen had resented the lack of equal access to the sport they both played because the primary responsibility for child care was hers. She also explained that, although her two children had been taken to tennis from the time they were young, if she and her husband played at different venues the children usually went with her. Because she and her husband played the same sport, she was able to make direct comparisons between their respective experiences.

Sharing tennis as an interest did not necessarily mean that child care was organized in an egalitarian manner, but it did usually mean that a wife expressed fewer feelings of resentment or ambivalence towards her husband's tennis, especially regarding the issue of child care. The disproportionate impact of child care on women's and men's tennis still reflected clear double standards. Women's tennis was frequently affected by their responsibilities for child care, whereas men's rarely was.

The greater proportion of women's tennis in Western Australia takes place during children's school hours, at times when the educational institution is in loco parentis, and structured on the assumption that women are not in full-time paid employment but do have responsibilities to children. Men's tennis, in contrast, takes place outside of those hours, structured instead to accommodate men in full-time paid work. The capital value of his paid work validates his access to leisure outside of it, and based on the assumption of gendered divisions of labor, also excuses him from the need to take on child care. As Karen explained,

> I have never played weekend pennants, since I've been [in Perth], more because of the kids, they have so much sport on the weekends and because [husband] can only play [pennants] at weekends.

In this way, women may provide the space for men's tennis by accepting its capital-based schedule and continuing to do the child care during the weekends.

Lorelle is an interesting case to highlight. Her husband spent the week running his own business. For ten years, from the time they were first married, through their three children's early years, he had coached tennis during weekends as well as played competitively. She explained how the children hardly ever saw their father because he spent all day Saturday and most of Sunday either playing or coaching tennis.

So the kids, unless they got up before seven o'clock on a Saturday or Sunday morning, didn't see him. The only time they really saw him was late Sunday afternoon, but by then, after coaching most of the time and playing on the Saturday afternoon pennants, he was fairly tired. It didn't make it easy, at that time.

She then related the many activities, mostly sporting, in which these children had been involved and how she had organized, transported, coached, and officiated in these various sports. She said she had done this because she had been a teacher of physical education before she had children and regretted not having returned to this work, but also, "I suppose I basically felt, like if [husband] wasn't going to put in the commitment, sportwise, to the kids, then I would." She discounted any impact their father's tennis may have had on the children because, she said, it had not prevented them from doing whatever they had wished to do. She had made sure of that. To illustrate how her children responded to their father not being there, which increased their demands on her, she talked about the children of her husband's best friend (also a tennis coach) and his wife, whom I have named Tom and Elaine,

> Like, as Elaine would say to you, if [the children] want something and Tom happens to be in the house, they are not used to having him around so they go to Elaine to ask for it. Well our kids would have been the same, it's sort of conditioning as well. They know that that's how life runs in your household, so that is it. My kids in summertime would be surprised if they came in on a Saturday afternoon and saw [husband] sitting in a chair watching television or reading the paper or gardening. The silly thing is they wouldn't dare walk up to him and say, what are you doing home Dad? They would walk inside to me and they'd say, Mum what's Dad doing out there? Because they would be so stunned at seeing him around on a Saturday afternoon, that it would be like, is that a mirage out there I see? And if I would say, oh look, your father's not playing today because he is sick or something, then they would go out and speak to him. But it's like, is that a mirage out there? Because they have never, ever been used to, in summertime anyway, seeing him on a Saturday afternoon.

His children discounting his physical presence, even when they see it, gives a bizarre twist to the "absent father" syndrome.

These women were asked about their children's involvement in tennis and several spoke of having strategically used their husband's interest as a way of engaging him, or trying to engage him, in child care. In some cases this strategy worked, but in others it did not. Sally explained that when her two children started playing tennis, her husband took responsibility for the organizational work involved. She said,

> He did most of that because I thought it was his job to do most of it, because I couldn't see why I had to do it. He was really interested in it, it meant a lot to him, and it didn't mean a great deal to me.

Marie had encouraged her children to play tennis because she thought it might be a good way of having her husband spend some time with them "since he played so much, he could help them." However, she said, "He wasn't very patient with them," and she suspected when he took them to the tennis club that he would leave them to play by themselves while he went off to hit with someone else. Tania explained how her husband would sometimes hit tennis balls with their son, "When I yell at him to spend time with [son], if I think the kids need to be separated for awhile, for example. He'll pack a sad but he'll do it." It seemed to be most successful if the woman also was a player, suggesting that there may be extra things she facilitated within tennis that helped. The six wives of tennis players who had tennis-playing children were all tennis players themselves, and conversely none of the children of nonplaying wives played the sport.

Trudi and her husband were both very keen players. His interest in his children's tennis illustrates an extreme case. He had purchased the house immediately behind where they lived, highly valued real estate in which his mother had lived for some time. Recently he had bought another home nearby for his mother and demolished her previous one to build a full-sized tennis court next to his. Although Trudi was looking forward to the "gatherings of tennis friends" they could then have, the main motivation was to provide somewhere private for their two children to play tennis, the oldest of whom was age eight and just beginning to play. It was not unusual for these women to credit the satisfactory relationship their children had with their fathers to their sharing his interest in tennis. I recall a friend, who was not interviewed but who assisted in the formulating stages of this research by answering my many questions from her experiences of tennis in all three of the roles on which I focused, saying how she did not expect her recently divorced ex-husband to pay very much attention to their four-year-old daughter until the child was old enough to play tennis. Five years later, talking about this book, I reminded her of the comment, and she said, "You know, that's exactly what's happened!" She then told me that the expense related to her children's tennis was one financial issue over which there had never been a dispute—their father always happily paid.

Rebecca had strategically utilized her husband's interest in tennis as a way of having him take some responsibility for child care arrangements. He usually took their son with him to the tennis club on Saturday afternoons because she was at paid work at that time. When he decided to play in a pennant team and therefore could not always take the child with him, she insisted it was his responsibility to make alternative arrangements. She explained how usually it was her job to find a baby-sitter but,

> When it's tennis I say, oh it's your problem, it's your tennis, you find a baby-sitter and straight away, no problems, he can find a baby-sitter. But that's the only real time that he has to do it.

To a large extent, because of the labor the women did as mothers and their primary role as homemaker, which aligned with being "at home" for the children, the ideology of motherhood generated the space clearing for their husbands' sport. The interviewed wives whose husbands appeared to contribute most to domestic labor and who got themselves organized for tennis were those either without children, such as Bronwyn, or those whose children had left their parent's home, such as Kerry. However, a wife's labor done to facilitate a husband's tennis was not always driven by her greater responsibility for child care. Anthea is a case in point. She and her partner did not have children. When speaking about his tennis schedule, she explained how he had been able to increase the amount he played because of the domestic work she did for him. She said,

> I suppose, because now we are living together, I can cook and everything, so I do all the cooking, the pressure is off him. Whereas he used to come home and have to do this, that and the other, now that pressure is off him so he plays more tennis.

She worked in full-time paid employment in a job that paid an equitable salary to his, but one that required shift work and frequently took her out of town. Since they had moved into the house they purchased together, she had taken on the bulk of the housework for both of them. Women's domestic labor that both facilitates and services men's sport is therefore also driven to some extent by the ideology of wifehood.

Meals: Pasta for dinner. Included in the domestic labor that Anthea provided for her husband was the responsibility for their meals. The planning and preparation of these meals reflected the way in which she catered to his tennis. She explained,

> The day before, if he's got an important match, he enjoys something like a pasta for dinner or some high carbohydrate meal. If I'm away, I've always got it in the freezer so he just has to choose it out and heat it up.

Her efforts went further than the consideration of single meals. She also was deliberately managing the dietary aspect of his tennis career.

> I did a catering course, before [present job], so I suppose I know a lot about different foods and nutrition. Because of that he has lost a lot of weight and looks a lot fitter since [we've been together] . . . I always do the high carbohydrate meals before a major tournament or whatever and cut it out if he is not playing as much tennis, he goes back down to a whatever meal.

Out of the fifteen wives interviewed, twelve did all or most of the meal preparation in their households. The three others, Bronwyn, Rebecca, and Sarah, said this task was shared with their husbands, although in the early days of Sarah's marriage this had not been so. Seven of these twelve women spoke of particular dietary considerations or special meals that they prepared in accordance with their husbands' perceived tennis-related nutritional needs. When June was asked if she saw ways in which she contributed directly to his tennis, she included her son's tennis also and replied, "Well, meals. They have a particular diet that they like to follow, prematch, and certain food that they like to eat when they're playing, and not eat." A belief in the benefits to sports players of "carbohydrate loading" had influenced these women's menus, with four specifically mentioning pasta meals. Lorelle said,

Before a tennis match, the night before, we will always eat high carbohydrate food, it is usually some form of pasta but the whole family likes it, so it is not a great trouble.

Lorelle's children all played different sports, including a daughter who played netball. She continued,

It gets a little bit much when you have a netball match during the week, and you have a something else and a something else, pasta gets on the menu an awful lot. Just as well they all like it.

The timing of meals and meal preparation also could be influenced by a husband's tennis schedule. Sally explained,

Well I have to think about when we are going to eat and what we are going to eat, and I have to fit in with things like [husband's training schedule] because quite often he is racing off to go somewhere else after he has done his training.

Squeezing lunches into a frantic Saturday was a common tale. For example, Karen described the "rush" between getting home from her children's sport commitments on Saturday mornings and getting herself and her husband to tennis on Saturday afternoons. Because her tennis playing was "social" rather than a pennant competition, she did not need to be there at a specific time, but

[husband] always does. I have got to have had his lunch ready, if he is going to tennis. That is about all that I have to do in a rush, make sure he has got lunch.

For most of the women, however, it was the impact on the evening meal that was more significant. Men's tennis training sessions, for example, usually took place during the early evening on weekdays, which the women would accommodate in one of two ways. Either they planned meals so all members of the family would eat together after the husbands returned from tennis, in which case their explanation usually included details about what this meant to any children at home, such as when they did their homework; or alternatively, as Pauline said, whose daughters were older and helped with the preparation of meals, "We just make them and leave them and he reheats them when he comes home." When Marie was asked if she had managed meals to accommodate her husband's tennis, she replied,

> No, he did his own thing. I figured if he was big enough to go to tennis he was big enough to do his own thing. Besides, I had six other mouths to feed, he could get his own food.

Although the women interviewed showed some variation in how they coped with meals in relation to their husbands' tennis schedules, there was never any indication that the opportunity that was afforded to these men to participate in their sport was constrained in any way by a need to be home to prepare meals for others, and most could expect their meals to be provided. This is an interesting contrast with the women players discussed in the following chapter, and the organization required of mothers servicing children's tennis detailed in the previous chapter.

Emotional and backup support: Being a "listening post." For Janet, meals in relation to her husband's tennis commitments had gone one step further. Since his retirement from paid work, her husband had taken on a key voluntary role in the administration of tennis which, she said, involved him "all day, every day" and was more demanding than his paid work had been. She explained how she had to be continually prepared for whatever this new role required of her, saying, "I sort of keep things in the freezer in case [husband] says I'm bringing so and so home for dinner tonight." She explained in more detail how she planned and prepared ahead in anticipation of major events, which included sewing her own clothes for the formal tennis occasions to which she would accompany him.

> Like I'm drastically thinking about Christmas because we have this tournament [at the club] three days before, then the Hopman cup follows straight on and then we go over to the Australian Open championships. I'm thinking now I've got to have clothes for these, so I can be at tennis all day and then rip home and wear something to the dinner at night. You do things like, you wash every day, so you don't have to waste a day having a wash day. . . . I feel if I want to enjoy it I don't want to be hassled when it is on. Think ahead, so you can be unhassled and enjoy it.

She added that she did not think her husband was aware of the extent to which she prepared ahead, "He just thinks that it all flows on anyway."

Janet perhaps provided the best example of how a wife's labor may become incorporated into directly servicing her husband's leisure interest. She explained how she had deliberately supported his activities and suppressed her own, saying,

> I think I backed off a bit so [husband] could be involved. I'm not a great, how would you say it, I'm not a great pusher for women dominating things and that. I'd suppose you'd say I'm not a great women's libber or anything like that. I sort of feel—I was happy to help him. I hate to be a bossy boots, saying women should have this and women should have that.

Her thirty-four years of married life had been lived with tennis being a major focus. She did not play the sport, however, having ceased playing before she got married. Instead she had been intensely involved in multiple servicing roles for the neighborhood tennis club she and her husband had founded, for her children's tennis, for other children's tennis, and for her husband's range of tennis-related activities. While she spoke very proudly of the administrative position her husband had attained, undoubtedly the support and backup labor she provided had made an enormous contribution to what he had achieved. She had been involved in tennis administration at her club for decades but, she explained, "This year I have dropped off the club committee. I find I've got to be free to cope with [husband's] side of it."

She described some of the things she did.

> Well you are [a secretary] in a way. You've got to sort of be the listening post. I sort of read all the information that comes through from the [Eastern States], and local, all the minutes and things, so that we can discuss it all. Sometimes he forgets things or I have a different idea, and it might be a good idea. Just giving him a bit of reassurance perhaps.

She spoke of these tasks not in terms of aiding the administration of tennis but simply in terms of being a "good" wife.

Several wives spoke of being involved in the tennis administrative roles of their husbands. Sally showed more ambivalence about it. Her husband had many roles in tennis and she said,

I'm the best telephone answerer. Fortunately I tend to know most of [the people who call], tune in to most of them. So I know who I'm talking to and what the relationship is and what they really want to know. . . . I'm the front line, and the sounding board, and I'll pass the information on to [husband], who blows up and explodes on me but he will be very nice to them on the phone!

The role she involuntarily played in diffusing any of his antagonism enabled him to proceed calmly and effectively in his interactions with others. Two of the veteran women tennis players interviewed offered other examples of assisting their tennis-playing husbands. Carol spoke of "his" position in their tennis club as requiring him to organize a large tournament and then talked at some length about how "we" organized the event. Brenda's husband was president of their club for "many" years, and in that capacity he organized "several" State tournaments. She did the selecting and purchasing of the trophies for those tournaments and said, "but I don't even know whether that was because he was president or not. Someone had to do it, so you'd go and do all that sort of thing."

The husbands of twelve of the fifteen wives interviewed had held administrative positions in tennis, most often as members of their tennis clubs' organizing committees. The wives of the three men who had not were the younger women interviewed, and all were nonplayers, Tania, Rebecca, and Anthea. Being a committee member required, at minimum, going to a meeting one evening a month. June explained what this meant to her.

There were times when he would be going off at night to a tennis meeting . . . and I would be left here with everything, all the homework problems, and all the dishes and all the organization.

She explained how he was "always on the committee, he's always had meetings," and that he had been awarded a life membership to their club for his many years of contribution. Later, when the children were "well and truly at high school," she too served for five years as a member of the club's committee. She made the comparison in the following way:

It was more difficult when the children were little, of course. Getting three toddlers to bed on your own is a lot harder than telling three teenagers to get to bed.

Many of the positions the men held required on going responsibilities. Three husbands had been pennant team organizers,
which Bronwyn described in the following way:

> It was a lot of work actually . . . and it is hard unless you play
> at the club every week, to know what people's standards are,
> especially as he was doing women's [teams] as well. . . . It's
> chaos trying to organize it because people say we want this
> team put in and then when it comes to the date, oh sorry she's
> gone on holidays, and he's left with only three people in the
> team. . . . A lot of time on the telephone actually, people
> would always be ringing up, they had to come and collect balls
> from the house, he has to get scorecards, he's running to
> WALTA for meetings, and ringing them up to make sure a
> team is okay, that sort of thing.

Four husbands had been State team selectors. This, according
to Sally, "requires lots of time. When tournaments are on he's
expected to go and watch these kids play." She spoke of how she
"happily went round with him" to all these tournaments. However, after having done this for "many years," her husband was considering resigning and, she said, "That would be nice because it has
taken up a lot of time, over the summer period in particular."

Other husbands had been their clubs' president, captain, secretary, treasurer, and grounds supervisor. Two, Janet's and Sally's,
had been extraordinarily involved in tennis, in a variety of ways.
It would add little to detail these here, but nevertheless, these
women were able to, being fully conversant with all of these
activities.

Sally described being "an ear" to her husband's tennis adven-
tures. This included her telephone answering skills but also concerned the way he coped with the stresses of competition. She said,

> He can come home and vent his feelings as a result of who did
> what, and what did who, to whom. So you are a sounding
> board in lots of ways. And also before he goes, you are a sound-
> ing board as to what he thinks he is going to do or what he
> hopes to do. . . . I listen, I'm quite happy to listen to those bits
> and pieces because I'm interested in the people who he is talk-
> ing about because he has played with and against them for so
> long that you feel you know those people, and you *do* know
> those people.

She told the following particularly quirky story:

> He would tell you about his game. I mean, [husband] replays his match, when he comes home, we'd all have it verbally. Say, for example, if he was to go for a run on a Sunday morning, which we used to do together, then he would be thinking his match through. He would run fast or slow depending on his winning points or losing points or just playing them out. I would run as I would want to run, but he would come and go, depending on what was going through his head at the time, as the result of the match the day before.

June also spoke of how her husband and son replayed their games.

> There's a degree of disappointment if there's a match which should have been won but which was lost, and there's after-match discussion sometimes when you think, oh, I'd just like to turn off for a little while. And that's when they go over it and over it.

Perhaps surprisingly, only three of these women spoke of tension in the house created by their husbands' competition stress. When I asked Anthea about this, she replied, "No, no, never, oh God, I couldn't handle that." She explained that if he was upset about the outcome of a game, he "took it out on the ball, not on me." Both June and Sally, however, talked about the nervous tension prior to their husbands' play. Sally mentioned how hers had to "let off steam" afterward, and "if he doesn't it's a problem situation for him. He takes it all very seriously." June denied having to manage the atmosphere in the house, but followed this by saying

> They have their times when tempers have been very frayed and perhaps on the odd occasion, you always like to send them off to a match relaxed and not having made them think about something that hasn't been done or something. And sometimes you haven't been able to do that, maybe there has been an upset and they will go out and perhaps not play as well and I always feel guilty. (laughs) You know, you do have to be careful. You sort of think, oh well, I'll yell at him tomorrow about that, not today.

Alongside their physical labor, women's emotional labor, the work they do managing emotions within the household (Hochschild 1983), allowed these men to be undistracted and focused on their sport.

What does he do? One of the questions I asked the interviewed wives was, "what does he do to be able to get to tennis," or words similar in intent. It seemed to strike many of the women as being a strange question, verging on stupid. I got the impression that sometimes it was as though I had just asked what he did in order to be able to breathe! For example, Anthea initially said, "Well, it sort of just happens," then, struggling to find something to say to answer the question, explained how he telephoned the people he had arranged to hit with to make sure that they could keep the appointment. Bronwyn also answered the question by speaking about the telephone calls her husband made to arrange practices.

Karen's response explained how her husband created space from his work in order to get to tennis.

> It's a simple thing, he just blocks his day off every Wednesday. It doesn't matter what comes up, he is not available after half past four, and he has done that for ages.

However, most of the responses involved organizing tennis equipment or specifically preparing for playing. Sally replied,

> Well he is always really organized ready to play well ahead of time, because that's him. He would have his racket handles taped and all his drink containers ready, his sweatbands, he would make sure he had enough of those, his towels and his bits and pieces and a change a gear . . . and he is particularly aware of stretching and making sure that his limbs are all in order to carry him through because of the way he plays. . . . He gets himself organized mentally and also his physical requirements he has organized, well and truly in advance. He is never staggering around at the last minute saying where have I puts this, he knows where he has put it and he has got it.

June talked about how her husband strung his own racket and made sure its grip was right, continuing,

All that's done the night before, or perhaps even on the morning of the matches. . . . They won't do anything strenuous on a Saturday morning, just relax and laze around the house, get their rackets ready, get their drink bottles ready, have an early lunch and they're gone by twelve o'clock.

Generally there was little appreciation of the "space creating"needed for husbands to get to that point, or their role in providing that space. Sally, however, did recognize this. She was one of three wives who said that the biggest demand on them of their husbands' tennis was their time. At this point in the interview, Sally said,

Probably my time, then once you have given your time and got him organized then your time is to yourself but . . . my time, I should think, in all bits and pieces, that you do to enable him to go and do, which he would never admit, and that you are not recompensed for in any shape or form, but are expected to give.

Those women who felt resentful about being left to do more of the child care because their husbands played tennis did recognize how this labor created the space for their husbands to play in that regard. However, other domestic labor was generally not considered in the same way, and Sally's comment about expectation and compensation was unique.

Pauline's reply to the question about what her husband did toward getting to tennis was, "Well, (long silence) I don't know, it's just that tennis is *the* thing. It's something you've got to do and you do it." She was referring to her husband's tennis, but the ambiguity of the "you" was interesting. It covered both the "he," in that he just "did" and went to tennis, and the "she" of "well," she just did everything that needed to be done. The high priority most of these men placed on their tennis drove it in such a manner that, in a sense, it did "just happen."

Priorities: "Number one." During the interviews, these women were asked how important they thought their husbands' tennis was to him. Their superlatives in response included "exceedingly," "extremely," "very, very," "right at the top," and "if he didn't play, he would die." Two women spoke of it as being an "addiction"; Marie called it "his magnificent obsession." Asked to put it on a priority list, Karen, Sally, Tania, and Pauline all said, "number one," and by this they meant that, in their impression, their husbands placed it ahead of their wives and children. Karen laughingly told a story about this, which she said was a long-standing family joke. It was about a photograph of her husband, having been discribed as showing the three most important aspects of his life, which included his tennis but not her. Marie replied to the question, "Well, first is his job, then tennis. Let me think, I used to have it all worked out, but I was so far down the list it wasn't funny." Others made ambiguous statements, such as Kerry, who explained,

> He would never sacrifice the family for tennis, I don't think, now. Like if the kids said they particularly wanted something he would do that but, like he wouldn't have helped [son] with the pergola on Saturday, because it could have been moved to Sunday.

In some instances, however, when "family" and tennis were firmly combined and family life was organized around tennis, the relative priorities between the two may not have been put to the test. This was the case for Janet's husband. She said of him, "He's a person who always said that his family came first," but she had organized her life to serve his interests and described tennis as having been a number-one priority "for the whole family." Anthea's comment also illustrated how her accommodation of her partner's tennis gave it priority status without challenge.

> Well, if I complained about his tennis he wouldn't do it, I know that, but it is very important to him, extremely important. I don't mind his tennis. I don't think we would have survived if I did. I know as well, he says, do you mind me playing so much tennis and I say no, and he says thank you.

Out of all the fifteen wives interviewed, only Bronwyn, Sarah, and Lorelle were currently unequivocal about their husbands' tennis being low enough in priority to be easily negotiable. For all three, this was a transition from an earlier stage in their husbands' playing careers. Bronwyn's husband had made a deliberate choice between seriously playing tennis and having a career in law, for which he had returned to university for a second time. Tennis had been important to Sarah's husband earlier in their married life, but this changed when his work transferred him to a country town where he could not play as competitively as he could in the city.

Lorelle's husband's health no longer allowed him to play as much as he had previously.

These women illustrated that being married to a man who played tennis intensively could make huge demands on their labor and impact heavily on their lives. As wives doing the domestic labor and child care, they created the space for their husbands to play the sport. The priority given to their husbands' leisure, especially if rationalized by the economic imperative of their status as the major income earner, excused their husbands from having to contribute to this but ensured that their needs were met.

YOU CAN'T BEAT IT, JOIN IT

When we look closely at the experiences of veteran women tennis players, as we shall in the next chapter, it becomes obvious that these women experienced tennis differently, depending on whether or not their husbands also were players. If a woman had a husband who did not play the sport, she was much more likely to keep her participation separate, and often hidden from her family. If, on the other hand her husband also played, she usually became more immersed in the tennis culture which overflowed into her domestic life. A woman's tennis, in these circumstances, no longer stood separate from her family relationships and responsibilities, but was immersed in and sometimes crucial to them. It also could mean that she played more frequently, and her presence in tennis gained a higher profile generally. Her immersion was further affected by the almost inevitable participation of her children.

The interviewed wives profiled in this chapter show how this immersion worked both ways. For the male players, having a wife who played tennis similarly contributed to a more intense tennis experience that incorporated family relationships and became part of family life. However, in contrast, if a man's wife did not play, it did not necessarily mean, as it frequently did in the reverse, that his tennis was limited to times that did not impact on his family. Men with nonplaying wives did not keep their tennis invisible from their families as did women players with nonplaying husbands. Male tennis players could be oblivious and uncaring about the impact their tennis had on family members. Having one's wife and children involved in the sport obviously made it easier to negotiate the space to play, but men's play was not necessarily constrained if their families did not condone or join his sport. In both scenarios, his interests prevailed and could be unaffected by those of his wife. Similarly, in both scenarios, her labor was co-opted to facilitate and service his interest, whether she was a tennis player or not. The experience of being married to a male tennis player, however, varied considerably, depending on whether or not she also was a player.

I shall now focus on these differing experiences and argue that both tend to show how the wives' interests were mostly of secondary importance to those of their husbands. If a woman was a tennis player alongside her tennis-playing husband, their greater involvement in tennis was enhanced and serviced through her multiple roles and the increased labor this multiplicity demanded of her. While this seemingly enhanced the rewards she gained from the sport, the effect of her immersion in tennis culture was to make invisible, to herself and other family members, the labor she did on their behalf. If a wife did not play tennis, the marriage and family relationships she valued were more likely to be abused by her husband, with her interests in the quality of these relationships often being of secondary importance to his tennis.

Wives as Players

When a woman and her husband both played tennis it was highly likely that their children would become players also. Tennis, in this case, became an activity that involved all or most of the woman's immediate family. Because of this, certain distinctive things occurred regarding the labor she provided to her family and their tennis.

Hidden labor: "I was doing it for both of us." To begin with, when a wife also played tennis and gained rewards from this activity, the labor she did in relation to the tennis of other family members became disguised as "doing for herself" and, therefore, was less readily recognized for the way it also facilitated the sport for others. It became hidden, in that it could not be easily separated from what she did for herself to contribute to her own leisure. Sarah illustrated this distinction by explaining, when she began to play tennis alongside her husband, that her labor did not change but her perception of it did.

> Well when we were first married, and in the city, I would have had his lunch ready and had afternoon tea ready and had his clothes ready etcetera, etcetera. But then as I say, not long

after we moved to [a small country town] and then the pattern changed and we both, I mean, I was only 'The Housewife' so naturally I did the laundry and the meals but I was doing it for both of us, getting ready to go to tennis, not the devoted wife sort of putting the tennis gear out and everything for him to go. We both went.

Her labor for tennis became immersed, not just within the ideology and practices of family care, but also within the framework of her own perceived pleasures and choices. Thus the demands made upon her by the sporting participation of her husband were no longer seen as such.

If a woman player was married to a player, her involvement in tennis was intricately tied up with serving and maintaining the conjugal relationship and family harmony. Tennis therefore demanded a great deal more of her commitment and labor, but this became hidden among the domestic work she considered to be hers anyway, and could be dismissed because it was connected to the rewards and pleasures of her own play and the organization required to make it happen. Ellen, for example, had some difficulty drawing a distinction between the labor necessary to facilitate her own tennis from that of her husband, and hers was a common response. To begin with, she could not comprehend my line of questioning. She was asked the question, "What sort of things does [husband] do that helps you get to tennis?" Her response,

> What sort of things does [husband] do? What do you mean? I don't think there is anything necessary for him to do, is there? It would bug me if he tried to organize me. I'm very independent.

I awkwardly attempted to rephrase the question, and in a way that could not be construed as leading, to which she replied, "You don't have to be tactful, just ask!" So I gave examples of the types of domestic work done by women that facilitated tennis for their family members and explained how the smooth running of a household created the space for leisure for those within.[1] She replied,

> But that is women's character. That's in their nature. You see, women can see six different things that need to be done, so you do a bit at a time. Men don't even notice them. You will be rushing around doing something and think, gee why does-

n't he give me a hand? But all you've got to say is can you do so and so, and they say, oh yeah, but they didn't notice that it needed doing. So it is our fault as women if we don't get as much help as we think we deserve because we don't ask.

I asked then if it would be a fair assessment of how the labor was organized in her household to say that she did what was necessary to enable her and her husband to get to tennis. She replied,

Yes, yes, but he is fairly good at organizing himself. Like if we are going to go somewhere he will pack the car, pack his own things. But he is not going to pack mine because he would never take the right things anyway.

The domestic labor that created the space for his tennis was not recognized as such because it also created the space for hers, but also was accepted as a normal, gendered arrangement with no expectations of reciprocity.

Multiple roles: "Down to a very fine art." The second characteristic of the tennis-related labor done by "immersed" women is that, not surprisingly, there was more of it. This was not simply because the volume of laundry, for example, was increased by the number of players in the household, nor because family meals needed to be organized around the differing playing/meeting schedules of more people. These situations did occur, but in addition the sport culture itself took on multiple meanings for the women, carrying extra labor demands that were inescapable because of their own participation. It became exponentially greater because of their multiple roles within the sporting institution. In particular, the extension of tennis into relationships with family members and friends required a level of engagement that was essential to the maintenance of those relationships. Once again, the rewards women gained through those relationships obfuscated the labor involved and the multiple interests it was serving.

An example of this was the common practice amongst tennis-playing families of going to tournaments in country towns on long weekend holidays. As a long-standing tradition, June, her husband, and their three children joined other tennis families, and they would all camp together at the town's local camping ground. She provided a detailed description of what this entailed, which illustrated the exponential effect on her labor of being immersed in the tennis culture as a player, the wife of a player, and the mother of players.

> The week leading up to a tennis tournament takes organiza-tion, like getting all [the family's] tennis gear ready for them. I say 'Don't wear that shirt if you want to take it to Bunbury. It's the last time I'm doing this washing!' So they wear differ-ent gear to train in for those few days so they've got a supply of shirts to go with them. It's a phenomenal amount of gear we take with us. We take the family car of course, and we tow a trailer. All the camping gear fits in the trailer which is just chocker. I mean, [son] will take perhaps three rackets, [hus-band] will take two, I will take two, [older daughter] will take one, [younger daughter] one. We have ten tennis rackets alone to go. Usually only one pair of tennis shoes each but you need shoes for after tennis. And when we go to Bridgetown we need more than one pair of tennis shoes each because they get wet . . . I hate getting ready, I mean we have to pack up half the house to go.

She detailed all of the clothing they took with them and what this meant in terms of laundry afterward, as quoted earlier. Then she described the labor required to clean up and put all the camping gear away. I commented that it sounded like a "mammoth effort," to which she replied,

> It is! But we have it down to a very fine art, because we've done it so many times. I know exactly what to take to the various campsites. I know what's there and I know what I need. I actu-ally have a camping checklist which is about six pages long, which I check off and that way I know I've got everything.

Sally and her family also had done this, although for the first time, during the year in which she was interviewed, she had not gone. She gave a similar account of the work it usually entailed and said of it, "That's my job! That's why it was fun not to go because it meant, if I wasn't going I didn't have to do it." However, remov-ing herself from this event as a player only reduced some of her workload. She could not remove herself from being the wife of a player or the mother of players, and hence the labor associated with those roles. She explained,

> The only thing I did, I pulled the gear out, I still pulled out the necessities [from] inside [the house] that had to go outside, but all the tenting things [they] organized.

And,

> I just put the food in the container and they bought what they didn't have . . . I just made sure they had a hot meal, a spaghetti meal or something like that for the Thursday night after they had driven down.

Then there was their laundry afterward, which she did. She continued her domestic labor associated with family care, which had long ago incorporated their sport.

Social networks: "We are fairly conversant, tennis wise." The extension of the sport into a woman's social life was an area where the lines between labor, family care, and leisure may have become especially blurred. However, it was possible to some extent to discern the role a woman played in enhancing the social aspects of the sport that made it enjoyable beyond the tennis court for herself and others. A wife's attention to the social experiences of family members also assured this within domestic life and friendship circles, such as when social activities and friendship groups became an extension of tennis playing. This occurred to a far greater degree for those women players who had tennis-playing husbands, and was an important feature of the rewards women identified from their participation in tennis. For example, both Sally and June talked about years of spending Saturday evenings after tennis with several other "tennis families" who had become a very bonded friendship group. On these occasions, adults and children would all gather at one of the families' homes to eat take-away food and socialize. They would rotate the home in which they would gather, and the "hostess" for the evening would provide dessert for everyone. Because of the social associations of this labor, these women recalled it as being a pleasure rather than a demand.

Again, there were patterns that indicated that a husband's involvement in the sport was a key factor in determining the form of social interaction and also who comprised a husband's and wife's social group. Lorelle, for example, explained how she and her husband's closest friends were tennis-playing people. More specifically, they were the men her husband had played tennis with since he was a child, and their wives and children. She described one recent social gathering to illustrate the pervasiveness of tennis in their social interactions.

LORELLE: But basically when we go out, it is nearly always with tennis people and then the conversation is nearly always tennis, . . . we went to [friends] for lunch yesterday and there were a group of tennis people, . . . and the whole conversation all lunch time, for about three or four hours, was all tennis, from the guys, just nonstop tennis.
Q.: And the women?
LORELLE: Well, I suppose we are fairly conversant with tennis too and we threw in . . .

She trailed off here and explained that there were lots of young children around because it was a small birthday party for one of them. This had kept the women busy, which explained why they were not so involved in the conversation on this occasion, but she continued,

We are fairly conversant, tennis wise, after all this time (laughs). If we went out to a restaurant in the evening the talk would still be mainly tennis, or people to do with tennis, and the women all know everybody, so we talk about it.

This friendship group, which Lorelle considered her own, was not only determined by her husband's tennis interests but the sport was also its focus and something in which the women were compelled to be engaged, in the interests of the social group as well as their own conjugal relationships. Being able to contribute to the conversation and to be part of the interaction was necessary as the wife of a player and was made easier if she herself played. Lorelle explained at length how she could not envisage a woman who was not "a sporting person" marrying a sport-playing man, because

If your social life is predominantly talking sport or going to sporting things, then that person wouldn't be interested in going on that social outing, so you can't visualize them getting to the stage of getting married, because it wouldn't last that long, do you get what I mean?

She also hypothesized that if "they" did get married, it would unlikely last very long.

Putting energy into the interests of their husbands was easier and more satisfying for the women if they themselves shared that interest. It also was considered a necessary part of maintaining good relationships and harmony, not only with husbands but also with children, especially if the children were male. Sally explained how she considered this necessary in order to remain visible as a "person" in her family. She described her home as an "all-male household," which by definition excluded herself. Tennis, she said, was "probably the pivot around which the family rotates," and she continued,

> Yeah, to be honest I reckon it is. Because I mean they talk tennis and tennis rackets, and strings and types of strings and types of shoes and all the bits and pieces that go with it. I know all about those. I mean, if you were to say to someone about a [name brand] this or a personally weighted tennis racket, most people would look at you like 'you've got to be joking lady.' Or if you talked about the tension in your strings, if they were increased or decreased then this would happen, you know, they'd think you were talking in a foreign language whereas it would be quite the norm here for people to talk about things like that and be understood. . . . I think also the fact they are an all-male household here and they pay attention to scores and to records that have been set and who played for what club and who does this and who does that. Not only in [tennis], they will do it for football, and in the cricket season with cricket players. I don't think girls do things like that, it doesn't mean anything to them. I think boys do . . . these two [sons] do. They are into sport, into all sorts of sport and that is probably because they have a father that is that way. I don't pay attention to those things. I think statistics are boring, I don't think they are interesting in the slightest. I'm amazed that they would bother to remember [them], . . . but I've made more of an effort this year to try and listen. . . . So those things probably have been forced upon me to a certain extent, otherwise you missed out. Like, you're a 'dumb mum' if you didn't know.

The imperative nature of men's interest in tennis, and sport generally, can therefore set the agenda for their wives' social interactions.

The expendability of her tennis: "I had other things to do."
Within this framework, a woman's tennis could easily become secondary to her domestic commitments and could be expendable if
demands upon her increased. While her ability to perform the servicing labor was enhanced because she was a player, the intractabil-
ity of it meant that her own play could become expendable if labor
demands became too great to maintain all roles. These patterns
were in distinct contrast to those experienced by male players. In
the following chapter, which focuses specifically on women tennis
players, examples are given of situations where both a wife and husband played tennis but the woman's involvement was more likely
to give way to the demands of caring for small children. For the
women players interviewed, their decreased responsibility for child
care as their children grew older usually meant increased opportunities for their tennis. There was not a similar correlation for their
husbands' involvement in tennis, which had been either consistent
throughout their marriages or was more intense when their children were younger. Two of the women players, both with adult
children, now played much more tennis than did their husbands.
When talking with Sarah about how much her husband had played
previously, and how at that stage she "didn't get the blues about
him going to tennis too often," she continued,

> It's actually got round to the other way. I play more now. It's
> funny that we're doing this interview because only a couple of
> days ago I said to him, what about playing tennis on Sunday
> this year, as well as your Saturday tennis. And he said he does-
> n't have the time to do it. And I said, well if you stopped doing
> so much cooking and cleaning and things like that in the
> weekend you could get out to it. He feels he likes to help me
> catch up on all the mundane household chores at home here
> and he feels that's his role in the weekend so he can only
> devote one afternoon a weekend to playing tennis.

Sarah's account of her husband putting domestic chores ahead of
his tennis was unique in this study.

Another example of the ease with which women's tennis
could be displaced by family responsibilities occurred when women
took up paid work during the week. If the greater proportion of a
woman's tennis had been played midweek, it was not easy to shift
her tennis to weekends, because domestic labor and family care
still needed to be done. Sally and June had both experienced this,

and in both cases their play had been considerably reduced while their husbands' had remained the same. June said during her interview, "I can't imagine my life without tennis because it *is* our life. I've said it so many times, tennis is our life," however she had completely stopped playing it herself. She spent weekdays in paid employment and explained of the weekends,

> The house is cleaned on the weekend. The meals are organized, I buy everything on Thursday night, I do most of the shopping and it's frozen for the various nights. . . . I work hard on a Sunday now, at home. All the washing's done during the week, but Sundays I'm cooking and cleaning and generally getting organized for the next week. But we've got it, as I said, we've got it down to a fine art.

This "we" is really "I," because during the weekend June's family members continued to play the same amount of tennis they always had. Along with her explanation of how she no longer had time to play tennis herself, June described her contribution to the tennis of her husband and son first as the special meals they required, and then as

> There's always their gear, their tennis whites. Apart from making sure their gear is ready, their shorts and T-shirts and track suits, washed and ironed, that sort of thing. And their meal and their drink and towels, that sort of thing. . . . But I've grown up with it! (laughs) It's just part of my life. I do it without thinking.

Not only was this service automatic, it also was nonnegotiable. After having moved into the paid workforce, it was June's leisure that "gave way" in order for her to maintain the standard of domestic care associated with her family, including that demanded by their tennis.

When Sally talked about the playing routines of her family members, it led into an explanation of what happened when, with her children as teenagers, she returned to paid work.

> The only times when [our schedules] clashed was when [husband] would play Saturday afternoon pennants, [son] would play Sunday morning pennants, [other son] and I both played Sunday afternoon pennants. And so to get everybody orga-

nized, fed, dressed, and water bottles and all those things that needed to be done. But to be fair, once I went back—no, not once I went back. That was wrong. After having been back at work for several years both [husband] and the boys then learned that they were capable of doing things too, and they didn't just have a mum to do it for them.

I commented on how I had noticed she changed the way she had said that and asked her why. She explained,

> It was not something that happened overnight. It took many, many tearful sessions, many tired sessions of, I can't do this any more. I've got other things to do and I've done other things, just like you guys have done, now you have to do it for yourself. I mean, they were still waited on to a great degree. . . . You had to lay it on the line, because it wasn't something they were accustomed to because previously I had always been here to do it, and then I wasn't.

She explained how she had tried to continue to provide the same level of domestic service, spending all weekend "whizzing round like Sadie the Cleaning Lady," but found she was "absolutely pooped." I asked if this had affected her tennis. She replied,

> Sure, because I didn't find then that I was as interested because I had other things to do and I wasn't prepared to put the time in as much. Yes, my tennis did give way because on a weekend my time was used doing household things. Previously I'd been very involved in the tennis club, . . . but then you find you just can't keep doing those things.

Kerry recalled a similar story in relation to her playing squash. She recalled how her going to college when her children were at high school had changed the division of labor within the household "dramatically," but that

> Actually it wasn't all of a sudden. The first year I got through college doing everything, absolutely everything. . . . Well I managed to get through the first year, and started the first term of the second year, and half way through that first term I just, I must have been very close to having a breakdown, I suppose. And I just started to cry and cry and cry.

From then on, she explained, her husband did "absolutely everything." At the time, she said, she was playing A grade squash and
did continue to play competitively one night a week, "but I can't
remember going to practices. If I did it would have had to have been
Saturday afternoons," which was when her husband was at tennis.
When asked at another stage of the interview if any special concessions were made in the household for her husband's tennis, she
replied,

> Yes, I suppose there were. I don't remember them specifically
> but I certainly know that he never ever missed out on tennis,
> but I must have stopped going to squash so that he went to
> tennis. Like if I was having a dinner party, they might be his
> friends but he didn't stay home, but I would, because I would
> be doing the cooking. . . . Tennis was standard. But I don't
> remember thinking he should be home with me. I think I just
> accepted that. I don't ever think that an issue was made, it
> was just expected that that is what would happen, you know,
> for him to go to tennis and really, anything else that, sort of,
> came up was just not [husband's] issue, I would deal with
> that.

She made two pertinent comments in relation to this. One was that
the situation she described would no longer happen because their
relationship was now more equitable, reflected in the current divisions of labor and the fact she was now able to value her own interests more highly—she would not now put her squash aside "for
anything." The second was that at the time "he was the breadwinner," and now she was also in full-time paid employment.

The priority of a husband's leisure is based in economic rationale and the controlling power of his role as "breadwinner." However, this did not always break down if his wife joined the paid
workforce and brought her own economic return to the household,
such as Kerry had experienced. A wife may still need to negotiate
her play from domestic and family servicing work, and, when
immersed in the sport through the participation of other family
members, it may be necessary to remove herself as a player in order
to discharge some of the work that involved. As the tennis-playing
wife of a player, her sport may still be played in unequal circumstances and her servicing labor made invisible by her own presence
as a player. This point is further illustrated in the next chapter,
which profiles women players.

Wives as Nonplayers

Of the fifteen wives of players interviewed, seven were not regular tennis players themselves. One, Kerry, played squash, and although this did not immerse her in the tennis culture it was possible to draw some parallels between her participation in squash and the tennis of the other wives. The remaining six women played little or no regular sport at all and did not have another leisure interest equal in intensity to their husbands' tennis. This group therefore provided an important contrast to the previous group of women discussed, whose marriage relationship and family life incorporated the sport played by their husbands. For the nonplaying wives, these areas were distinctly separate and frequently in conflict.

The major contrast between these women and the women who were tennis players alongside their husbands was the way in which his tennis was kept separate from family life and family relations. This does not mean to say that it had no impact upon it. On the contrary, many aspects of family life and marital relations had been profoundly affected by his being a tennis player, despite its separateness. His tennis could construct the lives of his family members just as profoundly as it did when his wife also was a player, only it did so in very different ways. The useful contribution to our understanding made by the nonplaying wives was that they allowed us to see that impact unclouded by the immersion effect occurring when wives were also tennis players. They made it starkly obvious how husbands can pursue a sporting activity regardless of the interests of their wives and children, and showed how that activity could nevertheless still demand wives' labor.

Of all the women interviewed, the nonplaying wives were the most invisible within the tennis culture. They had been difficult to identify and problematic to contact. Four had been found only by relying on network information, which I sought only after it became apparent that this group was not surfacing at random. When I asked June to help me identify women who did not play tennis but were married to men who did, she proceeded to go through her club membership list and identify the names of male tennis club colleagues whose wives she had "never seen" at the clubrooms. She called on her husband to help her. They were, in many ways, hidden women.

The group of nonplaying wives included the four youngest women interviewed, Anthea, Bronwyn, Rebecca, and Tania. It would be understandable to expect age or generational variation in the way women managed paid and unpaid labor, marriage, and child care, and for this to be reflected in such things as the impact of a husband's sport. However, this proved to not necessarily be the case. Just as Sarah, when she was a young wife twenty-odd years ago, had expected to "naturally" do all of the laundry and meals, as quoted earlier, Anthea as a young "wife" of nine months was currently doing all of the laundry, cooking, and cleaning, and saying,

> I don't mind doing the housework. I don't really mind it, I don't think it is really an issue . . . and if I do all that, the pressure is off [husband, to be able] to play tennis.

Furthermore, while Sarah, at the time, had young children and was not in paid employment, Anthea has no children and worked full-time in paid employment.

The two women interviewed (Bronwyn and Rebecca), who were married to men whose tennis apparently made the least impact on their lives, were nevertheless in this younger age group, and their own paid work contributed to more equitable divisions of labor within their marriages. However, the two who portrayed the most extreme examples of lives being affected by a husband's tennis were at opposite ends of the age range, Marie, at age sixty, and Tania at age twenty-seven. Both of these women gave accounts of having experienced colossal anger and frustration resulting from their husbands' tennis. Both had children, had worked in paid employment during their marriages, and both were, in my assessment, lower middle class. The major difference that could be attributed to generational variations was that Tania had considered leaving her marriage, while Marie had stayed in hers.

Denied interests: "It's not my idea of marriage." Three of the interviewed nonplaying wives will be especially highlighted as case examples of how it is possible for men to take the time and space for their sport against the interests of their wives and children. These women, Marie, Tania, and Pauline, had been living in marriages where their own hopes, aspirations, and expectations have been largely ignored and often deliberately denied by their husbands in order for them to play their chosen sport. At the same time, the women's labor was taken for granted as a means of creating the space for their husbands to do so. Because of this, their husbands' tennis became the catalyst for dysfunctional family relations, negating the women's desires for better marriages and family life. Furthermore, there appeared to be little or nothing they could do to change the situation, short of leaving their marriages.

Tania and Marie talked openly and in detail about the detrimental effect their husbands' tennis had had on their marriages and family life. Marie had been married for thirty-eight years and Tania for six. Pauline, who had been married for twenty-two years, spoke of similar outcomes but did not express the same anger or bitterness. Her interview, however, was strained and one of the shortest. I gained the impression that she did not wish to delve very deeply into the topics we discussed or confront the issues that my questions were raising, even though she had willingly agreed to having them asked. She laughed nervously throughout, particularly after making comments that made it obvious that her husband did precisely what he wished. While she talked lucidly about her husband's relationship with his children, she avoided discussing his relationship with her.

I found all three of these interviews difficult and disturbing because the focus was on something the women openly viewed as being a negative aspect of their lives. For Marie and Tania, it was obviously cathartic for them to be able to tell their stories; for Pauline, I did not think it was. It is difficult for women to admit to a stranger that there may be tensions and blatant inequalities in their marriages, and we both became increasingly uncomfortable with what my questions to Pauline were making obvious, yet remained unspoken. Marie's response to my initial letter was euphoric. Over the telephone, when I called to arrange the interview, she said of the letter,

> You made my day! It was better than winning lotto. I thought, well, every dog has its day, this is my day. I've been waiting years to have a go at this. I nearly jumped over the fence when I got your letter, I tell you, it was better than lotto.

However, she phoned a week later to cancel the interview appointment. Her tone was markedly different, and she was obviously very upset about something related to her husband's tennis. She explained how she did not think she was the sort of person I wanted to talk to because my letter had mentioned women's "contribution" to their husbands' sport and she said, "I didn't do a thing. I did everything to make it difficult for him." I explained I wanted to hear that too, that up until then I had only spoken with women

who were tennis players alongside their husbands and who mostly
thought tennis was "wonderful," but I suspected that there was
another side to the story. She confirmed that there was, and
explained,

> I suppose I should talk to you. When I got your letter I
> thought, well this'll be fun. It was a bit of a joke then you see.
> But I've had a crisis in the family and it's not funny any more.

Marie's comments about the impact of her husband's tennis
on her and her children illustrate how her concerns for the quality
of her marriage partnership were abused by her tennis-playing husband. Marie could not tell me exactly how frequently her husband
played tennis, because it had become such a sore point in their relationship that they no longer communicated about it. She said, for
example,

> I think he has a practice on Thursdays, I don't really know but
> he comes home late for tea on Thursdays in his tennis clothes
> so I think he goes to tennis then. You see, we don't communi-
> cate much. He doesn't tell me, he just comes and goes. He does-
> n't tell me so that I won't say anything about it. But I wouldn't
> say anything now, I don't any more. I used to, when the children
> were little I'd go off my brain. I was very, very angry.

She explained that her not talking about it was

> a bit of a family joke. Tennis is a dirty word. My daughter will
> say, "Is Dad at, oh, can't use that word." Over the years there's
> just been too much hurt and resentment.

This lack of communication concerning his tennis, Marie
explained, had over the years led to a general breakdown in communication between them. Although she did not wish to give
details of the crisis she had recently experienced, she attributed it
directly to the fact she and her husband had long since stopped
communicating about anything of significance as a result of their
antagonism concerning his tennis.

Her resentment had stemmed mainly from his being so frequently away from home and the ease with which he could do this,
in contrast to her responsibilities for the care of their children. She
explained,

It was just so easy for him. I just wanted him to stay here with me. I wanted companionship, some adult company after all week with the children. Or I would have loved him to say, I'll play one Saturday, you play the next. Just to give me a break.

When asked what effect her husband's tennis had on their children, she replied,

> Well, I was always there. But I was always in a bad mood and that must have affected them. . . . I was really strict on the children. I was always very cross and I suppose I took it out on them. I never hit them, but . . .

She continued, "They joke about it now, and it never stopped them buying him tennis balls and things like that for birthday presents." A source of deep anguish for Marie, related to the current crisis, was the lack of empathy from one or more of her children for how her life had been. They had "sided" with their father.

She explained how she stopped him from going to tennis once, saying she did not know how she did it.

> I must have been really cross. Nothing else would stop him . . . I'll never forget it. He spent the whole afternoon sitting on the back step with a face like this, sulking. He said it was either put up with him playing tennis or he'll go to the pub!

She continued, "He wasn't a drinker, he wouldn't have gone to the pub," but it was an effective threat because she said she hated drink, her father had been a drinker. While she knew she could not prevent him going to tennis, she continually protested in the only ways she felt she could.

> [I did] all sorts of things. He's a great man for leaving everything around and he'd leave his tennis shoes out [at the back door]. And I'd be watering the pot plants there so I'd water his shoes. And I'd take out the laces so that he'd have to thread them all through again. He'd be sitting out there on the step, threading the laces back into his shoes and making these huge sighs, but he never said anything. I unpicked the seam of his shorts once, at the back, so they'd split when he was playing and embarrass him. I used to saw through the strings of his racket with a nail file, just part way through, so they'd go ping

when he hit the ball. I don't think he ever realized that one. I think he just thought they broke. Sometimes I'd take his racket out of the car, and he'd drive all the way down to the club, discover it not there and have to come back. Then I'd think, oh God, he'll be back for it now. He'd say, "Don't you ever do that again, just don't you ever do that again." It was all silly really.

Marie related contradictions she experienced between feelings of frustration and her commitment to him as his wife. For example, after she spoke of how the children gave their father tennis-related gifts, she said,

And I've done it too. When I went to Singapore I bought him some shorts! I remember standing watching this little Chinese man climb up a rickety ladder stretching right up because he thought he had a size 42 up there, and thinking, what the hell am I doing? (laughs)

When asked what had been the biggest demand on her because of her husband's tennis, she replied,

The demand it's made on our marriage. I've spent most of my married life feeling very resentful. I'm a Scorpio, I've mellowed over the years and it hasn't spoiled our marriage, but it hasn't been what I expected marriage to be. It's not my idea of marriage. I wanted companionship. I just wanted him to be here, to give me support, I expected that. That's what I regret. I don't think any game is worth that. You only get one chance in this life.

And then she said,

I became nasty, and I don't really like that. I say to him, I wasn't nasty when you met me, I was nice (laughs). But I don't think you can live with resentment for so many years and not have it effect you. I've mellowed, it's just a big joke now, I can laugh about it, although [husband] can't.

In contrast to Marie, Tania had been married for six years. Her story was not so much a retrospective view as was Marie's, whose story had elements of a kind of resolution. Tania's was more of an exploration of the frustration and anger she was currently experiencing. She admitted in the interview that she was considering leaving her husband and that talking to me about the situation was a way for her to clarify the issues and her options. At one stage she asked what I would do if I were her.[2] The major sources of her frustration, however, were identical to those Marie expressed, such as companionship within the marriage and issues concerning child care. She said,

> I see things black and white, there are no gray areas with me any more. I've decided if it doesn't improve this coming year, then that's it. I've given him an ultimatum. There's no relationship, why stay with him?

His paid job required him to work one evening a week and Saturday mornings, and she felt that his tennis dominated all other time.

> The only times we see him are Monday nights, Wednesday nights, Friday after tennis, and Saturday after tennis. And then he's so tired he goes to bed at the same time as the kids do! He's asleep early. I really miss out on the company. I definitely don't feel like I have the partner I need at the end of the day. I don't have the partner I expected and the children don't have a father.

She said she did nothing to directly assist her husband's tennis, but did recognize that her doing all of the child care and housework provided him with the space to play. This, however, had been a rationalized decision. She explained,

> I don't go out of my way to do it but I sort of, well, if he didn't play he'd be impossible to live with and I don't want the confrontation so I just go along with it. . . . I've made it easier for him to go out to tennis because I can't handle the confrontations.

> Like Marie and Tania, Pauline also commented on her husband's noninvolvement in parenting and the consequential lack of relationship with his children. Their three children ranged in age from fourteen to nineteen, and she said,

> It was pretty much me that was with the kids all the time, . . . they got used to him not being there, basically. I guess now it's

a little bit harder for him to have a close relationship with them. He tries to. It varies as they get older, but the younger one, he finds it hard to get close to her.

She continued to say she could not be sure that this was a result of his playing tennis, because

> When it's the way it's always been, it's hard to know. . . . The girls are used to it. I mean, they're used to him not being here I suppose. It's been that way since they were little.

Child care in relation to a husband's tennis had been a source of some conflict for Rebecca but was not what she identified as being the major issue. Her husband had recently announced that he was joining a team from his club to play in the Saturday pennant competition for the first time. She said,

> So when he said he was playing in the pennant team I was annoyed really. Because he didn't even tell me. He just came back and said, "I'm in the pennant team, we're going to play every Saturday." I said, 'Oh that's great, that's every Saturday now until whenever.' There was no, "oh how do you feel about me playing?" He just did it, so I was a bit annoyed about it all.

She explained how much more "complicated" Saturdays then became, such as his new need to use their one car (her car) conflicting with her need to get to and from her paid work. It also meant that he would no longer always be able to take their six-year-old son to tennis with him on Saturday afternoons. However, what concerned her most about her husband's pennant play was that it also meant that he would be going to practice sessions on Thursday afternoons.

> Oh, and of course Thursday afternoons, that was just decided. Because you see, my days off are Wednesdays and Thursdays and all winter I might say to him, Oh let's go to lunch or let's do this or let's do that and he couldn't because he's been working all winter, on Thursdays. And all of a sudden [summer] tennis starts and he doesn't work Thursday nights any more. He can finish at 4 [P.M.]. So I was really peeved about that because that's my day off. We could have been doing something together. So that really annoyed me.

According to Rebecca, "The biggest demand [of husband's tennis] would be that we forfeit time together."

The two women who did not have children, Anthea and Bronwyn, expressed the least resentment or frustration over their husbands' tennis participation out of all the women in this group. Not being left with the responsibility for child care while their husbands pursued their leisure was undoubtedly a key component contributing to these women's more moderate attitudes. The amount of labor it created for Anthea, for example, did not concern her. If their partners' tennis was or ever had been a source of frustration, it was because of its impact on the times available for them to spend together, and the women's lack of control over that. For example, Bronwyn said that early in their relationship

> I didn't have any time for [husband's tennis]. I used to get very grumpy with him taking up all day Saturday and coming home at seven o'clock at night and I wanted to go out at night and he was too tired. I didn't understand that and I used to get a bit cheesed off. You just cope with that, . . . you just organize your life differently so you are doing something while he is doing something, or you go along and watch him.

Coping with or adapting to a husband's tennis schedule meant that the women arranged their own schedules around it. Anthea spoke of the frustration of coordinating her paid work schedule with her husband's commitments to tennis and how it meant very little time together. She worked shifts, and at her husband's request, she had once organized her timetable to have a block with weekends free so she could travel to a country tournament with him. She commented, however,

> When I had the weekends off and he was playing tennis I saw a lot less of him than when I worked having Tuesdays and Wednesdays off. A lot, it was amazingly so. Like, I could see him on the court, this sort of attitude, or I'd see him at the club, but we didn't spend any quality time together, because it was tennis, tennis, tennis.

She described her own leisure activities as being "singular," being things she did on her own during her days off, when he was at paid work, such as gardening, walking, and reading.

Guardians of "the family." The concerns expressed by all of these women, which refer in some way to the quality of the partnership with their husbands, casts them as "keepers" of family life and "guardians" of their marriage relationship—those who put in the effort to maintain communication, harmony, and commitment. The women's efforts in this regard forced them to accommodate their husbands' tennis, but it also was frequently thwarted by the men's tennis interests, becoming a major source of frustration. Tania explained,

> I don't want him to stay home just because I demand it. I don't want him to do it just to appease me. I shouldn't need to demand that he spends time with me and the kids. But it's all secondary. We go to the beach and I see other couples having a picnic and enjoying themselves. [Husband's] idea of going to the beach is twenty minutes, not even going into the water, just squeezed in to appease me, then rush home so he can get changed and go to tennis. It's costing me my life just for him to have his tennis.

Family outings and holidays were a related issue. Pauline talked about going as a family to her husband's tennis tournaments. As she did not play in these tournaments, she said she "amused" the children while he played. Also,

> We did go to Queensland once and there wasn't any tennis involved, that was something that we did together without tennis being the end to it, but a lot of times tennis is the purpose of going away. . . . We've only had about two [family holidays] where tennis hasn't been involved.

Marie had recently taken her oldest child on a holiday, but her husband was not interested in going. She said,

> We never had a family holiday. For the last fifteen years we've gone away with friends to Geographe Bay, during the long weekend in January. I never wanted him to take his tennis gear but he's always looking for someone to play tennis with. He met some people there one time, from the country, who like to play, so now he takes his gear just in case they're there. I think it's mean. We're only there for three days. He knows I like to go to the beach and swim. So it ends up I go to the beach and he plays tennis! Sometimes I think he does it just to annoy me.

Concern for family relations was not confined to their immediate households. Marie volunteered, "We've had family gatherings that [husband] hasn't been at, he's been at tennis, and that's really hurt." Tania said,

> [Tennis, to him] seems to be the most important thing. If there's some sort of situation or something that means he has to give away tennis he's really upset, really angry about it, even if it's [something] big. I'll give you an example. My Mum remarried this year and he didn't come to the ceremony. He went and played tennis. So it seems, he says it doesn't, but it seems to come before family.

When Pauline explained the sorts of concessions that have been made for her husband's tennis, she said,

> Oh there might be some birthday or something, if tennis was on, that came first, I suppose that's a concession. I did have a baby during the tennis season. He had to cut short his tennis to come and see me in hospital. (laughs) I remember that because my Mum said the same thing. She said, oh Dad came to see me in hospital in his tennis gear and said, "I had to cut short a game of doubles for you," or something or rather. I thought, oh it's history repeating itself. (laughs) That's probably why I remember it.

Significant family events such as births, deaths, or marriages were not immune to being surpassed by the greater importance the men placed on their sport. Marie recalled,

> When my mother died I was in hospital having a bladder operation. . . . I'd just had the operation so I was in a bit of a daze when they told me. My daughter came in that afternoon and she said, "You know where Dad is? He's gone to tennis!" I was really hurt by that. I thought at least he could have come and sat with me at that time. But that's the way he copes. He was very close to my mother, they got on well, and I suppose his going to tennis was his way of coping, but that was cruel to me.

Socializing in tennis circles. In comparison to the tennis-playing wives, whose main circle of friends was usually other tennis players, nonplaying wives generally did not socialize with tennis people. In some cases, this was not for lack of trying. These women did not wish to remain hidden or excluded. It was often forced upon them, being something that, one way or the other, depended upon their husbands. Pauline explained, with little enthusiasm, that her husband's tennis interest dominated their social activities, "It all revolved around the tennis club sort of thing." She described her social life as

> basically it's mostly to do with tennis, tennis people, things for the tennis club, quiz nights, socials for the tennis. Most of it, except if it's for work. Once a year we go to [his work] do.

Bronwyn had deliberately joined her husband's tennis club. She said,

> I did say I would become more involved in tennis, when we met, and I joined the tennis club and I was on the social committee, I *was* the social committee, for what is a pretty large club, and I found that a bit too taxing so I resigned this year and I haven't joined the tennis club again either.

She said she had done this because "I wanted to, because that was his interest. I thought well, it being so important to him I had better get to do something about it." She enjoyed the company of his tennis friends. Anthea was also being drawn into her husband's tennis circle, although somewhat reluctantly and only by accompanying him on the social engagements he was required to attend because of some sponsorship he was receiving,

> It is sort of expected of [him] to do that, to make an appearance. . . . There was a function last night that we had to go to, but it is more out of duty than anything. It is really fluffy to have to do all these things, just to get into the tennis, but it's one of those things you have to do.

Both Marie and Tania felt that their husbands had deliberately kept them out of their tennis lives and thus any social contact with tennis friends. Marie said, "It's something he shuts me out of." Tania explained how there was no pressure on her to go to his tennis club, but "the opposite really, he doesn't want me there." She gave an extraordinary example of exclusionary treatment by one of his male tennis friends, recalling how she, her husband, and child had gone to this man's home one day for lunch. She had been attending to her young child and realized the friend "had served some food and had set only two places, for him and [husband]. I was ignored!"

Kerry told of an event that had upset her immensely and made her feel as if she had been harassed out of the group of her husband's tennis friends. She explained how one of his male tennis colleagues had humiliated her at a barbecue she had attended when, after he had finished eating, he wiped his filthy hands down the front of her skirt leaving it covered with grease marks, and had laughed at her subsequent anger. She speculated he had deliberately picked her because she was an "outsider" to the tennis group. Since then she had refused to socialize with this group, even though her husband continued to do so and wished her to join him. These two examples show how the behavior of male tennis players may marginalize and exclude nonplaying wives from tennis circles.

Marie described how her husband's tennis had contributed to her even greater social isolation, and explained how her interaction with friends had been limited by his absence from home.

> Another thing that happened because of tennis is we stopped having visitors. Because [husband] wasn't here, he was always at tennis, visitors would come but the man would be at a loose end. The woman would be alright, we'd chat, but there was nothing for the man, no point, because [husband] wasn't there, so in the end they all stopped coming. It curtailed friendships. Because of the kids and having no car it was easier for them to come to me than for me to go visit them. We never visited anyone. [Husband] was at tennis and I had no car.

In various ways, the social inclusion or exclusion of nonplaying wives into their husbands' tennis circles occurred more or less at the discretion of their husbands and their husbands' playing colleagues. Husbands' involvement in the sport did not necessarily enhance wive's social networks and could instead contribute to their social isolation.

Reciprocity in leisure: "Very little really." As another contrast, the tennis-playing wives generally had a greater sense of leisure fulfillment. Regardless of how immersed their own tennis was with that of other family members, and not forgetting its expendability, their own participation in the sport and a perception of it being "shared" provided them with a feeling of satisfaction with their lives not generally experienced to the same degree by the nontennis-playing wives. The exception in this latter group was Kerry, for whom squash fulfilled a similar role as tennis. By contrast, the nonplaying wives were more aware of discrepancies and inequalities between their own leisure and their husbands' leisure. These discrepancies were huge in some instances and were a source of discontent not similarly experienced by the former group.

Rebecca stated, "He automatically gets to do his leisure activity." Even though she gave a detailed account of the things she did and enjoyed as leisure, she was frustrated by, and struggled to express, the way her leisure time was perceived by her husband as belonging to "invisible" time, thus not involving him. She continued,

> I've got [son] all the time when he's at tennis, or I'm working. He says I've got two days off during the week while [son]'s at school. But the point isn't trying to get away from [son].

The activities Anthea described as leisure she did on her own, mostly at times that were invisible to her partner. She described the pressure she experienced to make her husband's tennis a priority in her off-work hours.

> He really doesn't like it when I'm not there to watch him play tennis. Like I'll say, I'm sorry but there's an auction on and I'd rather go to that, and he'll just, he can't understand that. . . . I enjoy, I got into antique pottery when I went through Asia, and he couldn't understand why that [auction] could be more important than watching him play tennis. . . . And so in the end I will say, oh okay I'll come, sometimes. That's happened quite a few times, so I turn up [to watch him play] half way.

Unlike their husbands' leisure, Marie, Tania, and Pauline's leisure was much more elusive. Marie considered herself only having had leisure time since she retired from paid work. When asked about her leisure, she said,

> I never did anything until I finished working. I was always running. I'd come home from work to do everything here, although the girls helped. We had a roster on the fridge. Now

I walk, I go to exercise classes twice a week, I listen to music, I have a little organ here that I play. I read at night. I used to sew for the girls. . . . Life's good now. I was thinking it's the best it's been, until this [crisis] happened. My sister's here now. We go for walks, play scrabble, do the crossword, I don't have to cook etcetera if I don't want to.

When Pauline was asked what she did for herself, what her leisure was, she replied, "At the moment not much, very little really."

Out of her growing frustration, Tania provided immense detail of the gross inequalities she experienced in all aspects of her marriage. She said, "It's double standards all the way, that's the best way to describe it." When asked about her leisure, she exclaimed, "Leisure? I don't have any." One of her pleasures was dressmaking, but it took second place to her children's needs. When explaining how she felt she was "like a sole parent really," she said,

I spend every other moment with the kids. I just don't want them to be affected by [husband's behavior]. I want them to be well balanced. I have to manage my time well. Like I now do my dressmaking on a Saturday night, when they're in bed.

When asked if there was any form of reciprocal arrangement between her and her husband concerning their leisure activities, she replied,

Definitely not. Like last night I went out to a work function. A girl from work was leaving. I came back here for half an hour to get changed and all through that time he did things to show how displeased he was that I was going out. And it's the first time I've been out like that for four years! I came home early, left half way through, to avoid his confrontation, but I got it anyway. Or he'll do something to upset me. Once I was out and he was looking after the kids and when I got home he told me [son] was in hospital. He wasn't, I found him in his bed asleep, but [husband] had done that just to upset me.

She continued, "He's always expected me to stay home though, even before the kids came along. I wasn't supposed to go anywhere."

These women considered that it was the quality of their marriage partnerships that had been most seriously abused by their husbands' insistence on playing tennis and, as part of this, their concerns for child care and shared parenting. The situation was colored by the fact that some women had tried but discovered they could do little or nothing to bring about change and were forced to accept and adapt to marriages that denied their expectations. They offered a distinct contrast to the tennis-playing wives whose positive attitudes toward their husbands' tennis came from their own involvement in the sport and the way this was perceived as enhancing their marriages, family, and social life. It contributed to their feelings of leisure reciprocity and marital satisfaction. For all of the interviewed wives, however, their husbands' unnegotiable leisure interest was a major factor that organized their lives and was predicated on their unrecognized labor. The double standards upon which men's tennis acquired this status are further illuminated when we consider the status of women's tennis in the next chapter.

SUMMARY

In her work *Married to the Job* (1983), Janet Finch discussed how the structures of men's jobs affect the lives of the women to whom they are married. Parallels can be drawn between the ways in which Finch describes wives' incorporation into men's work and how they also may become incorporated into men's sport. Finch classifies the two prongs of incorporation using the phrases "hedging her in" and "drawing her in" to differentiate between the structural impact on wives of their husbands' paid work and the labor it may demand.

The first of these, "hedging her in," refers to spatial and time elements and the characteristics of men's work that constrain or impede wive's ability to control aspects of their lives for themselves, such as its location or temporal organization. For example, Wolff's account of her husband's Australian Rules football schedule includes,

> . . . then when football actually begins in late March, training changes to [only] Tuesday and Thursday nights. Sweet temporary relief, one less day tied to the washing machine. (Wolff 1989, 6)

Published biographies by women married to sportsmen include Barnes' (1973) account of the upheaval in the lives of women whose husbands were traded around the Canadian Football League, Bouton's and Marshall's (1983) description of the constant relocating experienced by wives of professional baseball players, and Edmond's (1986, 1987) tales of international travel with her husband's cricket team and how she waited until he was retired from the sport before she conceived her first baby (Herd 1989).

The second form of incorporation Finch describes, "drawing her in," refers to the work wives do either for or in association with their husbands' work. Finch highlights studies that focused on wives of doctors and clergymen, public figures whose work is considered especially important. She characterizes these as "noble endeavors" and says,

> Men with wives who *believe* that they are engaged in noble endeavors may find that the potential competition between work and family, far from being expressed in conflict between husband and wife, results in the husband being given *more* space to get on with the great work. A wife who sees work taking over her husband's whole life, and who endorses the legitimacy of its claims upon him, may well respond by taking on *all* responsibility for domestic tasks, leaving him free to concentrate on his work. (Finch 1983, 28, original emphasis)

The cultural potency of men's sport, and the sometimes huge public profile of individual players, casts it easily into the realm of "noble endeavors," forcing a similar response to that which Finch describes and which wives would similarly find difficult to resist. Kathy Botham recalled, when she became engaged to her cricket-playing husband at age eighteen, being taken aside by a male friend of her father's, who said to her,

> Ian is a bloody marvelous cricketer. He will play for England some day, Kathryn. You mustn't do anything to stop this. If you interfere with his career in any way I'll tan your arse. He must be single-minded and dedicated. You'll have to accept this. (Botham 1988, 51)

The threat of violence was not necessary, however, when Botham later described how she nursed her husband through a fever prior to a major international competition. She continued, "This continued for forty-eight hours. I didn't sleep at all. Feeling much like Florence Nightingale, I was proud of myself when he was pronounced fit enough to do battle in the Madras Test" (Botham 1988, 138).

The impact of men's sport on their wives has been long recognized and often problematized. Early feminist analyses of women in Australian society highlighted the relationship of men's sport to the oppression and frustration of the women to whom they may be married. Dixon (1976) argued that the importance Australian men attached to their sport (especially football) and their gathering together to drink beer was in such contrast to the way in which they ignored and excluded women that it led to deep feelings of anger and bitterness in Australian women. In the same year, Summers, while dismissing the accuracy of current stereotypical representations of Australian males, suggested they did nevertheless persist and described, with some cynicism, male behavior associated with horse racing and football and its implications for Australian women. Of football, she said,

> The role of footballers' wives is on the sidelines, cheering, probably with some bitterness since they cannot but realize that every success for the team is a setback to their hopes for conjugal enjoyment. They must acquiesce in having a conglomerate husband, a man who lives and breathes in an induced environment of competitive unity, who brings the rest of the team home, even to bed, with him, and whose inadequacies socially and sexually are to be endured as a necessary sacrifice to sportsmanship. One could conclude that it is the wives who have to be good sports. (Summers 1976, 77)

Wives of sportsmen have been portrayed as contributing background labor and support (Edwards 1988; Ehret 1988; Freh 1990; Ganahl 1979; Heyman 1987; Nix 1978); staying at home with the children (Cameron 1989; the *Sunday Times* [N.Z.] 1993); dismissing their own careers and homes to be "on tour" with their husbands (McIntosh 1990; Parker 1994) and to be their managers (McMahon 1990; Wilkison 1986); enjoying the reflected rewards (Lasson 1989); and coping with the marital strains from a professional sportsman's lifestyle (Paviour 1992). These specific examples come from Australia, Canada, Great Britain, and the United States, representing seven different men's sports.

Journalistic treatment of sportsmen's wives generally ennoble self-sacrifice and glorify gender-prescribed behavior. For example, the *West Australian*, in a full page feature article (with color photograph) of the wife of the coach of the local (men's) Australian Football League team, stated,

Stand by your man. It sounds corny when Tammy Wynette sings it but it is a rule of faith for Mrs. Malthouse—and no one would dare say there's anything corny about her. Other superlatives spring to mind: strong, efficient, organized, chic, nice. (Burns 1992)

Often emphasized is the national importance of wives who accept background roles and provide the space for male sporting victory. Commenting in 1989 on the win by the Australian men's cricket team of the traditional competition against England called "The Ashes," an Australian journalist stated that "the best tactical move of the campaign" to win that much coveted trophy was the male administrators' decision not to allow the players' wives and children to join them in the United Kingdom until after the fifth test (Jones 1989, 122). After such victories, wives (and children) are shown radiant in self-sacrifice (Cameron 1989). Such portrayals are common in New Zealand surrounding men's international sailing competition. One specific example related to the start of the 1993/1994 Whitbread "Around the World" yacht race (the *Sunday Times* 1993: 41). A photograph showed male crew members aboard a sailboat about to depart, while alongside, farewelling them from on shore, were four young women, each holding a baby. The image is strongly reminiscent of photographs associated with the departure of Australian and New Zealand Armed Forces in both world wars, when troops sailed in large numbers from home ports to the war zones, leaving women and children behind to maintain home and country. Similar connotations of forging a "noble" history, and with immense capital and national interests embedded in men's international sporting competition, such wives would find little room to resist. It contrasts the experience Hochschild highlighted when she quoted a woman from the United States, saying,

Whenever my husband leaves on a trip everyone smiles and says to me, "Aren't you excited?" My husband is a gymnast and he was nationally ranked last year. Just recently he went to Japan, to the Center for Men's Gymnastics. With all the work of getting him off and my feelings of being left behind, I'm not excited or happy but often depressed. There he is going off to all these exciting places, free, and here I am holding down the fort, doing everyday things. When he went to Japan I felt depressed and deserted when everyone else thought I should have been happy and excited. (Hochschild 1983, 82)

While drawing parallels with Finch's (1983) thesis of incorporation works best if the sport is men's work, such as when played professionally, they also can be drawn when played as leisure. What is crucial, Finch insists, is that the servicing work is done by the men's wives, precisely *because* they are the wives of these men. She says,

> . . . the general point can be taken. Wives' domestic labor produces male wage laborers, and capitalist employers benefit thereby. In providing for her husband's well-being, and taking on most (if not all) other domestic tasks, a wife presents her husband's employer with a worker who is fit *for* work, and able to give his undivided attention *to* work. This process is not restricted to particular types of employment, and it occurs whenever a wife takes on the sole or major responsibility for domestic tasks. (Finch 1983: 80, original emphasis)

Producing men who are fit and attentive to their leisure interests carries a similar capital-based imperative. Further to that, however, it stems from ideologies of wifehood and family harmony. To provide for a husband's needs and interests, whether or not these interests are condoned, is to be a "good" wife. In the case of the women I interviewed, the interest was tennis.

FOUR

Being a Sports Player

I never let my chores go down.

—Molly

A s described in the previous chapter, the work done by women married to men who played tennis created the "space," the freedom from responsibilities necessary for these men to play sport. Women's child care labor, domestic work, and the diverse range of supportive and backup tasks done as "good" wives and mothers contributed directly and indirectly to husbands' lives as sports players and not only enabled husbands to play but fostered and contributed to the satisfaction and success experienced as players. It is an interesting comparison, therefore, to consider the experiences of the women who were players of the same sport, and to ask how their sporting careers were facilitated.

A total of thirty-one interviewed women had played tennis on a regular competitive basis. Fifteen, who were members of the Veterans Tennis Club of Western Australia, had been specifically interviewed for this reason. Another sixteen were the interviewed wives and mothers of players who also were tennis players. This chapter, however, draws mainly on the experiences of the veteran players, all of whom were over forty years of age and had been playing tennis for decades, some for most of their lives.

I discuss the labor required of women to create the space and opportunities for their own sport. There are two main issues. First, there is the work required of women to be able to be a tennis player. Following similar themes to those in previous chapters, I shall consider how women managed domestic and child care labor in order

"SOMETHING DOESN'T SEEM RIGHT HERE?"

FIGURE 4.1
CARTOON BY DONN RATANA.

to be able to play tennis themselves. Second, there is the additional work, done by women players for tennis organizations, which contributes to the structure and continuation of the sport.

WHAT WAS REQUIRED

Domestic Management

When women play tennis, the conditions under which this is done are quite different from those described in the previous section by the wives of male players. In contrast to those men, the women players interviewed created for themselves the space and opportunities to participate in sport, fitting it around the lives and needs of others. While playing tennis frequently provided the men with an opportunity to abdicate responsibility for child care, for the women players, it did not. And whereas the men would, by and large, have their personal needs such as meal preparation and tennis-related laundry done for them, the tennis-playing women did these tasks for themselves as part of providing for their entire families. Whereas men's tennis assumed a priority in their lives to which other family members adapted, the opportunity for the women to play tennis depended on their successfully meeting all other family needs first. The interviews with the women veteran players, all of whom had played tennis for decades, provided a clear picture of the conditions by which their tennis participation took place. All of these women had had primary responsibility for the care of their children and for the domestic labor and management of their households. This in itself had an identifiable impact on their tennis careers, although there were varying accounts of how it was managed. Furthermore, being in paid employment did not necessarily change this responsibility or alter patterns of labor.

Managing child care: "If a baby cries, someone picks it up." Because all of the women players interviewed had played tennis while being primarily responsible for the care of their children, none of them considered having children an impediment to participation in this sport, nor was it anything special for them to have done so. Eight of the women described themselves as having played tennis continuously throughout their adult lives, starting from when they were children. They did not recall pregnancy and childbirth as having markedly disrupted their tennis careers or, if it had, the disruption was considered insignificant overall. For these women, if tennis-playing routines were established prior to pregnancy, it seemed unquestionable that they would not return to playing soon afterward. Alice recalled,

> I remember I started playing tennis again when [son] was six weeks old. We'd just joined [tennis club] and they said, "Right, play in this tournament, we're having a handicap tournament." I remember playing singles against one of their main persons, and beating her and coming in with all the milk just flowing down (laughs). And so they said, "Right, onto the next round," and I said, "Look, I just can't, I just have to go and feed a child."

In this case, Alice was talking about her third child. She had not played tennis for five years, when her first two children were babies. It was considered the norm by these women players that at least some tennis-playing time would likely be "lost" to the care of their babies, but they had all played tennis when their children were toddlers.

In several instances, having children and being "at home" caring for them had been the catalyst that had motivated women to begin or return to playing tennis. Four of the veteran women players who had played tennis as children but stopped as teenagers or young adults returned to it after becoming a mother. Dorothy, for example, explained the resumption of her tennis career "because I was home, you see . . . once I had a child."

Another four women, who had not played previously, actually began their tennis careers when their children were very young. Molly, for example, said,

> Well I started off [playing tennis] probably about seventeen years ago. The kids were little and I was staying at home doing nothing and I started with a little group [of women playing] at the school, . . . I had to have something apart from just work bringing up children.

Being "at home" with full-time responsibility for child care and domestic work, and finding this situation lacking, had been the impetus for Molly, and most of the other women players interviewed, to become involved in tennis.

Patricia explained how she had made a deliberate effort to continue playing soon after the birth of her first baby, when she became aware of how divergent her and her husband's lives would quickly become if she did not do so. She recognized this profoundly, because to that point their sports careers had followed parallel courses.

> People say, oh you're lucky to have the same interest, but when we were first married it wasn't as good as it sounds because someone had to stay home and look after a new baby, or have it anyway, [husband] certainly couldn't do that. So he was still playing in tournaments for a little while. I could see that I was obviously going to be the one that was home and I didn't like it. Even going to play golf and things like that, we both played golf, we both played squash. It wasn't good that

we had the same interests because I wasn't really happy to stay at home and because we had the same interests I could see a direct parallel. So it was really, you know, I had to sort of get out and get into it if I wanted to, otherwise I was going to be left home with the children.

Most significantly, these women could play tennis while caring for their children because their children could be taken with them. All thirty-one women players in this study had taken their child or children to tennis at some stage in their playing careers. This was usually when the children were of pre-school age, although older children were also taken if the women played during the weekend. Being able to take their children, of any age, to the tennis club when they themselves played was a key factor in making participation possible for these women. Not only did this facilitate their participation in sport, but three women explained how the ease with which child care could be arranged had influenced which particular sport they played. Making comparisons to other sports they had played, Alice spoke of the length of time it takes to play a golf match and "you can't leave children" for that long. Ruth said, "With [field] hockey, you couldn't get off the field to go do things for them," and Carol said, "It's not as healthy for kids, sitting at the top of a squash court."

The relative ease and acceptability of taking their children to tennis was mainly based on the understanding that all of the women were, or had been, in the same situation. Hence, having other women with whom to play meant sympathetically recognizing and accommodating each others' child care responsibilities. Ruth simply stated, when asked about playing while her children were young, "[I] used to play with mothers' clubs. No bother, . . . another mother minded them while you played." Alice described this in practical terms, saying, "If a baby cries, someone picks it up." She recalled a specific incident where another woman helped facilitate her play.

Tennis hasn't been a problem with the children, except the youngest one. Even though he was taken [to tennis] from the time he was four weeks [old] or something, he just sat and yelled every time I went on the court, for about a year. He'd just stand at the end of the court and scream his head off, it was just amazing. . . . And one of the women I used to play with one day went and really told him off. We used to just say to her "just tell him off," because he'd stop immediately [when] she told him off.

Rather than being critical of her "unmanageable" child, Alice's tennis colleagues sympathized and helped facilitate her play.

For all of the veteran players interviewed, child care within tennis clubs when players' own children were young had been an informal arrangement, such as that recalled earlier. Some described various more structured arrangements that had since developed in clubs but that nevertheless still assumed women could and would bring their children, and that child care arrangements were an integral and a necessary part of facilitating their sport. Marilyn's club had a crèche, costing one dollar per tennis day per child, which paid a woman to look after the children. In Molly's club, the women members who were rostered for the day to arrange the playing schedule (the sets) and make the tea also were responsible for keeping an eye on any children who were brought there. Both of these arrangements were only applicable to women's mid week social days and arranged on the assumption that the mothers were nearby, playing tennis.

While it was the usual practice to take children to tennis clubs when games were sociable and the competition less formal, if the women became involved in structured competitive play such as pennants this arrangement was not always as easy or acceptable. Reasons given included the need for players to be able to concentrate on their games without distraction, having to travel to other, sometimes unfamiliar, clubs and the tighter, more formalized playing structures that left fewer women uninvolved and thus able to keep an eye on any children. Molly told a story about members of her pennant team, some of whom were many years younger than she, which showed how child care arrangements still tended to remain informal and ad hoc.

> One day one of the ladies in my team, she . . . had a bad heel, so all the others that have got little kids all went to her place and gave her the kids. . . . It was like a kindergarten when we arrived back there. She said she didn't know whether it was better to play with the sore heel and suffer, or have all those kids there. (laughs)

It was a very common scenario for the women to wait until their children went to school before they became involved in formal competition, and then to limit their competitive play to the midweek pennant competition that was deliberately scheduled during children's school hours. Nevertheless, even if their children were of school age, it was recognized that mothers were always "on call." Patricia coached women's teams and spoke of the advantages of having a female coach who understood this reality.

> So I would sort of say to them, 'Now, Wednesday morning you've got to forget that you're a mum and you've got to not worry about everyone else. It's your day and you've got to make it your day.' And get them into different ways of thinking about the day, to get the most out of themselves and to enjoy the day. Whereas [a male coach] is going to be saying, "Don't forget to keep your grip right on your backhand," things like that, you know what I mean? It's their whole emphasis. Now I sort of say, 'If anyone's got the measles or mumps, have that covered, know that someone's going to be able to look after that child so you can go to tennis on that day,' whereas he wouldn't have even thought of that.

Obviously clubs varied in the way in which child care was accommodated. The women knew which were "good" clubs for children, describing assets such as playground facilities, fences with gates that closed to the road, having plenty of other children to play with, and a general tolerance for children. Patricia described the difference between two clubs with the same size membership where she coached, one with "no little kids around at all," the other with "masses and masses. If you can't play with kids yelling and screaming up and down the back of the court you may as well forget it." She attributed the latter to the fact that it had been a very good junior club years ago, and those players had now returned as adults with their own children. Marilyn told a story about her club that implied that tolerance of children at sporting clubs was a gendered characteristic. It concerned a time when the local government authority had suggested the tennis club amalgamate with the adjoining lawn bowls club. Marilyn explained one of the reasons this did not eventuate.

> One guy, we know this because his wife was a member of the tennis club, didn't want the kids around. I'm sure this was a big reason. The bowling club women never complained about the kids but the men did. They were just next door so of

course they could see all the kids around. We didn't have our own clubrooms so we used to go over there for drinks and of course the kids came too. This particular guy would be at the bowling club while his wife was over at tennis with their children. It was his way of getting away from them and he didn't want any kids around.

Assistance with child care from outside tennis circles also was provided by other women, invariably female relatives and most usually mothers and mothers in law. As Ellen said,

> When they were babies, I played, but I was in [a country town] and my mother lived 100 yards away. So it was, "See ya, Greg, see ya Steve, see ya when I get home," whoosh. It was lovely. . . . They stayed with Mum.

Carol also explained how she was able to travel to State representative tournaments after she had children because of her mother's help with their care. For both Marilyn and Patricia, however, this assistance was provided to enable their involvement in paid employment, but was extended to include their tennis. For example, Patricia's tennis was associated with a professional coaching business of which her mother heartily approved, having been a business woman herself. When asked how her mother helped, Patricia told the following anecdote:

> Oh she pushed and pushed me. She never wanted me to get married. When I was walking down the aisle she said, "Now if you don't want to go ahead with this you don't have to." She thought it was the most dreadful thing to do, to get married when I had a whole life in front of me to do what she thought I could do. But what I wanted to do was get married and have a family so she pushed in the best method she could think of which was, "I'll mind the kids, you go out and do what you need to do." So it was great.

Frances, who looked after her grandchild three days a week while her daughter-in-law was in paid employment, now took him to tennis with her as she had done with her own children years before.

Only one of the thirty-one interviewed players described having used private, paid child care to play tennis, and this, Trudi explained, had been in exceptional circumstances, "Just when nothing else worked, you know, when my mother-in-law was on holidays and [husband] didn't have time and no one else was available." On this occasion, she had employed another woman.

These women do not play tennis under the same conditions as men. A major difference being, for the women in this study, issues concerning child care were central to the way in which they organized themselves in order to play tennis. For the men, child care was largely irrelevant. While the men played, their children were being cared for by their mothers. The next question is then, what did the fathers of these women's children do in terms of providing child care to facilitate women's tennis?

On one level, it is argued that the fathers maintained gendered divisions of labor by being in full-time paid employment. They therefore provided the capital base for the family unit, an arrangement that ensured the women were "at home" with children and thus able to "choose" to play tennis during weekdays. Husbands' paid work, done under the conditions of capital relations and gendered divisions of labor, facilitated the space for women to play tennis. This will be discussed in more detail later.

Given such divisions of labor, however, what exactly are the divisions of leisure, and how is leisure facilitated for women? Jean's recollection of her return to tennis when her children were young illustrates how husbands may support women's "leisure" without actually recognizing how it is bounded by child care.

> Someone convinced [husband] to join the club and asked him about me. He said, "Oh yes, she can play tennis, but she has three young children." So this guy said, "That's no problem, the tennis club is like another kindergarten." So I went along and took the kids. [Husband] fixed up one of those playpens so that it undid one side, so I could put it around the net pole and do it up again, and the kids went into that.

Whether or not fathers took care of their children to facilitate their wives' tennis depended, in almost every case, on whether or not they also played the sport. If they did not, as was the situation for six of the veteran women, they were not involved in child care while the wives played tennis. Betty, for example, worked full time during the week and played tennis on Saturday afternoons. Her husband typically attended horse racing meetings on Saturday afternoons. She said, "I'd get him organized for that and [son] used to come to tennis with me." Four other women restricted their tennis playing to weekdays, within their children's school hours, until the children were old enough to not require supervision, at which point the women felt they were able to play during the weekend. The one exception was Ruth, who recalled that her husband would take their children to watch football on Saturday afternoons when she went to tennis (before which she always cooked them a roast dinner!).

The eight veteran women players interviewed whose husbands also were tennis players were more likely to talk of child care being shared, at least on the occasions when both parents went to play, such as during weekends. It was in the context of weekend play, for example, that Brenda explained, "I would sit out with the children and then I would play the next set and [husband] would sit out with the children. We did that for a couple of years." And Marilyn said,

> It was a great club for kids, there was always older children around to look after them while I played and rarely were [husband] and I on the court at the same time.

Several women mentioned how this was very common in tennis clubs and becoming more so, which they saw as evidence of the progressive, egalitarian nature of tennis compared to other sports.

This arrangement for child care, facilitating each others' shared interest, seemed straight forward and equitable when the tennis being played was at a social level within their own club. Once again, though, when it involved structured competitive tennis, the situation became more complex. Whether or not both parents could play competitively depended a lot on the scheduling of their respective competitions. Both Alice and June recalled how weekend competition schedules had at times worked for them. Alice described how, many years ago, her pennant competition was held over one three-month block and her husband's over another. She said, after explaining this, "He was the one that encouraged me to play because he said, 'I'll stay home and look after the children.'" June explained,

> I used to play weekend pennants myself in the winter time and that was generally on a Sunday afternoon. The women played Sunday afternoon, the men played Sunday morning. So when the children were little [husband] would get home, we'd do a swap over and I'd take off.

There were some subtleties to negotiating "shared" child care, however, and frequently they meant that in the final analysis, mothers did more and played less.

In the situation where both parents played tennis, several issues were raised in discussions about who played, when, and how frequently. Again, one of these issues concerned the scheduling of women's and men's competitions, coupled with perceptions of entitlement to leisure time and when that could occur. If the women were not in full-time paid employment and played competitively during the week, they would very likely forego the women's weekend competition with the justification that this was the only time the men's pennant competition was scheduled and therefore the only time their full-time working spouse could play competitively. In this case, the women would then be responsible for the child care arrangements during the week, to facilitate their own tennis, and during the weekends to facilitate their husbands'. They would likely limit their tennis during weekends to social play in their club, which more easily accommodated this responsibility, perhaps until their children were older. Husbands' paid work, along with their roles as the major financial providers for the family, rationalized the priority of husbands' leisure and wives' greater responsibility for child care.

Another rationale used to prioritize tennis concerned comparable playing ability. If husbands were perceived as being better players than their wives, or played in a higher competitive grade, it was frequently considered that they had more right to play. Barbara said,

> I stopped playing pennants then for a couple of years and [husband] used to play, because he was better than me (laughs). So he used to play on the Saturday so I would mind the children.

Similarly, Alice explained a regret she now felt about the years she had not played.

> Well, when I had children, particularly when I first had them, . . . [husband] was very good, but because he was playing A Grade I didn't play very much at all, which was five years of the best years that I would have had. And because he was playing, it was much more difficult [for me to].

This did not necessarily occur in the reverse, however, as Trudi illustrated. She had been a far more accomplished tennis player than her husband before their marriage, but following the birth of their children her husband had played more and had since achieved championship titles as a veteran player.

When Karen and her husband both played in weekend competitions, their two children went with her. Her reasoning for this arrangement included a comparison of their abilities. She said,

> And I was playing a lower level of tennis so if I had to run to the back of the court to say [to a child] "get off that thing and back down on the ground" or something, it was better [that it was me].

Arguing the right to play, and to play uninterrupted, based on perceived comparable ability, is a potentially powerful rationale for inequities between men and women. Ten of the twenty-four women players interviewed who had tennis-playing husbands specifically stated in some way, and without being asked, that their husbands were better players than they. Alice, reflecting on her own tennis career, advised young women today to continue to play competitively through their childbearing years. She then went on to explain the difficulties they may meet, including how the most competitive women's competition was scheduled at the same time as the men's. This meant, she explained, that a baby-sitter would be necessary and, ". . . so invariably, I'd say, because they probably can't afford that, it's the man that plays rather than the woman, unless she happens to be a top player." Thus a rationale of achievement and success is applied to justify women's leisure.

The issue of comparable ability had another, more subtle, side to it. Alice explained that because her husband was a better player than she, when they went to tournaments together she would be out of the competition earlier, which meant,

> He played a lot more competition. We used to go to tournaments and things and he always got to the finals and I'd be out much earlier. So, yes, I looked after the kids, so he could play more.

Another rationale concerned comparable ability at providing child care. It is easy to see how gendered notions of who is good at what can become reproduced. The logic seemed to be, if the husband was considered "better" at tennis, he played more tennis; if the wife was considered "better" at child care, she did more child care. Karen's explanation of child care arrangements when both she and her husband played pennant competition at different venues concluded with an explanation of how she felt more relaxed if her two children were with her.

> I also probably tended to take the boys with me to pennants much more than [husband] ever did, . . . that was probably my choice, I probably worried myself sick if he had taken them. He would have got so involved in his tennis one could have run across the freeway and he wouldn't have noticed. I tended to always take both of them and yet I was playing pennants too. . . . I think [husband] preferred it that I did it. I don't think he would have demanded. If I said, 'Look I'm getting absolutely fed up with taking the kids every week,' I'm sure he would have taken them, but I think in all honesty I was happier taking them.

This lack of faith in the ability of the children's fathers to provide adequate supervision of children while involved in tennis was something that had contributed to Pauline's, a non playing wife of a player, giving up on an attempt to become a tennis player. She explained,

> I did play, yeah, for a little while, when the oldest one was fairly small. [Husband] used to baby-sit when I was playing, but you know, a few times she galloped away, out towards the highway. I'd be out on the court and see this kid running towards the highway and think, aghhh! that's my girl! What are you doing?

The notion of "shared" child care also needs closer scrutiny. Karen explained how it was she, rather than her husband, who had responded to the needs and wishes of their children when they all went to the tennis club together. For example, at the end of a Saturday or Sunday of tennis, when her two young children were tired and hungry, she would take them home to feed, bathe, and put them to bed while their father stayed at the tennis club to socialize. At the time of the interview she expressed considerable frustration because of his recent decision to play in the pennant team of another, more distant, tennis club and thereby become a member of that club. This meant, she argued, he would be spending his time at this new club, and not with her and their children at their local club, of which they had been members for many years. She had no interest in changing clubs and was angered by what his change would therefore mean in terms of his time with his family and his lack of consideration for their interests.

Trudi was giving reasons why she and her husband had changed tennis clubs to one closer to their home. She explained how they had considered the previous club too far from their new home and how the driving was especially uneconomical when they went in two separate cars. This they had done frequently when the children were young because she would wait until they had woken from their afternoon nap before going to tennis, while he went earlier. She gave a detailed account of the preparation required to take the children to the club with her.

> I have to pack their lunch and I'd have a little [cooler] with me and when they were smaller I had emergency things like twistees because I knew as soon as I give them something new, or something to eat they would settle down. I always kept lollies or twistees or something in my bag in case they would become a bit unsettled or whatever. And I took toys along, and things for them to draw.

Overall, child care was a major concern for the women players interviewed who could not always assume, as the male players had, that it would be done by the child's or children's other parent. Women players managed their playing in ways that took this responsibility into account continually, relying mostly on other women for assistance. Only in cases where the child's father was also a tennis player did he undertake child care to facilitate his wife's tennis, and this was usually restricted to short periods of time when they were both at the tennis club together. His responsibility for this was limited, however, especially if the children were very young and it frequently meant that, when tennis interests competed, Mum's was more expendable.

Managing housework: "Just a little bit of organization." It was usual for the interviewed women players to talk about child care as being their accepted and "rightful" role. It was even more so concerning the domestic labor of maintaining households and their families' welfare. For all fifteen of the interviewed veteran women players, this had been, and usually continued to be, entirely their responsibility. June and Brenda told me that their husbands now cooked some of the meals, a development that had occurred since the women had returned to paid work when their children were older. For most, however, maintenance of the household was taken for granted as something that they did. When we talked about what they did and how they managed in order to be able to play tennis, the strongest theme to emerge was the women's perceptions of themselves as being well organized. They made comments such as, "I'm a very organized person" (Alice), "I'm an organizer" (Marilyn), and "Just a little bit of organization" (Ruth). Molly was the only veteran player interviewed who willingly provided any form of detailed account of what this entailed.

> I had to be organized otherwise I don't think I could do it if I wasn't organized. I had to work to a routine and sometimes I might let something go and catch up the next day. And if that day of tennis wasn't really important, I'd still go, but I'd only stay for two sets and come home and catch up on the chores because the day after that, that was a more important day for me at tennis which was going to be a whole day . . . Sometimes we'd go down and have a hit up on the Tuesday and I'd come home and I'd cook tea and I'd put on something for Wednesday night because I found that playing tennis, if you had a really hard day, there's nothing worse coming home to have to think, what are you going to give the family for tea. Well, if you'd got something organized, it's easy to sort of just warm it up and it's never been a burden really.

Being organized was necessary, however, in order to ensure that playing tennis did not have an adverse affect on women's ability to get the housework done. It could take considerable effort to maintain a high standard of household orderliness as well as to play tennis, as Betty highlighted.

Betty had played tennis for fifty-four years. She was now retired but had worked full-time in paid employment for most of her adult life. She spoke of frequently being up until midnight on Friday nights doing housework so that she could go to tennis the next day. She said, "I was terribly fussy about the house in the early days. I used to polish the front verandah and things like that." During the interview, her husband Des came into the house, and she called him into the room to meet me. She initiated the conversation with wry humor. It went like this:

BETTY: Des, Shona just asked me a question you might be able to answer. How did I manage to organize my personal life, doing housework and looking after you and [son] and working and also playing tennis. She asked me how I organized all that, fitted it in. Can you answer that?

DES: Well I'll tell you, she used to come down and pinch the car off me when I had it down at the pub and drive off to tennis and leave me stranded without a motorcar.

BETTY: I did not. I always walked to tennis anyway.

DES: You did this day. We all came out of the pub and hey! where's my car gone? (laughs) Well, I think you're pretty methodical with what you do especially. . . . Well, you did have a lot on your plate, but the tennis court's not far from here and we didn't do much other than that. We'd go to work and Betty would play tennis. . . . But, I don't know, I think a lot of the mothers were in the same predicament, you know. They'd have to do everything and scramble a bit. There'd be some days when we probably had to wear the same shirt twice.

BETTY: Oh fiddlesticks! I don't ever remember either of you saying "I'll do the vacuuming this weekend, Mum." Who would've ever said that?

DES: Ah well, we men are not born that way. That's a different generation. Well, got to go.

Despite Betty's years of effort to single-handedly maintain the house, provide domestic service for her husband and their child, and not have her tennis impact upon them, Des still wished to record a singular incident where he had been inconvenienced.

These women did not generally expect assistance with housework from other members of their families. Only Frances and Molly spoke specifically of how their children did things that helped them get to tennis. In both cases, these children were daughters, and in both tellings, it seemed laughter was being used as a way of offsetting a hint of guilt over having put their tennis ahead of their children's needs. Frances spoke of her daughter cooking meals at age ten.

> I don't remember it but she does. She tells me I was off playing tennis and left her to cook dinner. She really likes cooking. I was being a good mother wasn't I, encouraging her, giving her all that opportunity! (laughs)

And Molly,

> I used to say to the kids, 'Right, it's Mum's tennis day!' They
> knew that they just could not get sick on Mum's tennis days.
> They knew that you just don't ask questions on Mum's tennis
> days and you got out of bed early on Mum's tennis days and
> that's how it was always. (laughs)

Four of the veteran women had had paid help with domestic
work, but the extent of this varied considerably. One woman had a
woman "come in" on average about once a week for more years
than she could remember, and she described it as "a godsend." For
another it had been only once a month for about a year. She did not
view this as necessary but had decided it was worthwhile only in
that it motivated her children to tidy up their bedrooms. All of
these women had been in paid employment themselves, and the
assistance they employed was with housecleaning and for two,
some laundry.

Middle-class affluence benefited these women in other ways,
such as in their levels of material comfort and their ownership of
household appliances. Linda gave an example of how she used this
to organize her domestic responsibilities around her tennis.

> Then you have to get special stoves that will turn themselves
> on when you're not home. I had to do that, so the dinner
> would go on while I'm at my tennis on Saturday and it's get-
> ting late talking and mucking around afterwards. . . . I didn't
> tell you about that, I just bought an automatic stove. It turns
> itself on, it cooks the dinner, it turns itself off, as long as I
> remember to put the food in it before I leave (laughs), which is
> great, and you've got microwaves that help too.

Paid work: "I'm lucky, I don't work." The availability of time
and the degree of organization required to get to tennis would, of
course, be compounded if the women were involved in paid
employment. However, of the fifteen veteran players interviewed,
six had not been in any form of paid employment since the birth of
their first child. The tennis of these women was predominantly
played during weekdays and they would likely play most frequently, perhaps three or four times a week. They might also play
during the weekend, if their husbands also played tennis or had
another interest during that time, such as Dorothy's husband, who

played lawn bowls, or Linda's, who was a musician. The women's playing time was possible because they all were, or had been, married to men who had been employed full time in paid work and who financially provided for them and their families. One of these women, at age seventy, was widowed, working class, and not well off. The remainder, however, were middle class women and financially comfortable. While they considered that their work was caring for their homes and families, there was the perception that this gendered division of labor somehow privileged them, in comparison to their husbands, in terms of allowing a more flexible lifestyle that could accommodate playing sport. Carol had played tennis, squash, and golf. She was explaining how women's golf, like tennis, is scheduled mid week and said, "I'm lucky, I don't work so I can play then." A remnant of the historical, classed association of tennis as a sport for "ladies" with leisure (Hargreaves 1994; Stoddart 1986) remains today. The larger proportion of women's tennis is scheduled inside what are normally paid working hours, and women's tennis is still officially termed *ladies'* tennis.

Three of these veteran players had coached tennis professionally, thus shifting their tennis involvement from what could be defined as leisure to being associated with paid work. For two, Patricia and Anne, this had been a long-term commitment alongside their husbands' and contributed further to their immersion in servicing tennis. Anne spoke of it as "helping" her husband in his professional coaching role, and how they had done it for the promotion of the sport rather than for any great financial reward. She said, "We had enough without having to make a great deal of money out of it and so our fees were very reasonable compared to the present ones." Patricia was part of a successful tennis coaching business that she and her husband had set up in partnership when they got married. She laughingly told me how it was called "[his name]'s School of Tennis," and said, "I didn't even put in my name. I never thought about it . . . I was quite happy with that. Well I was home, as I say, a lot more than he was." For these two women it was difficult to draw distinctions between their own work and sport, their husbands' work and sport, and the work required to service them all.

Five of the interviewed players had worked in part-time paid employment and spoke of the ways they arranged it alongside their tennis. Marilyn explained how she had started her job when her first child was three months old, saying, "I needed to get out of the house and not be tied to the house with kids." Then,

When the kids went to school I played mid-week pennants. I worked at [firm's name] on Fridays and Saturdays and as I gained seniority at work I didn't need to work Saturdays so started playing Saturday pennants as well.

A degree of choice and flexibility was made possible by the financial security of having a full-time working husband. For Sarah, her tennis took priority. She explained,

That's why I work four days a week, I play mid-week tennis (laughs). It's very hard to get a job too, I can tell you. I must have applied for hundreds in my day, and I'd say no I don't want to work Wednesdays.

She joked about how her work colleagues referred to Wednesdays as her "religious" day. Although Alice had worked full time, it was in a profession that had allowed a certain amount of flexibility and autonomy. She had organized her schedule to work one evening of the week, hence, she said, "I had some Wednesday time off and I played mid-week pennants then."

Brenda had worked full time for seventeen years but still managed to play tennis on both Saturdays and Sundays. She explained this by referring to her organizational skills and her "luck." She said,

I feel if you want to do something, you'll organize the housework. The same with work for me. That doesn't upset me. I'll get up and I'll do the housework before I go to work so I don't have a hassle at all. And then I'm lucky in as much as I've got a husband who will help which is good. I mean, he doesn't mind cooking a meal or that sort of thing.

Being in paid employment did not substantially relieve these women from responsibility for domestic work, from which time for their tennis had to be squeezed. As some of the women married to tennis-playing men later showed, if these labor demands became too great it would likely be the women's tennis that "gave way." The veteran players who were or had been in paid work were obviously "survivors" of these sorts of multiple demands, in that they had found ways to cope and were still playing tennis. It could be, however, at considerable cost to themselves. Molly described her work routine leading up to a serious health problem.

I never used to let my chores go down. We used to have a farm up at Gidgegannup [distance approx. 35 km.]. We had sheep on there and I used to get [husband] up for work at 4:30 [A.M.]. He'd shoot off to [work] and I'd be not far behind him, shoot up to Gidgegannup, . . . checked the water, checked the stock, chucked out twenty bales [of hay] and zipped back in the car, come home and have a quick shower and by then, [children] would be moving and going to school or wherever they were off to. Zippy round, clean up and about 9 [A.M.] I'd be off to tennis. Or I'd do it the other way round. I'd water all the garden, do here first, go to tennis, finish at tennis by 12:30–12:45 [P.M.], come home, get changed, zippy up there, feed out and come home, be home by 3:30–4 [P.M.], and off to tennis again the next morning. Sometimes I wonder how I did it. . . . There was only one time there, just before I got sick. We were playing this game at [club] and I thought, now next year it's either the farm or tennis, it's one or the other, something's got to go, because I found it was draining me a lot to keep the pace up. . . . When I got sick, I'd say my body was telling me that I've been overloading, but I just wasn't taking any notice.

I could not help but be impressed at the often incredible lengths to which these women went in order to find their own leisure time and pursue an activity of their choice. It took an enormous amount of organization and hard work for these women to get themselves to tennis. On the other hand, tennis was structured in such a way as to accommodate many of these demands.

Keeping it invisible: "My house and my husband had to come first." For tennis-playing women, an important explanation of how they maintained a playing presence was that the sport accommodated their roles as mothers and wives in a relatively unproblematic manner. The gendered and class structure of tennis provided the support necessary so that it was a feasible leisure activity for women that neither disrupted nor seriously challenged expectations of normative roles or the women's ability to function acceptably in them.

Keeping their sport contained within school and normal paid work hours was necessary so as not to have it challenge their ability to be good mothers and wives. In one sense, being "at home" caring for babies and pre-school children had already positioned women invisibly so that playing tennis was inconsequential. This social position allowed the space for it. Dorothy explained the beginning of her midweek playing.

> I worked for three years after I got married so I couldn't play then, and weekends I spent with my husband because he didn't play tennis, but then once I had a child and I was home, that's when I went back to playing tennis.

Another issue raised here by Dorothy is the relationship of women's tennis to the schedules of their husbands. Dorothy's going "back to" tennis meant playing mid week, whereas before her marriage she had played during weekends. While the women interviewed spoke mostly about how the midweek tennis schedule accommodated their responsibilities to their children, it was also important that it located their play conveniently during times when their husbands were in paid employment. This meant their tennis simply did not impose in any significant way on their partners. There is strong evidence to suggest that married women's tennis could be as much, if not more, restricted by responsibilities to husbands as to children. Children could more easily be, and were, inconvenienced by their mothers' tennis, if only by the fact they were taken along and, as Alice described, could be left to scream their heads off at the end of the court.

Quite definite patterns emerged from these interviews concerning the influence on the women's tennis of whether or not they were married to men who also played. If a husband did not play tennis, it was most likely that his wife's playing would be restricted to times that were kept hidden from him. Thus, it would remain predominantly during the week, when he was in paid employment, and generally not involve much weekend play. The logic of this rationale was given by Sally when she was explaining why some women in her club might only be midweek members. She said,

> [Women players] could have played on the weekend, but many of them had small children and maybe if their husbands didn't play then of course they wouldn't play on a weekend because it would interrupt family routine.

This implies a situation where a woman's leisure time, in which she may pursue a chosen sporting activity, is defined as that time when family members, especially husbands, are not at home. This time, therefore, is largely determined by her husband's paid work. Molly summarized,

> Like with this Vets thing, I don't go to any of those because I try to keep my weekends with my family and my husband, because I feel that, because he doesn't play sport . . . I just feel that if I go to play tennis and he's left home here, it just doesn't seem right. He doesn't complain about me going during the week. I've got all week. He said I can play from Monday to Friday, it wouldn't worry him, but weekends, he likes you to [be home], and that's the same with the family.

The women's participation in other aspects of tennis, such as social gatherings or out-of-town tournaments, could similarly be limited by their husbands' interests. Dorothy explained why she did not travel to such events.

> I'd never go on my own and leave my husband home, but then he's not interested in it so we wouldn't go to that. I think, like I said, I'm lucky to still have my husband. A lot of women haven't and that's why they go.

Four of the six veteran women players who were married to nonplaying men did, however, play during weekends, if only locally. Mostly they explained this as occurring because their husbands had consuming interests of their own in which they were involved at the same time, thus creating space for wives to increase their tennis participation. For example, Dorothy had only recently begun to play during weekends following her children leaving home. She explained, "See, he bowls at the weekend so I sort of said, well he's playing bowls, I might as well play tennis." She explained how he had wanted her to join him at lawn bowls, so she became a member of his lawn bowls club for a brief time. However, men and women did not generally play bowls at the same time, so the objective of sharing weekend time with her husband was not satisfactorily fulfilled by this sport. Instead, she joined weekend tennis.

Linda's husband played in a musical ensemble; Frances, although now divorced, spoke of how her ex-husband had been involved with cars. She was the only one of these four women who had gone away to tournaments outside Perth, and had done so while she was still married. She explained how she had left her children at home, saying, "That's the only time their father looked after them." However, she also referred to times when the children went to stay with cousins, thus freeing her husband from that responsibility.

Betty spoke of how her husband went to the horse races on Saturday afternoons and she took her son, while young, to tennis with her. However, Betty's situation has a different logic that highlights the economic imperatives underlying the positioning of women's and men's leisure and the rationales that tend to keep women's hidden. Betty had been in full-time paid employment for virtually of all her adult life. Her paid work during the week "earned" her this entitlement to leisure on Saturday, and thus her tennis, in much the same way as men in full-time paid employment, are considered entitled. Women not in paid employment, who work as "housewives," are not considered to have earned their leisure in the same manner, and therefore their tennis becomes a somewhat illegitimate pleasure to be undertaken secretively. Trudi described a friend of hers whose husband was "a bit touchy" about the amount of tennis she played. Trudi recounted,

> She said, as soon as it's nine o'clock and he's out of the house she quickly grabs her tennis gear and out she goes, and quickly washes everything [afterwards] so that he doesn't see that she played tennis.

Housework is not considered "real" work, or at least, not demanding work, characterized by flexibility and autonomy. For this reason, "housewives" are frequently deemed as "leisured." Within this conceptualization, the hidden nature of women's tennis compromises both women's work and women's leisure. "Hidden leisure" is a contradiction in terms for the way it denies agency. Central to this dynamic are the gender-based divisions of labor that deem housework and child care as predominantly women's work. However, this division does not necessarily break down with women's involvement in paid work, and thus women's entitlement to leisure must frequently be earned through diligence to domestic work as well. Recall Betty's description of being up until midnight on Friday nights before tennis, doing the vacuuming.

Another way in which the interviewed women strove to keep their tennis from becoming overly conspicuous to their families was in the considerable lengths to which they would frequently go to make sure it had no detrimental impact on their ability to do the housework. Frances commented,

> Do you know, I played sport and I played a lot, but I can't bear leaving my house untidy. Always had the beds made, everything was done before I'd go out. I would never go out and leave beds unmade and dishes not done. But my children say I drive them mad with my organization.

There is a sense that these women had to continually keep their tennis within narrow confines, which meant on a priority scale below children, husbands, and households.

Molly is a worthwhile example to highlight. She illustrated well the contradictions and difficulties experienced when trying to maintain an equilibrium between what are frequently conflicting roles as sportswoman and wife/mother/homemaker. Her account showed how she juggled priorities and at times lived a charade so as not to lose grip on the delicate balance she was maintaining, or make it conspicuous that these roles were sometimes in conflict. At one point in the interview, she stated,

> I've always managed. I always have my theory that if I went to play sport, then my children and my house and my husband had to come first and I've got myself organized for that. I had to be organized, otherwise I don't think I could do it if I wasn't organized.

Although she expressed this as being unproblematic at the time, she had previously acknowledged the difficulties of living this way. When I initially spoke with her on the telephone to arrange an interview, she told me how much she enjoyed playing tennis and how important it was to her. She laughed and said that at times it was her number one priority, but "I'd never let my family know that." During the interview, she inferred how she had pushed the limits of her family's tolerance of her sporting schedule, recognizing that these were her boundaries and needing to test them. "I started off with one day, then two days, then three days, and I've gone as high as four days and there was strife over that as well." She explained how her husband had tried to limit her play and how she had resisted.

He used to whinge a bit. . . . But the more he whinged, the more I thought I'd stick at it (laughs). He just thought, "She's not going to surrender and that's it." However, he constantly niggled at it. He'd say to me Tuesday night, and with all these years I'd been playing tennis he'd still say, "Are you going to tennis on Wednesday?" And I'd always say to him, 'Yes, I'm off nice and early in the morning.'

When her husband came into the room briefly during the interview, Molly described him as "a very understanding husband." However, the practicalities of maintaining this balance depended on her ability to continually perform the domestic work expected of her and reaffirm her control and agency within the understood parameters. She explained,

I had to work to a routine and sometimes I might let something go and catch up the next day. And if that day of tennis wasn't really important I'd still go, but I'd only stay for two sets and come home and catch up on the chores because the day after that, that was a more important day for me at tennis which was going to be the whole day. So I worked around that. I worked around the kids, the husband.

She also explained that she "did the roast" dinner on Monday nights, to "get it out of the way" before tennis days, which started on Tuesday. In a quite explicit way, Molly described the common conditions by which these women experienced their tennis, playing it around the needs of "the kids," "the husband," and the housework.

The process that rendered women's tennis invisible was most obvious at three interconnected levels. Individually, women organized their own time and labor and managed their respective households in order to fit this into their lives. Collectively, they assisted each other, especially with child care, so as a group they could play. Their tennis stayed hidden through their own ability to be well organized and through help from other women. Structurally, the administration and infrastructure of women's midweek tennis provided the opportunities for women to play without compromising or disrupting their expected domestic duties. At all three levels lay the assumption that women's leisure was prescribed by domestic and caring roles and could not impact on others.

The "Midweek Ladies Shield Competition" had been organized in such a way as to specifically cater to women who were not in full-time paid employment, but were predominantly home-makers with husbands and children. Furthermore, it acknowledged, by its structure, that a woman's responsibilities to a male partner and her children was the first priority, thus creating a leisure opportunity that was unproblematic and unchallenging to those responsibilities. It took its very logic from middle-class heterosexual coupleness and gendered division of labor, assuming the male was in full-time paid employment during a "regular" working week, while female work was caring for a husband and children. A woman's "free" time, thus the opportunity to play tennis, was constructed by this definition.

Immersed in families: "Tennis is our life." The definition shifted partially for those women who were married to tennis-playing men. A woman's tennis became more visible, it seemed, both within tennis administration and among other family members, if she had a tennis-playing husband. If this was the case, the women players would be more likely to play during weekends as well as midweek; to travel away to play in country tournaments; to have children who became tennis players; and to be involved in administrative positions, particularly within the more "integrated" tennis structures. To varying degrees, this was the situation for twenty-four of the total group of forty-six women interviewed: nine of the veteran women players; eight of the wives; and seven of the mothers interviewed.

June was perhaps one of the more extreme examples, although other women interviewed had similar stories. She found it difficult to express how enormously significant tennis was to her family and said repeatedly, "Tennis is our life. I just could not imagine life without tennis now." This seemed to summarize the amount of tennis June and her husband had played; the contribution they had both made to demanding administrative positions in their club; the sports' relevance to their three adult children, who had all played continuously since they were young; its significance to the way all family members related to each other; the family's long-standing commitment to tennis-based holidays; and the importance of other tennis-playing families to their friendships and social life. While players such as June obviously had a higher profile in tennis and their playing was much less confined to "invisible" hours, they nevertheless illustrated how women's tennis could become immersed in family care and responsibility, rendering it invisible in a different way and casting doubt on the extent to which individual agency motivates the leisure choice.

As with most of these "immersed" women, June's competitive tennis was mostly played during the week, in women's midweek pennants. When she could no longer play at that time, she had ceased playing tennis completely. Her priority on weekends, therefore, remained as it always had been, centered on the welfare of her family and the interests of her husband. In marked contrast to a man's tennis, a woman's tennis could not, in itself, disrupt "family routine." However, if he also was a tennis player, weekends would become the time when tennis frequently *became* the family routine and her responsibilities shifted into that realm.

Having a tennis-playing husband could mean that a woman's tennis no longer remained invisible to her family or separate from her responsibilities to their care. Instead, these responsibilities were incorporated into the sport and became so integral to it that her own involvement as a player was an extension of those responsibilities, extending that care into a further dimension of family members' lives. Tennis, family life, and relationships with family members and extended social groups all became intertwined, and the sport became pivotal to this. Their work, however, did not cease once they got there. Further labor was required for the administration of tennis and the continuation of its structural and cultural practices.

Sport Administration Labor

Traditionally, sporting clubs and organizations in Australia operate on the voluntary work done by their members. In most clubs, the only professional worker might be a tennis coach and/or a groundskeeper, which may not be full-time positions. The traditional development of sports clubs in Australia was first based upon the provision of public land by the local government authority and then administered by the volunteer labor of those people who made up the sports club membership. Some tennis clubs, those that have grown in membership and financial resources, may eventually employ some additional professional services, but most clubs in Western Australia function almost entirely on the voluntary labor of their members. For such a club to run smoothly, and the sporting and social objectives to be satisfactorily met, an immense amount of work is required. From the experiences of the veteran women players, this work was predominantly done by women.

The players interviewed were unanimous in their agreement that, within tennis clubs, women did more of the work. Betty had been editor of her club's newsletter. She said,

> Women do far more work in the club. I worked it out once exactly what positions they had and the percentage of men and women were in it. I put it in the [club] newsletter but nothing was said about it.

From the interviews it became obvious that there were three major areas where women's work was concentrated: supplementary fund-raising, social facilitation, and catering. As well as being highly interrelated, these tasks were mostly continual demands that also had strong associations with women's domestic and caring labor. Men, on the other hand, were more likely to hold key official positions within the club administration, and the women interviewed associated the men's labor most frequently with the maintenance of courts and grounds.

Fund-raising: "In lieu of a lamington drive." It has been a long-standing practice in Australian culture for women to work as supplementary fund-raisers for male-dominated institutions, and it is not just confined to sport. Women's "auxiliaries" are part of hospitals, schools, and charity organizations, as well as sporting organizations, and account for huge amounts of women's voluntary community labor (Baldock 1983). In those sports where the players have traditionally been almost exclusively men, such as in Australian Rules Football, there will invariably exist women's auxiliaries to provide backup support for men's and boys' play. In tennis, the inequities in this practice are softened a little by the fact that women are also active players, but nevertheless, men remain the policy and decision makers, holding most of the administrative positions. Women's auxiliaries function with the primary role of raising funds to augment the coffers of the "main," male-dominated organization. The Western Australian Women's Auxiliary of WALTA is one such establishment.

One of the veteran players interviewed, Marilyn, was the president of the Women's Auxiliary at the time of the interview, and had been for three years. She explained its history.

> The Women's Auxiliary was originally commenced to raise money for WALTA, as a women's auxiliary body, to raise

money when they needed it, to organize the cups of tea and all that sort of thing originally and raise a bit of money to send the kids [to tournaments] interstate. That's how it started.

Marilyn related how, in the past, the women predominantly baked cakes to sell to raise the money, but in 1962 the committee of five women "came upon this brilliant idea that they'd have a midweek pennant competition" for women and charge each player a dollar. This money would be given to WALTA.

So that's why the Women's Auxiliary members pay a dollar for their [pennant program] book, which the weekend pennants [players] get free, . . . But it is in lieu of a lamington drive, which they used to have! (laughs) Isn't that typical? Going back in time they used to make hundreds and hundreds of lamingtons to raise money for WALTA.[1]

Thus was the origin of the "ladies" midweek shield competition, which began in 1962 with six teams. By the summer season of 1989, there were 161 teams. Marilyn commented it was likely that very few women now playing in this competition knew of or remembered its original purpose, but nevertheless, "It has never ever changed and Women's Auxiliary is still seen as a fund-raising group, and every year we hand a check over to [WALTA]."

The Women's Auxiliary's concern with and support of children's tennis had also continued. Every year this organization runs a major tournament for schoolchildren. The food catering they do in conjunction with this tournament also is a fund-raising effort. Linda, who was treasurer for the Women's Auxiliary, commented,

We cater for the school children's tournament and we send the ladies out and they have to be there, do all the work, all day, It's hard work, and raises the money that we give back to WALTA.

Catering at tournaments and other tennis functions is one of the activities the Women's Auxiliary has traditionally been called upon by WALTA to provide. Recently, Marilyn explained, the Womens' Auxiliary suggested that the members of the club hosting each tournament be given the option of doing the catering as an oppor-

tunity to raise funds for their club. At this level, the work would
still mainly be done by women. Marilyn thought about her own
club.

> Not being a big club, we don't run many tournaments at all,
> but when we get them it's mainly the women, and a few
> retired men who have the time to do that.

While the traditional role and purpose of the Women's Auxiliary is to raise funds for the "main" Association, for WALTA these
funds are actually peripheral. The Association does not need to rely
upon them in order to function. As Marilyn said,

> We are only there as a supportive group to WALTA . . . because
> they do have a separate fund-raising member of the WALTA
> executive who runs fund-raising functions and that sort of
> thing. It is a bonus to them.

For this reason, the Women's Auxiliary is able to designate how the
funds will be spent.

Women's work toward providing service and financial support is
built structurally into tennis. It proliferates at all levels of organization, from the formalized auxiliary structure to the work women do
collectively within clubs, as well as the individual roles they take on
in the administration. The gendered assumptions of this role, that it
is women's work and the work that women do best, mean that it is
not only understood as the purpose for a women's organization such
as the Auxiliary, but the logic extends to determine which offices are
designated to women within the tennis organizations generally.

The "fund-raising member of the WALTA Executive Committee," to whom Marilyn referred was likely to be the position considered most appropriate for a female member of the Committee.
Marilyn described an example of how the perception of "women's
work" and fund-raising was conflated in administrators' eyes. She
explained how the Women's Auxiliary was not officially represented on the WALTA Executive Committee, and in her capacity as
president of the Auxiliary she had written to the Committee "suggesting that perhaps they would like to add a women's representative." She commented on the response.

> They thought I was being all very ambitious and that I was the
> one who wanted to be on the executive, so they offered me a

position on the executive, which I said I didn't want. They offered me the fund-raising position, which I thought was brilliant (laughs) and I said no, that wasn't why we wrote the letter.

Jean had been a member of the WALTA Executive Committee for more years than she could remember. For some time she had been responsible for "promotion" of tennis. She recalled how she "got sick of that" and threatened to resign.

So [the president would] say, "Well you can have another job." So then I did fund-raising, which I quite enjoyed actually. I did that for many years and really liked that, it was good. I mean, you've got to raise a hell of a lot of money every year.

Within the clubs, fund-raising, was also women's work. Some of the larger clubs, those with more affluent members and a valuable resource base in amenities, are not so reliant on the fund-raising efforts of members, or approached it in a different manner. For example, members may be levied if extra funds are needed. Jean explained how this had become a more common occurrence at her club and expressed disapproval at the club moving away from practices that relied on the voluntary work commitment of members. However, according to Marilyn, "There's very few really financially well-off tennis clubs. They are around, but not many."

Betty and Noelene were both founding members of the same club that was established in a working-class area of Perth. Betty spoke of the fund-raising.

We had to do a lot of fund-raising. We held major raffles. We've had cake stalls, and socials, things like that. We have a lotto thing every Saturday now. The midweek ladies do a good job. They have a gala day and invite other clubs and they make money that way. I was involved in the beginning, well I am now too I suppose, midweek, because we always have to have stalls and everyone makes cakes. I've got a raffle book out there now to sell. . . . We have a little raffle every Wednesday, thirty cents a ticket for a pot plant or a pair of tennis socks or something like that. . . . But I think the women, in any organization that men and women are involved in probably, are predominant in the work they do. Well they do in our club, I'm sure about that. And raise more of the money.

Noelene and her husband had both been awarded life memberships to their club as a tribute to the work they had done. Noelene's was awarded five years before her husband. Her account of her involvement in the fund-raising and social activities of the club was phenomenal, and difficult to convey in a few lines. The following is an attempt:

NOELENE: I'm fund-raiser this year again, mainly raffles. I'm not the social organizer now, I used to be, I'm not now, I'm just the fund-raiser. I was social organizer off and on for about fifteen years.

Q.: And the fund-raising?

NOELENE: Well, my husband, if I haven't done it, he's done it. So that's why we fund-raise all the time. Well we have to, to keep the grass courts going. . . . We had to start from scratch. We had nothing up there at the club. . . . Now we have marvelous facilities, which is a huge hall, big bar, big amenities room, lovely kitchen. I do the hall bookings, and we've also just put in four hard courts and I do the letting out of the courts, those are my jobs. . . . We've got to keep raising money all the time to keep our club viable because [another club] has just closed up. They weren't able to keep it [going]. It costs us a lot of money a year. We've got a permanent groundsman and his wages and his superannuation to pay. So you really do have to work very hard . . . I think we've been very good for the club. I'm still collecting cans for the blessed club and taking them in. I might only make eighty dollars in about six bags of cans, but I still collect them.

As well as this, Noelene had been social organizer/fund-raiser for the social committee of her husband's employment, the social committee of her own paid employment where she had worked full time for twelve years, for her husband's football club, and for her church.

When Marilyn was asked who did the fund-raising in her club, her response came in such a way that, by the time she had finished speaking, her answer was a revelation to herself. She said,

Well, I would say, at [club], when we wanted something we have a special fund-raising drive. When we wanted the pergola built or a new lawn mower bought or something like that, then it's a fund-raising group, which is run by the social committee, which is 90 percent women! yeah! (laughs)

Social facilitation: "It falls on women's shoulders." Marilyn's response highlighted the strong connection between fund-raising work and the activities of those responsible for the "social" aspects of tennis culture. Linda observed that these were both tasks done by women when she said,

> I've discovered that in some of the clubs in the city, it seems to me that there's a lot of ongoing fund-raising, and it predominantly falls on the women's shoulders in terms of their greater involvement in the social committee, their running of raffles, running of Gala Days. Everything that will happen like that will fall on the women's shoulders. It just does, men just don't do that.

Many social activities in a tennis club were organized specifically to generate revenue for the club. Furthermore, many of these involve food, the catering of which was also women's work. These connections help explain the extent to which women were involved in the continual labor that maintained a club.

Much of the regular, ongoing fund-raising activities such as raffles and gala days was carried out within women's tennis, and thus it was women who were making the financial contribution as well as doing the work. Gala days, for example, were traditional fund-raising events held by most clubs every year. They were organized by women tennis club members for women guests from other clubs, and occurred within the calendar of women's midweek tennis. All of the interviewed veteran players spoke of Gala Days, either being involved in them when hosted by their club or attending them as visitors to other clubs. In terms of the work involved, Dorothy explained,

> Like we have a Gala Day once a year, where you invite people from all other clubs to come and pay a fee and play for the day. And we have to all bring cakes and sandwiches, or we make sandwiches actually for sale, but we bring cakes and that sort of thing for morning and afternoon tea. We provide those for visitors and there's always a lot of work to be done for that, organizing that day. You take on a job on the day. You might be the gatekeeper or you might be the score taker or something like that. That's just the one day a year that we have fund-raising like that. This year we handed $950 over to the club from our day in November.

Across Australia, Melbourne Cup Race Day is observed as a special festival. This horse race, traditionally held on the first Tuesday in November, has become an event that tennis clubs, like hundreds of other work and leisure organizations, take on as a special event. In the club to which both Noelene and Betty belonged, it was celebrated with a luncheon catered by Noelene. She explained, "I do that by myself. I do the catering fully and the girls help set it out in the end, but I've been doing that as a fund-raising thing for the last six years." She described how she provided three different meat dishes, thirteen to fourteen different salads, garlic bread, five different desserts, cream, and ice cream,

> and that costs you six dollars for that . . . [This year] I charged seventy-one people six dollars and I made $210, and I thought that was brilliant for the tennis club because if I make it too dear, the older people that are on pensions can't come. . . . Now people say to me, "Oh how can you do it for six dollars?" But all the plastic spoons and that, I rewash . . . I might lose so many, but then I don't have to buy them all the time. The only thing I buy now, I never used to, I used to use china plates, but I do buy paper plates now to save the girls washing up and I've got enough cutlery myself . . . that would supply 100 people, so I really don't have to buy knives and forks.

Being the "social organizer," that is, the person who is designated as being responsible for social activities, is a position most likely to be held by a woman in both the club administration as well as the WALTA Executive Committee. It is this role that cements the connection between fund-raising and catering. However, it also means that women create the social atmosphere, facilitating the friendliness or "familiness" of tennis culture. This is an important aspect of sporting club life, while at the same time being actually peripheral to the main objective, which is playing the sport. In this respect, it can be viewed as an adjunct, a "trimming" to the sport. However, it is a trimming that helps bind together the members of clubs and organizations, facilitating the interpersonal contact that makes a voluntary organization possible, effective, and enduring. Thus women provide the social fabric upon which the sport depends for its continuation in the community. The organization of social events is a vitally important part of a club's continued health.

Another important aspect is communication among members. Betty, as she mentioned earlier, wrote and distributed the newsletter for her club for several years. Jean and Frances were similarly involved. One of Jean's tasks was "dispatcher" of the newsletter for the Veteran's Tennis Club. This contained details of all of the playing fixtures, such as who played whom, where, and when, and it was distributed four times a year. Jean had a "team" of women who helped her with this.

> We sit around this table and we swear at one another and carry on. There's 600 or so [newsletters], because they go all across to other states and seven go overseas. They spill into the other room, envelopes everywhere.

Frances was a member of the team, and she explained how she and Jean had been doing this distribution for many years. "The dispatcher gets changed but the actual group who does it stays the same." The Veteran's Club president (who, in the history of this organization in Western Australia, had always been a man) was responsible for the content of the newsletter, but it was the "nitty-gritty" work of these women who compiled, folded, addressed, and posted it, which maintained the communication network upon which the organization depended. Jean commented about the men in this organization. "Give them their credit, they'd be the first to tell you they'd be lost without the women, in getting things done."

Catering: "Women have always done the teas." The relationship of food to special social/fund-raising events, such as Melbourne Cup luncheons and Gala Days, has already been highlighted, along with the role women play in its provision. However, the provision of food and drinks also is an everyday aspect of tennis culture. Serving refreshments for other club members, extending hospitality to visiting players, and generally facilitating the social ambience within the club through sharing food and drink is work done almost exclusively by women members. Within the all-women sphere of midweek pennant tennis, women provide food for each other, as Molly explained.

> The home team always takes a plate. I might take sandwiches and the other ladies take fruit and we pile them up together, and make a cup of coffee. We entertain the visitors. We never used to do it at first but we found that some of the ladies used to come and not bring their lunch because they just didn't

have time. They were getting the kids off to school and that, and we would feel, well to make a plate of sandwiches, you can do it the night before.

Within mixed tennis, women do it for themselves and for the men. Alice was describing the Veteran's organization when she said

the women do all the catering sort of things. . . . The women organize the booze and organize some salads and spread the crockery and things like that, all the womanly sort of things.

The connection between catering and social convening was consolidating as these jobs often were the responsibility of the same woman. Frances explained,

Like, for arguments sake, tomorrow afternoon there's a [Veterans' tennis] afternoon at [club]. So therefore the social convenor, or whatever you like to call her, she'll organize what we're going to eat, whether it be cheese and bikkies or whether it be [chicken and salad].

She added that this would be for about 100 people.

Brenda described how her position on the committee of her club had recently been, along with other administrative positions, "restructured" to give the club a more "professional" approach to management. She illustrated that such changes do not necessarily break down gendered labor divisions.

Now I have the wonderful title of being the 'catering manageress' (laughs). I've been doing it for about three years now, I suppose. It's just that you get the afternoon tea . . . well you organize the afternoon tea down at the club. . . . It was alright when it was just doing the afternoon tea because I could just buy all the stuff when I was doing my own shopping and just take it down. . . . It used to be just called the tea manager and then this year they decided on this 'catering manageress' business. You're supposed to organize the catering for when we have functions. Like when we have a barbecue you have to do all the salads and that. That's not so good. I really didn't want to do that, but. . . . It's when they have a barbecue or a champagne breakfast or, what else we have, a function at Christmas, something like that, you're supposed to organize all the food.

She explained how there was no constituted group to call upon for assistance, "You just sort of say to someone, would you mind making me a salad, that sort of thing," a system that relies on women's friendship networks and the work of people, more usually women, who are approachable, willing, and competent to contribute food in this way. She did say, however, that there were men in her "help network."

> Funnily enough, it's always the guys who come rushing in to wash up which is wonderful. . . . There's about three guys who really enjoy grabbing the tea towel and coming in and having a natter. And they do it every Saturday. People pitch in, particularly the ones that you're friendly with. I mean some people, which is a terrible thing to say, would never dream of coming in to do the afternoon tea, or lifting a tea towel, they just sit there. I don't know how they think it all happens.

"Afternoon teas" carry significant importance as a focal point to club social life. It is a time when all club members will usually break from their play to enjoy a cup of tea together during weekend club tennis. The preparation and serving of this, and the washing up required afterward, is similarly a significant focus for the assessment and perception of the club's management of labor. As the interviewed women spoke of this, they used it as a "signifier" of the club's relative liberal progressiveness, organizational sophistication, or affluence. For example, several women described how this work used to be done voluntarily in their clubs but now it is a rostered duty. Or, as Marilyn said about one of the city's more richly resourced clubs,

> At [club] you don't do anything, you don't make a cup of tea, you don't get on the bar. . . . They have a tea lady and someone who organizes the drinks and that's their socioeconomic scene.

However, whatever the form of modernization, it was still mostly women who made the tea. There is an interesting issue here, highlighting a gendered association with certain beverages. While women served tea, men have traditionally worked in the bar at tennis clubs, serving alcoholic and other cold drinks. The bar is an additional source of revenue for the club, and often a substantial one, which gives it a certain importance. The gendered demarcation between who poured tea and who poured beer was apparently breaking down in tennis clubs in Western Australia, mainly because more women were becoming involved in bar work. Betty explained the system for these duties at her club.

> It's rostered now. . . . You're either rostered for bar or for making tea. There's usually a husband and wife team if possible on the bar and women usually make the tea.

This redistribution of labor, however, seemed to occur in one direction only. More women are becoming involved in bar duties, but men are not as readily taking on tea duties. In Alice's interview, she said,

ALICE: You have turns behind the bar down here, and the women do it as equally as the men do.
Q.: And the teas?
ALICE: No. Well they employ someone to do the tea. Well that's on Saturdays anyway.

Changes in the allocation of work at the tennis clubs can be difficult to bring about, as Betty discovered.

> Well, women have always done the teas. Once last year I was doing the newsletter so I put in the newsletter that the men were going to get the tea on a certain Saturday. And there they were, they got the teas alright but that's the only time they've ever done it. I can't see why men can't go and get the tea.

When change did occur, it more often than not reduced the involvement, or expectation of involvement, from the men, such as when someone (a woman) is hired to serve afternoon teas, or ready-prepared food is bought. The women were not relieved of the work they previously did by the men taking it on. For example, when Ellen became club captain she introduced a policy by which everyone was to wash their own cup and saucer after tea, something that women were previously rostered to do. Men then acquired a portion of the work, but they were not asked to do it all.

Economic value: "It seemed silly to pay for it." Women's labor has economic value. It is given at times when men will give money. Linda explained,

I mean, if we have an interclub match, the women are always doing all the cooking. The men put in five dollars, you know, to cover some drinks and that, and the women do the baking and they lay the tables and make the tea.

Women's labor was given freely to tennis by women players and made a huge economic contribution to the sport. Their fund-raising activities contributed to keeping it financially viable at several levels, from the thirty-cent raffles sold at a women's midweek social club day to the structured "purpose" of the Women's Auxiliary. On the other side of the ledger, the work women did voluntarily actually saved money for the sport by reducing operational costs. This included, as Betty and Linda described having done, the "courtesy driving" and "hostessing" service that women provide for major international tennis extravaganzas held in Perth, such as the Davis Cup and the Hopman Cup competitions. It was most obvious though in relation to catering, which again ranged from women members making tea at their local clubs to the Women's Auxiliary doing the same at an event such as the Western Australia Open Championship tournament. This role in clubs and organizations, obviously considered important, seemed to provide the passport for women's inclusion into decision-making groups. For example, at Ruth's club, there were three men and three women members on the club's committee. When I asked if this had been deliberate, she answered, "Oh they've got to have it, because they've got to have so many women to have their say. They run the afternoon teas and things like that." Jean recalled how she became formally involved in junior tennis development, beginning when she replaced the paid caterers at junior tennis training camps with her own, and other women's, unpaid labor. She explained,

I went along one year, WALTA had hired cooks, . . . and we thought, we could do that, just cooking up a meal and serving it out. So the next time we did it. Have done it for years, stupid [of us] probably, but it seemed silly to pay for it when it was something we could do.

This work had led to her voluntary position on the WALTA Executive Committee, where she held the "Junior Tennis Development" portfolio.

Formal administrative positions: "No woman will ever make president." Every one of the fifteen veteran women players interviewed had held some formal position in the organization of tennis. All had been, to a greater or lesser extent, directly involved in the administration of the sport. The least involved was Ruth, whose sole administrative position had been captain of her midweek pennant team. Arguably the most involved woman was Jean, who had held key offices in her community tennis club, the Women's Auxiliary, WALTA, and most recently, the Veteran's Club.

Seven women specified having held positions as social facilitators and five specified fund-raising offices. Three women had been the secretary for their clubs. The bulk of women's representation in administrative offices was in gender marked areas, those in which women's work was traditionally done.

Two women, however, had been presidents of their clubs, the top club administrative position. In both cases they were the first woman in their clubs to hold this position. To enable her appointment to take place, Marilyn recalled how the club's constitution had to be changed to allow a woman to hold that position. She was very proud of this accomplishment and considered it one of the highlights of her tennis career. Anne became president of her club reluctantly, but did recognize the substantial experience she brought to the position. She explained how she had "stood" for the presidency because the club was about to appoint a man considerably younger than her, a man she had coached when he was a child and did not consider capable of running the club.

> . . . so rather than have that boy as the president, I offered to stand and so I was made president of the tennis club, and I did that for two years. . . . I'd always run things at the church I'd belonged to, I'd always been president there, of the ladies group. I was used to the business of being president and that kind of thing and I knew I could do it, but it had never been done before. There'd never been a woman being the president before. I didn't know that at the time but I thought, I'd had that much experience that I would be better and I proved it too.

Along with Marilyn and Anne, Jean was the only other veteran player interviewed who had held positions of any reasonable status and influence within "mainstream" tennis administration. Jean had served on five different WALTA executive subcommittees and had been the chairperson of three—promotion, fund-raising, and junior development. At the time of the interview, she was no longer a member of the WALTA Executive Committee, and there was currently only one woman member of the total thirteen Executive Committee body. This woman had refused my invitation to be interviewed, explaining that she was too busy. Jean related how this same woman had been the president of the Women's Auxiliary for three years, but immediately followed it by saying, "No woman, I don't think, will ever make president of the [WALTA] Executive [Committee]. I doubt it, might after my life time but I can't see it ever happening."

Five of the women interviewed had been members of the Women's Auxiliary Executive Committee, and three had held the office of president. Another had been vice-president and the fifth, treasurer. It was not unusual for women to hold these sorts of positions for very long periods of time. According to Marilyn, the original group of five women who ran the Women's Auxiliary did so for its initial fifteen years. Jean spoke of one secretary of the Women's Auxiliary who had been in the position for twenty-four years. Frances had been a delegated representative to WALTA for a rural zone for twelve years. Considering the number of years many of the interviewed women had been tennis players, it did not surprise me that many who had been thoroughly involved in administration had actually lost track of the positions held and for how long.

However, most of the women's involvement in administration was within the separate structure of women's tennis. There were numerous positions the interviewed women recalled having held within the midweek women's tennis organization. In addition to social facilitator and fund-raiser positions, these included ladies captain, ladies vice-captain, pennant supervisor, and captain of pennant teams. Four women had been involved only in midweek women's tennis administrative positions, and it is interesting to note that all four were married to men who did not play tennis. This was another area where women's involvement in tennis was related to whether or not their husbands also were players. Those women with tennis-playing husbands were far more likely to be involved in tennis administration, especially within the weekend or "main" club administration. As Molly, whose husband did not play tennis, explained,

> You always find that the ones that've got the kids off to school and their husbands are involved in the weekend down at the club, you'll find that they're the ones that will put a lot more time in it and take on a lot of the [administrative] jobs.

Furthermore, having a husband who held a high profile administrative position in tennis could mean that his wife became more involved in organizational work as a backup to his position. When Brenda was asked if she had been involved in running her tennis club, she replied, "Yes, my husband was president for many years at [club]. In fact he's a life member of [club]. He ran big State tournaments a number of times." This was when she went on to talk about buying the trophies for the tournaments.

CAROL: I was on the committee for one year I think, and I helped, my husband was involved on the committee for a few years and I helped him run certain things.
Q.: What sort of things?
CAROL: Well he ran, we ran, they run an Easter tournament there, and I helped run tournaments, and junior tournaments. We put in about five or six years helping.

Women's labor, which supports tennis structures, is further extracted through women's partnership with tennis-playing husbands, and completes the immersion effect of tennis-playing wives.

REMAINING MARGINAL

Although women tennis players, as members of tennis clubs in Western Australia, did more of the work that kept the clubs functional, this work was unlikely to be widely recognized or highly valued. Commonly, it was background work, low profile, often hidden and unrecognized, done as peripheral support but was work that was necessary for the smooth and cheap running of the institution. Linda drew a contrast between the profile of men's work and that done by the women when she said,

I suppose the major running of big tournaments, the national tournaments and international Davis Cup, the men of course are pretty involved in that and they do that part. But never with the catering, never the nitty-gritty work. It's always the ladies.

The undervaluing of women's labor within tennis parallels their marginalization as players and members of the institution per se. A closer look at the relationship of women players to the structures and practices of tennis culture follows.

Of all the major sports played in Australia, tennis is popularly understood as being one of the more egalitarian in terms of gender. Tennis clubs have always been open to both male and female members, and mixed play is a formalized tradition. A close analysis, however, exposed the myth of this perceived equality. The conditions under which women played tennis illuminate the contradictions and inequalities that existed, despite a conception of egalitarianism. Tennis is no less characterized by patriarchal practices than other sports, but these practices are muted and disguised by the presence of large numbers of women as active players. On the one hand, women players provided visible evidence of apparent equal opportunities offered in tennis, and were seen to be experiencing the joys and rewards of participation, as did men. Simply by "getting out" and being active, women players defied notions of female disempowerment and illustrated a heightened level of agency in the management of their lives. However, double standards persisted and were reflected in the multiple ways in which the tennis played by women in Western Australia was marginalized and hidden. The women's participation was defined by gendered notions of domestic responsibility, which not only determined the conditions under which they played but also their roles within the sporting institution. Both of these conditions restricted women's play far more severely than men's play, and demanded more of women in terms of their labor.

Domestic Marginalization

Formal tennis playing opportunities for women in Western Australia were organized within two main structures, one a separate organization of and for women players only, the other nominally integrated with men players. The former, separate structure is that which was organized for women during weekdays, either as midweek pennant competition or informal midweek social play in clubs. Examples of the latter, integrated tennis included the Veteran's Club competition, the weekend pennant competition administered by WALTA, and weekend play based in tennis clubs that could be tournaments or informal social play. However, even within the so-called integrated structures, the more competitive aspects of tennis playing remained gender divided into women's and men's competitions, which do not have equal status. The two structures interrelate of course, as many women were involved in both, but it was the separate structure that was more significant in Western Australia, impacting on the practices and perceptions of women's tennis in several ways.

The larger proportion of women's tennis was played within the separate structure. Greater numbers of women were involved in midweek play than during weekends. However, despite the larger numbers of women players in the midweek competition organized by the Women's Auxiliary and other midweek competitions, the women's weekend pennant competition administered by WALTA had far greater public profile and prestige. To be taken seriously as a champion player and to receive "mainstream" recognition, women players needed to be involved in the weekend competition. Singles match play was emphasized, State representative selection was based on these results, and it was only within this structure that women players were likely to receive sponsorship and media coverage. Tennis clubs themselves may have provided a sponsorship package to lure competent women players into the club to represent them in the WALTA competition, although this did not happen anywhere near the degree it did for men. This practice did not occur for the midweek women's competition. Of relevance to this discussion is the comparison that women who play in the top grades of the WALTA weekend pennant competition usually are the younger of the senior-level players and are less likely to have husbands and/or children. For example, most of the daughters of the mothers interviewed for this study played in this competition.

The veteran women players interviewed had all played in a midweek competition, although Betty had done so only after she retired from paid work. For most, it was the main opportunity for their tennis participation and one in which they had been continuously involved for decades. While certainly not the only structure for women's tennis, it was the one in which the majority of women players were involved, and it clearly encapsulates the predominant conditions by which the sport is experienced by women in Western Australia. In a complex manner, it provides the definition by which women's tennis is understood and valued, and highlights the contradictory interplay between women players as agents making individual and personal choices yet constrained by expected normative behavior.

Outside "mainstream" tennis. The major women's midweek tennis competition in Western Australia was run, not by the "mainstream" State administrative body (WALTA), but by the

Women's Auxiliary to that body. This put the women's competition outside of "mainstream" tennis in several ways. It was administered separately, by an independent group of women whose only formal connection with WALTA was through its definition as being an "auxiliary" body, with its historical raison d'être providing the "mainstream" organization with funds. Some of the regulations and practices of the Women's Auxiliary-organized competition have varied from those of the WALTA organized competition, however, when changes to these occur they inevitably bring the Women's Auxiliary practices more into line with WALTA's. The Women's Auxiliary does not have official representation on the WALTA Executive Board. One woman from the Auxiliary committee attends WALTA executive meetings to serve only as a "reporter" of its activities, and presumably as a messenger for WALTA's requests.

It is this administrative separateness, and the scheduling of women's tennis during weekdays, which contributed most to a form of structured invisibility of women's tennis and women as tennis players. However, it is argued that this structure has deliberately evolved to accommodate and not to challenge the roles and duties expected of women first and foremost, that is, their supposed domestic responsibilities to men and children. The women's weekday competition developed from an assumption that its participants were not in full-time paid employment, but were most likely to be associated with men who were. Furthermore, it assumed that the women player's main role was the care of children and maintenance of the home. Being a sportswoman must remain secondary to these responsibilities, and should not be seen to disrupt them. The existence of women's midweek tennis therefore relied on the fact it occurred apparently invisibly, not only to "mainstream" tennis but frequently to the women's families as well. It asked virtually nothing of, and made no demands on, those who were directly serviced by women's domestic roles, such as their children and husbands.

Hidden to families. To begin with, playing tennis did not necessarily negate women's ability to provide child care. Babies and young children were taken to tennis with their mothers, and tennis was recognized as a viable sporting option simply because this was possible. Nor did tennis generally provide women with a legitimate reason to shift that child care responsibility to someone else, as was commonplace for male players. In the few situations where this did occur, it was other women who took over the task, such as other women tennis players or female relatives. Many women limited their tennis until their children were of school age, restricting it to social play prior to that, which meant the needs of young children could be more easily accommodated. As Connie explained, "I would take [children] with me, but I wasn't interested in competitive tennis. As long as I had a game I was happy."

The major factor that prevented the women's competitive tennis from disrupting child care and other domestic responsibilities was the schedule adopted by the Women's Auxiliary. The "Ladies Shield Competition," commonly known as "midweek pennants," took place on Wednesdays between approximately 9:30 A.M. and 2 P.M. and thus did not impinge on weekends when both husbands and children could be expected to be at home. It was deliberately scheduled to begin after husbands would normally have left for work and children for school, finishing in time to allow the women to be home again before their families returned. Dorothy explained what this schedule meant to her when she said, "It was easy, because you didn't leave 'til after they went to school and you were home again before they were."

Social functions typically associated with women's midweek tennis, such as Christmas parties, Gala Days, or end-of-season socials, were invariably planned as luncheons, again staying within school hours, and as June explained, "It breaks for the school holidays. Over the summer holidays there's no pennants."

It should be noted here that when women suspended their own play during school holidays, it was then easier for them to service junior tennis, among many other activities in which children may be involved. Many junior tennis tournaments were held during school holidays, especially those planned for weekdays. The Women's Auxiliary took responsibility for running one of these junior tournaments every year, with the work being done by women from clubs with teams entered in the midweek pennant competition. During the six weeks of the 1989–90 summer school holidays, the WALTA calendar of events included twelve junior tennis tournaments. Such tournaments can make enormous demands on the time and labor of mothers of junior players, as detailed previously. Recall Peggy, for example, saying how everything went "on hold" during junior tournament weeks. The expendability of women's tennis at this time, to allow for easier servicing of junior tennis, was therefore important for the reproduction of tennis. Out of a total of thirty-one women players interviewed, twenty-one had children who had been or were currently involved in junior tennis tournaments.

Structural Marginalization

Tennis club membership. Because women tennis players who were married to men who played tennis were more likely to play during the weekends as well as midweek, they were also more likely to be what is usually categorized as "full" members of a tennis club. Membership categories, and the capital imperatives surrounding them, offer another set of complexities in sports clubs that have in the past served to both limit women's access to resources and confine them as marginal participants. Despite the number of women who play tennis in Australia, this sport has not been without a tradition of two-tiered membership, structured predominantly on gendered lines, which has contributed to the devaluing of female members within tennis culture.

Within Western Australian tennis clubs, there usually are various types of possible memberships, with different fee charges. A traditional option for women was a membership known as "ladies midweek," which costs less than a "full" membership. This lower fee only entitled the holder to use the club facilities on "women's" days during the week, and a woman may also join a team to play in the midweek pennant competition run by the Women's Auxiliary. Full membership, an option available to both men and women, has a higher fee. Such members could use the club facilities at all times, but organized play and other activities occurred on weekends.

There is a long-standing tradition in Australia of access to sporting club resources being based on a structure of differing fees, which is predominantly gender based. Prior to the passing of the Sex Discrimination Act in 1984,[2] a very large number of sports clubs restricted all women to "associate" memberships. The flawed assumption behind this was that all women who applied to and would be acceptable to join the club were "associated" with, that is, married to, a male, "full" member. Furthermore, that this man would be paying the membership fees for his "associate" and, having paid fully for his own rights and privileges, does not need to pay the same sum for hers. Associate members of sporting clubs do not have full privileges or voting rights, ensuring that control remains with the "full," male members.

With the passing of the Sex Discrimination Act, it became illegal to restrict women's access to sports club in this way, although at the time of the interviews the practice still existed, notably in some golf and lawn bowls clubs. Carol and Alice both described how women in the two different golf clubs to which they belonged were still restricted to "associate" memberships without full constitutional rights. Carol, whose club was one of the largest, most affluent, and prestigious golf clubs in Perth, explained how the women members of her club voted in 1984 to retain the status quo because they did not wish to pay the higher, full membership fee. With the way the Sex Discrimination Act is applied, to change this situation now would require women from within the golf club to legally challenge the membership structure, and none were prepared to face the inevitable ostracism to do this. Alice's explanation, although lengthy, is worth including here because of the way it highlights the traditional and intransigent gendered dynamics of these sports clubs.

ALICE: With tennis, women have equal rights. With golf, women don't have equal rights, anywhere near. You can't be a full member of a golf club here.

Q.: Isn't that now illegal?

ALICE: I know it is and I would love to get a group of women who want to join the golf club and I would sponsor them and they would apply for full membership. It would cause an absolute riot. It needs someone to push it and what annoys me is at the Golf Club, you cannot get the women to support women having equal rights. They say "Oh, but we would have to pay the same as the men." Now the women down here pay about eighty dollars less than the men a year, so that's one thing, and the fact that they are there playing [midweek], they can't see that there is any need for women to be able to play on Saturday. Now, the big thing in golf clubs is that men, because they work, they have Saturdays. The fact that women work and Saturday might be the only day they can play, you cannot get the women to see that. Now some clubs will let women play on a Saturday. In fact a lot of the clubs now, and I think we're going to get it through at [my club]. But they really have not got equal rights. And all the money, the men decide what's being done with all the money. The guys have no intention of letting the women have equal say, absolutely none. They had a building levy last year and they had a meeting which the women could come to, but we couldn't vote, and we had to put in our extra $135 each or whatever it was, and we had no say in it. And I upset one ex-president very much (laughs), I didn't know he was an ex-president, by slinging off about . . . he was saying something, we were sitting there, he just jokingly said, "I don't know why we did all these additions. The men could have just taken over the women's rooms and we would have had plenty of room." I said, "Look, that wouldn't surprise me one bit. I mean, when you can have a meeting and vote to take $135 from me and I have no say on it, yes, the men would do anything," and did he bite! I said afterwards, "Who on earth's that old boy?" We had a quite a battle there. But yes, whereas a tennis club, women have absolutely equal rights and they always have.

Q.: With equal say?

ALICE: Equal say. If you want to go on the Committee, there's no reason why you can't. You can have a woman president or anything, but with [golf], you have a Men's Committee and you have a Women's Committee, and the Men's Committee make all the major decisions. And I say "What about if we have such and such?" and they say "Oh, I don't think the men would give us the money for that." I said "Look, we pay the fees, why can't we? Where does our money go to?" You have no say at all in the Golf Club, which really riles me. . . . And a lot of them bowl. At [lawn] bowls clubs it's the same. Women raise all that money for bowls and what really gets me is that, I was going to start playing bowls at [club], when the men bowl, every Saturday, the women have to take turns in getting afternoon tea for the men, dressed in full uniform! They're not there to play! No, it's Men's Day. So bowling clubs are coming into it because they did have a case with the Discrimination Board, but the thing is that when you get in, everyone treats you like a leper. That's why the women won't do this test case with golf. It's that, if they win their battle, they really can't ever play in that club again because most of the women will ostracize them. Some of the younger ones are coming around to that way, a small group, sort of coming round to that way of thinking.

It was because many of the women interviewed could make comparisons between their tennis clubs and other, more discriminatory sports clubs that they concluded, as Alice did, that women in tennis had equal rights. Nevertheless, the membership categories and fee differentials have remained, and although theoretically open to both genders, the old patterns still dominated and traditional economic rationales prevailed.

"Associate" or "midweek" memberships in sporting clubs were

cheaper. Within marriage relations, expenses for leisure interests may be laden with gendered economic politics. For example, if a husband is the sole or major income earner, he may have considerable influence over how that money is spent. If a wife has no discretionary income of her own, she may be reluctant to spend "his" money on her leisure activities, such as a sports club membership. For these reasons it may be easier for her to find the lesser amount for a midweek membership, especially if he does not also play tennis. Husbands who play the sport themselves are more likely to sanction the payment of full membership to the club for their wives. An additional incentive is the fact that many tennis clubs have a "married couple" membership category for cohabiting heterosexual couples, at a lower price than would be paid by two adult members but which gives both partners full membership status. On the other hand, if a woman is in paid employment, her earnings, even if less than her husband's, may be her discretionary income to do with as she pleases.

Implications to women's tennis. Traditionally, although this has recently changed in some metropolitan tennis clubs, only women could become midweek members and all men were full members. Along with limited access to the use of courts and other club resources, midweek members had no input in club administration and decision making beyond the organization of women's midweek play. For example, they did not have the right to vote on club administrative or policy matters, or to be elected to office outside of the separate women's structure. Dorothy summarized this when she explained why midweek members did not have any say in how the clubs were run.

> Because they pay lesser fees you see, they just pay a midweek fee. Well of course, you're entitled to play less times with that than the weekend members. They can come down and play during the week, but when you're a midweek member, you're only allowed to play Tuesday mornings, pennants Wednesday, and I think you can go into the club's competitions, like the championships, but otherwise you don't play the rest of the time. But you know that when you join, you're told that.

While lesser club fees helped make the sport more accessible to women, it also gave women's participation a lower economic value, which further undermined its credibility and status. Following this, because the larger proportion of women's tennis was played midweek, women as players became conceptually associated with separate and cheaper membership fees, even when most were full members. None of the interviewed veteran players had limited their club membership exclusively to the midweek category for all of their adult tennis playing, although six had moved in and out of being a midweek or full member at various transition points in their careers.

One of the major implications of such a capital-based imperative for membership in tennis clubs was that women's midweek tennis was treated as marginal. Sally at one time had held the club administrative position called "Ladies Midweek Captain." When asked how this position related to the club's administration, she explained

> It was never a part of the weekend tennis. It was completely separate and you were sort of a second-class citizen as far as the tennis club committee were concerned.

In her club, there had been recent changes to the structure of membership categories, and Sally was talking about how it had been.

SALLY: The tennis club was different to the way it operates now. The ladies were "The Ladies" and the tennis club was "The Tennis Club."
Q.: Meaning ?
SALLY: The men!

Dorothy explained, "With the Midweek Ladies, you are only sort of an auxiliary." Following this, I asked if she felt midweek women players had any say in the way the club was run. She replied, "Well, we don't think so. We don't think that they consider us to be very important members of the club."

Sally's response to the same question was,

> No, [midweek members] didn't. At one point in time they didn't. They were just part of the club that brought in . . . ladies from the area to play and enabled the membership numbers to be as it was, which brought in a certain amount of fees.

After Molly had outlined the fund-raising done by women in her club, I asked her if these women had any say in how the money was spent. She replied,

No, well "midweeks" never, "weekends" do. Midweeks, because we never ever really made a great deal, we didn't have a great deal to put into anything.

These attitudes toward women's midweek tennis have ramifications for all of the women involved, whether they have paid for a full or a midweek membership. While the different, inferior status of midweek as compared to weekend tennis had a greater impact on the women who were midweek members only, it was perhaps more clearly recognized and understood by those who were full members, who played at both times and were thus in a position to make comparisons. Sally and Dorothy were both full members of their clubs, although most of their tennis had been played midweek. They both provided illustrations of the secondary status of midweek tennis by recalling experiences where women's interests had been in conflict with, and disregarded by, the male-dominated club administration. Dorothy gave the following example:

At different times, we've tried to alter the groundsman's order of doing things, tried to get him to get the courts marked earlier so we can start playing earlier on a Tuesday and this sort of thing. But they don't consider that's very important.

She went on to explain why this was important for women's tennis and for the strength of midweek club membership.

Like, any young mums that, say, have got children at kindergarten, they want to leave at 11:30 [A.M.] to go and pick them up and some of them think it's not worth coming down, if they can't start playing 'till 10 [A.M.] and they've got to leave again to go and pick up the children at 11:30 [A.M.], and we've lost a few members like that.

During the discussion with Sally about the relationship of midweek members to the administration of her club, she recalled, "[It was] interesting because actually conflict arose in several instances." These instances concerned practices that the women were not permitted to do during midweek play, but that could be done on weekends. Sally elaborated,

For example, if the court was wet on a midweek situation you weren't allowed to play on it until it was deemed to be playable, yet on a weekend, because there were many more people playing, they would just go and play on it whether it was wet or it wasn't, and this of course caused conflict in lots of instances. . . . It was a bit poor really.

The courts were being saved from wear and tear during the week for the benefit of weekend players. However, she explained this as being a result of the greater demand on the courts on the weekend. Because she and other women played on the weekend as well as midweek, it was difficult for her to clearly argue that this sort of conflict may have been gender based. Thus economic rationales such as the differing fee structure would likely be presented. Furthermore, Dorothy added,

. . . and then they say, 'well really, there aren't all that many purely midweek members anyhow.' Because quite a lot of us are full members that play weekends as well. So that, because there's not really that many just midweek members in the club, they don't think they're very important and it has been quite a beef with the ladies over the years.

Three of the veteran players were quick to point out that in their clubs, midweek membership was no longer exclusively for women. Dorothy said,

These days, we get quite a few men down on Tuesdays as well—retired men and husbands with rostered days off and so on, they come down. We don't call them midweek "ladies" anymore, they're midweek "members" now.

The extent to which this change had challenged long-standing and rigid conventions of gendered divisions in tennis was evident in the way it was expressed. Two women humorously evoked images of men cross-dressing as the only way they could fit into midweek tennis. Sally explained how there was now some flexibility possible in her club.

. . . which wasn't there before, it was quite rigid. You couldn't be a man and go down there and play Tuesday morning. That just wasn't on, unless you had frilly pants on and a skirt.

Molly's version from a different club was

the men can come now, because [the club is] all one now. . . . We give them a bit of a raspberry. We're not used to this "men coming" business. We used to say to them, "Where's your skirts?"

Despite the recent flexibility in membership options, mainly resulting in increased playing opportunities for men, the number of men playing at this time was very small and even less would have only a midweek as opposed to a full club membership. Midweek members remained predominantly women, and it continued to be viewed as a women's culture. Grbich, for example, reported in her study of "househusbands" in Australia, that these men most "suffered" in this role around access to informal daytime activities. She quoted one male respondent who said, "Women at home can go and play tennis because other women are playing tennis, but being a man, you just can't go and play with the girls (Grbich 1992: 88)." There was obviously a certain amount of resistance by the women players to having men encroaching on "their space."

As with many areas of social life, scholars have long debated the advantages to women of separate versus integrated sporting and physical education structures, mostly concluding that women's interests are better served when these activities are not mixed.[3] However, a major concern has been for the way in which women's separate structures become undervalued and marginalized within the institution, thus not advancing the cause for equality or change. Within this study there also was an understanding by the women interviewed that men's interests could be best served by a separate women's tennis structure, and that in fact women policed each others' competence in the sport with this in mind. Betty explained,

> This lass came along and said she was interested in joining but she wasn't strong enough so we had to ask her if she wouldn't mind taking coaching lessons or coming on a Tuesday when there aren't any men there. See it's Tuesday Ladies, that's our social day. So she would be better with a lot of ladies than coming at the weekend and having mixed doubles where she'd be up against men who would complain about her.

Linda began playing tennis in Western Australia as an adult, having been taken along to a club by a female neighbor who carefully "managed" her introduction to the sport. She recalled when she first started.

I enjoyed it and I kept going to the midweek ladies. It was a very low key, easy, happy kind of thing, nobody worried very much and it wasn't a big club in those days. . . . Then came the time when they said, "Right, now you've got to go and play on Saturdays, you know, mixed, with men!" I said, "No way am I going to play with men," but I did, eventually.

Female players remained hidden from mixed tennis structures until they were acceptable by male standards. Molly added,

We were very much separate for years and years and years but now it's supposed to be all one. But with the weekends, because they have men playing, it's definitely run differently. Midweek only have women. I'd say the midweek would be a lot more friendlier, not as bitchy as the weekends would be because you've got the men coming in and you've got to be a really good player to play with the men because the men won't play with someone that's not.

Reference was made to how many men tennis players did not generally like playing mixed doubles, although women did. There is no formal pennant competition for mixed doubles in Western Australia, and it only occurs in selected tournaments. However, on club days it is a standard form of organized social play. There were clear double standards in the implication that male players would be accommodated, no matter what their standard of play.

Control and influence. The positions of administrative leadership office held by the women players interviewed have been described earlier. All of the interviewed players has been involved in administration and held some definable role, but the majority of these positions had been within the separate sphere of women's tennis. Only three women had held positions of authority within "mainstream" tennis, that is, the tennis structures in which men were involved. These women, as well as the others, recognized that holding such a high-powered position was unusual and exceptional.

Executive positions in the administrative structure of the sport have decision-making and controlling authority. When women do not hold such positions, they do not have the opportunity for direct control or influence within the institution to which they belong and give their labor. Their "say" in organizational procedures is severely limited when administrative control is held by men, as is a characteristic of Australian sporting organizations generally.[4] These women, therefore, had very few legitimate channels of power through which to influence the shape and direction of the institution, despite doing the greater proportion of the labor for its maintenance. Controlling positions are mainly held by men, which gives men's labor a higher profile and tends to bias the perception of labor divisions. This misconstruction is well illustrated by Dorothy's response when she was asked if the jobs done in the club, those that keep the club running, were well distributed between the men and women. She replied,

> No, I suppose they'd be more men on the Executive [Committee] because you've got your captains, they're men, the grounds committee, they'd be men, the social director is actually a man now, but we have had lady social directors, but our pennant director I think is a lady this year. The clubs change around, but there would be more men than women [running them].

What formal avenues of control and influence the women did have were limited mainly to the separate sphere of women's tennis. Yet, even as a collective body, the Women's Auxiliary had very restricted influence beyond itself and remained clearly within the paternal power of WALTA. Marilyn, as president of the Women's Auxiliary, found it difficult to define its parameters of influence and control. She recalled a situation that illustrated the strange and ambiguous relationship between the Women's Auxiliary and WALTA. As mentioned earlier, and in keeping with its purpose, the Women's Auxiliary ran an annual junior tournament as a service to children's tennis, from which the proceeds were given to WALTA. All clubs with teams entered in the midweek pennant competition organized by the Women's Auxiliary were asked to provide two women to work from the Monday to Friday to assist with the junior tournament. Such assistance was organized on a roster system so that each club was asked to provide helpers only once every five years. This particular year, one of the rostered clubs refused to send anyone. According to Marilyn, the reason given was that the women in the club felt that they already did plenty of fund-raising for their club, and they believed the club received few benefits from the affiliation fees they paid to WALTA. Why, they therefore asked, should they also work to fund-raise for WALTA? The Executive Committee of the Women's Auxiliary, realizing it had no other means of ensuring this form of support from club women, considered banning that club's teams from the midweek competition they administered. The women in the club then threatened to write in protest to WALTA. This did not eventuate, mainly because the Women's Auxiliary Executive Committee did not carry out its threat to ban the club, but nevertheless, Marilyn had no confidence that WALTA would have supported the Women's Auxiliary in this conflict. She said, with tones of skepticism,

> I'm interested to see what the [WALTA] Executive's [Committee] position towards Women's Auxiliary would be. Like, about this particular club which refused to send anybody to help at the school children's tournament. I'd like to see where the power would come from, because we really don't have any power. . . . I would have been interested to see what power the [WALTA] Executive [Committee] would have used, in support of us.

Marilyn provided another example of the Women's Auxiliary's lack of authority by recalling how it had wished to commemorate the long service of its members. She explained,

> We don't have any power as such. It stems back twenty-seven years of the constitution. It's never been updated or changed. We asked on our twenty-fifth year if we could appoint life members to our association. Our constitution makes no provision for anything to that effect because we are only an auxiliary, we have no powers as such. WALTA has all the power and we couldn't have life members of our association, of Women's Auxiliary, because we are only an affiliate, well we're only a lower body in the whole overall concept. . . . We could as a group submit names to the Executive [Committee] of WALTA for life membership but, I mean, life membership is something extra, extra, super special at WALTA. So there's no way to recognize the long-term work done by women.

The implication was that women's work would not measure up to the male-dominated WALTA Executive Committee's criteria of "extra, extra, super special." The one area in which the Women's Executive Committee felt they did have some say was in nominating where the money they contributed to WALTA would be spent. Linda, who was the Auxiliary's treasurer, explained, "At the moment it's used towards the Hard Court Center, which we hope to have in a few years." While there was unanimous agreement that the Hard Court Center was needed and would be beneficial to tennis in Western Australia, it is interesting to contrast this priority for the Women's Auxiliary with Connie's comments about how older women much prefer to play on grass courts. With the increasing expense of maintaining grass courts, more clubs were opting for other surfaces. In response, Connie had attempted to arrange a competitive league for women over forty-five years old, playing only on grass courts. She said,

> I thought that, well I am older myself and I could see that it was going to be something that would keep the older women longer in tennis, longer competing, which they loved, and they have put a lot of time into tennis, a lot of those women.

The women interviewed were asked if they felt they had any "say" in how their club, and tennis, generally was run. Their responses were diverse, based on how much say they expected to have. Both Betty and Noelene, members of the same club, in a working-class residential area, were apologetic about how much say they felt they had had and how constructive it had been. Betty called herself "a big stirrer" and said, "I'm always putting my foot in it." Noelene said, laughing, that she probably had "too much" say, "But we're never right, we'll never be right." Patricia expressed guarded frustration about how, as a professional, her ideas had not been valued by a volunteer-based sporting organization, but how this had been the same for her husband. The areas in which the women spoke of having had influence were gender inscribed. Two explained how they had been responsible for their clubs' uniforms, another two for the interior decor of their clubrooms. Patricia and Linda both gave lengthy explanations of cases where the interests of women's opportunities to play tennis were overridden by male-dominated administrative groups. In Patricia's example, it was an initiative to encourage more women to return to higher levels of competitive tennis after having taken time off to have babies, but which after a year's "trial" was dropped. Linda described being asked, as the "ladies captain," to select a team of women from her club for a special, mixed, competitive and social event with another club. Having done so, she was told by the men's captain that the team could not include all of the women she had nominated because the members of the men's team wished the women's team to be made up of their wives. She had "stuck to her guns," and her team did not change but, she said, "I wasn't very popular for a while. The men's captain just sat there and said, "What am I going to do with this woman?"

Women's equality in tennis is, at best, debatable. Women play the sport in large numbers and provide most of the labor that is fundamental to its organization. This gives them some visibility within tennis culture and contributes to the popular perception of gender equality, enhanced by comparisons made with other sporting codes that women of the same age group and class readily participate in but are not seen to have as good a "deal," such as golf and lawn bowls. However, there are double standards and contradictions within and outside tennis that place women as marginal and expendable players, keeping their play defined by domestic roles, limited by capital relations, and controlled by patriarchal structures.

SUMMARY

Women's involvement in sport has been characterized by contradictions. Historically, women have been discouraged from taking part because such activity was considered beyond their physical capabilities, yet at the same time many women were involved in the strenuous labor of childbearing and the immensely physical work of sustaining their families (Lenskyj 1986). Women's sporting endeavors have been trivialized, and yet we have often been banned from taking part in competitions because to do so would be considered to undermine male achievements (Dyer 1982). When, despite all of this, women have engaged in sporting activities requiring skill, strength, and endurance, they have been expected to maintain an appearance that conforms to masculinist definitions of feminine vulnerability and beauty (Hargreaves 1994; Festle 1996). Such experiences are explicable when one recognizes that the institution of sport is overwhelmingly regulated by and oriented toward male interests. It is an institution readily and regularly described as masculine, male dominated, androcentric, and patriarchal (e.g., Bryson 1987; Cameron 1996; Birrell and Cole 1994; Hall et al. 1989; Hall 1987; Hargreaves 1994; Kidd 1987; McKay 1991a, 1992a, 1997; Messner and Sabo 1990; Nelson 1991). This has meant endless problems for women who have insisted on participating throughout the centuries.

Nevertheless, these tennis players provided an understanding of how some women negotiated their sport and allowed it to become a "motive force" (Talbot 1988b, 113) in their lives, and how sport and leisure became a vehicle by which they moved beyond restricting notions of gendered behavior similar to the young mothers Wearing (1990) studied in eastern Australia.

The sportswomen interviewed for this study played tennis as a highly valued leisure activity. For most, it was facilitated by classed capital and gender relations in which divisions of labor deemed women's work to be primarily "at home," but from which space could be negotiated as long as this work was not noticeably compromised. They did not, however, experience leisure under the same conditions as male tennis players. Opportunities came about as Barrell et al. (1989) also found in their study of men and women runners—the sportsmen "took" time for their participation, the sportswomen "negotiated" theirs.

The women tennis players in Western Australia serviced their participation for themselves, both individually and collectively, and kept it within restricted confines. They described ways their leisure could be subject to direct or hegemonic control, being as Woodward and Green argued of women's leisure, "one of the aspects of life in which women's behavior is most closely monitored and regulated" (1988, 130).

From an analysis of national figures on leisure activity from the Australian Bureau of Statistics, McKay pointed out,

> Leisure has a history that has been characterized by hegemonic struggles over *whose leisure activities count* more than others, and is situated in a wider social and historical context of structured, social inequality. (1986, 358, original emphasis)

While these inequalities persist, the contradictions remain that, despite the confines and marginalization of women's tennis, these veteran players displayed a heightened level of autonomy and agency by maintaining lifetimes of intense involvement in the sport. It is important to note that such opportunities are still afforded by capital and social relations that in this context privilege white, middle-class, heterosexual women who live in a culture where public displays of women's physicality are approved and sport particularly valued. It also is important to note, however, that despite all of their apparent privilege, and the rewards expressed in the following chapter, gender inequalities were still embedded in women's experiences of the sport.

FIVE

REWARDS AND RATIONALES

It's a lovely sport.

—Sonia

When they're happy, you're happy as well.

—June

HAVING AGENCY

An analysis of the ways in which the interviewed women found rationales for their actions and gained affirmation and rewards is usefully framed in a discussion of agency. Such a frame allows consideration of the dialectical relationship between the women as individuals who are able to create the details of their lives, and the social structures that determine their actions and thus the way those lives are lived (Berger and Luckman 1967). The conjunction between these is a continual contest and reformation, being a "fault line" along which women understand social structures, assess, review, redefine, and reassert themselves. Agency depends on both consciousness and action as a means of negotiating a path of control through constraints from social structures. However, as Scott (1992, 851) maintains, the concept is

> less one of opposition between domination and subordination, control and agency, than it is a complex process that constructs possibilities for and puts limits on actions undertaken by individuals and groups.

An important way to understand the processes of rationalization and the dynamism of agency is to focus on what the women viewed as being the rewards for their labor. In other words, why did they do it? Once again, it is necessary to discuss this question as it pertains to each of the three interviewed groups, as the basis for their behavior varies even if the details of their labor do not. For the mothers of junior squad players, the stated rewards reflected their concern for the upbringing of their children and the mothers' ability to facilitate what they saw as valued experiences. For the wives and domestic partners of adult male tennis players, rewards were based on a concern for the husbands' well-being and a commitment to the quality of the marriage relationship. Women who played tennis saw rewards for themselves inherent in their own participation. In that respect, their sport was itself a reward negotiated within the social conditions of their lives. There were women interviewed, however, who expressed ambivalence about the rewards, who reluctantly conceded them, or who struggled to find any at all. Their sense of having agency was less.

While each of the interview groups will be discussed in turn, it takes place in three sections. The division between the sections is based on the notion of "sacrifice" and the extent to which the women expected or sought rewards. For example, the notion of self-sacrifice as an ideological tenet of motherhood mutes the expectation that any rewards for the mothers are a necessary consideration. On the other hand, for women relating to adult male partners, "sacrifice" tends to hinge on expectations of reciprocity. Rewards are therefore more likely to be sought, and tension results if they are found absent. Therefore, the basis for rationalizations of servicing labor differs quite considerably between the groups of women, and it is this difference that the chapter seeks to highlight.

Mothers: Rationalizing Sacrifice

It could be argued that mothers have a certain amount of choice about the labor they devote to their children's activities, not just in terms of how much they do but also where it is placed. If we take as a given that raising children requires a great deal of labor, moral, and material support, and that the activities in which children become involved as they grow up are many and varied, then parents must exercise some selectivity in deciding on which of their children's activities to concentrate. Howard's and Madrigal's (1990) research in the United States concluded that it was mothers who most influenced the decisions about which recreational services their children consumed. What is it about sport generally and tennis specifically that provided the mothers interviewed in Western Australia with reasons for supporting their children's tennis to the extent described?

During the interviews, the reasons mothers gave for their labor were mainly expressed in response to a question that asked what the best thing was about their children's tennis. Not only could they clearly identify rewards from their labor, but they also were keen to articulate them. It seemed they were familiar with the need or desire to rationalize this behavior.

The question phrased as "the best thing" produced responses that tended to conflate children's and mothers' interests. Some mothers took this opportunity to talk about themselves, but most talked about the interests of their children. In some interviews I probed further about rewards for themselves, depending on the initial response, but many replies showed the extent to which, in the mothers' minds, these interests were conflated. For example, when Rosemary was asked what "her" rewards specifically were, she said,

> I feel he is growing up to be a well-adjusted young teenage boy and hopefully he will continue on as an adult. I think those things are very important to me, in all my children. I think if we're able to rear three children that grow up that way, I feel I have done my bit.

Rewards therefore were related to successful mothering, measured by the quality of the adult the child becomes. The rationales given for devoting their time and attention to their child's sport were mainly to do with what they considered this experience contributed to the development of their children. These included the personality attributes developed or enhanced by experiences in tennis, the social control of teenagers provided by tennis structures, the specific social contacts it afforded, and the perceived health benefits. Along with these, the mothers interviewed spoke of their ambivalence about possible professional tennis-career outcomes for their children, disputing a popular perception that this may be the "real" motivation.

Giving them confidence. The most frequently cited reward, by thirteen of the sixteen interviewed mothers, was given as retrospective comments about their children's character and personality attributes. For example, Beth said of her daughter's tennis, "It's given her a bit of confidence in herself, I think that's the big part, confidence." Six mothers, five of whom were referring to daughters, spoke of the confidence their child had gained through successfully playing tennis. Kath said,

> She'll survive because she is that sort of kid, but thanks to tennis. I mean she could get up and talk to a room full of people without any hesitation at all, she has done it at the club, when she won the [tournament], she got up and spoke there and we were extremely proud, said all the right things.

Jill spoke of how this alone had made all of her efforts worthwhile. Her reply showed how she had faced the question many times before. She said,

> When people say to me, I don't know how you manage, or why you are doing it, or whatever, you see there are obvious advantages and rewards. . . . [Daughter] in particular as a youngster was very nervous and very low in self-esteem. Now she is not supremely confident but her self esteem is very, very good. She's developed social skills that she would never have developed had she not been involved in tennis, in that she's had to hop on planes by herself, meet strangers, and go and stay at their houses, adapt to all manner of people and situations and she has been able to do that extremely well. She is very much an extremely mature, confident, personable sixteen-year-old, which I don't think she would have been had she not had this range of experiences that she's had through tennis. It has also developed her self-esteem enormously, so that she will aspire to things now that I'm sure she would never have aspired to four or five years ago, simply because she didn't think that she was worthwhile or capable of doing those things. So from that point of view, I think it has been wonderful.

Other traits attributed to their children's experiences in tennis included being "sensible," "capable," "independent," "disciplined," and "mentally tough." The latter three were described by mothers of sons, one of whom also explained how her son was learning to control his aggressive temper and hide his feelings. There is a suggestion here, although not a strong one, that the traits the mothers valued in their children were gender prescribed, but there was also some resistance to a too-easy gender stereotyping. Yvonne felt ambivalent about what her son was learning through tennis. She explained how she was mainly concerned about what sort of man he grew up to be and thought that in order for him to continue to be successful at the level of tennis competition he was embarking upon, he had to become more "cocky."[1] She did not like this characteristic and therefore had reservations about how he would develop, saying, "Some of the top [tennis] players are absolutely awful."

These women approved of, or felt pride in, the kind of people their children were becoming. This was often expressed in terms of how other people perceived their children. Trish said of her child, "The way she's admired for her placid attitude, I think that's the greatest highlight." Kath said, "We have been very proud, in that we have had people ring us and say that we should be congratulated on [daughter's] presence on the court." Such pride is the reward of having parented successfully, and provides affirmation of a mother's labor.

Getting to travel. Four of the mothers attributed the commendable traits their children had developed, such as confidence, independence, and maturity, specifically to the travelling they had experienced through their tennis. Jacqui said,

> To me, the best thing about [son's] tennis has been just getting to travel and being independent and seeing different things, not just live here and go to school. He's got a lot of diversity in his life. He has learned to deal with other people and personalities. He goes over to Germany and learns to deal with a German family. To me that has been a thing that he has got out of it more than anything. He is a very intelligent kid, as in common sense, judging people's characters, that sort of thing. And I think that's from his tennis, travelling around and dealing with other kids at the other end of the court, just dealing with all that and dealing with having to cope with a loss, a disappointment of a loss. To me that has been the greatest advantage of his tennis. As a person I think he will be very street wise.

Travel opportunities were one of the more tangible rewards, cited by seven of the mothers. Kath said,

> Whatever happens from now on is a bonus because she has been very lucky. She has seen far more than what [husband]

and I have seen. . . . She has been to every [Australian] state except the Northern Territories umpteen times. She went to the United States last year for two weeks, to Germany again, to Asia, so she certainly has had a lot from it.

Di spoke of how her son had had "some wonderful trips, so I guess that has been our reward," but, like other mothers, she mentioned how much this had cost the family financially, saying,

[Al]though, out of that reward we have had to cough up say, $500 or something. You win State selection but by jeez you pay for it. You buy your own tracksuit, you pay for everything, for this 'honor.'

Some mothers had reservations about the young ages at which high-achieving, tennis-playing children in Western Australia were expected to travel. Trish's son had traveled to the United States to play tennis at age eleven. Di said of her son,

I really feel they went away far too early. He was nine when he went on their first trip. They went to Brisbane. Now, [son] had never been on a plane before. Thinking about it now, . . . the kid must've been terrified. But we were so thrilled that he had been picked in his first State team, at nine, and we just took him to Perth Airport, showed him the plane, kissed him good-bye, sent him through the thing, and off the kid went. He said he was frightened.

Although the team had been accompanied by a young "manager" and "manageress," she said, "We probably should have gone with him, I don't know." Trish talked about having been recently asked if her twelve-year-old daughter would join a team to travel to Europe. She explained how she had said no and had not even mentioned it to the child, saying to me, "She's far too young. She's never even been away from home without us before." Reservations aside, the travel opportunities made available through tennis for children from West Australian were generally highly valued. Their parents, however, had to finance most of the associated expense.

Keeping them off the streets. The second most frequently cited rationale had to do with the social control and behavior of teenagers. It was perceived that as long as their children were playing tennis, and caught up in the intensity of the junior tennis lifestyle, they were controllable and not involved in behavior that could be construed as problematic. Eleven of the mothers mentioned this, with five phrasing it in terms of keeping their kids "off the streets." For example, Di said, "It's terrific, it keeps them off the street," and Trish, "They never had time to be street kids." Four other mothers spoke of how their children had been too busy playing tennis to get into trouble, such as Peggy, who said, "He has never had time to get bored, which means he has never given us any problems."

Eight of these eleven women were mothers of sons. One of them, Sonia, elaborated with reference to school vacations. She said,

> I think it's mostly because I don't have to worry about him. He's happy doing what he loves. He's picked a beautiful sport. It's a lovely sport, there's no danger to it. . . . It's great, isn't it? You don't have to worry, oh, the holidays are coming and what am I going to do? What if I have to go to work tomorrow? What will become of my child? Where is he going to be, in the middle of the day, day after day during the holidays? It's fantastic, it just takes care of itself. That's the biggest reward.

There was obvious security in the knowledge that their child, particularly a teenage son, could move from one institution of social control (school) to another (sport). Sonia and two other mothers spoke of their children's avoidance of drugs, alcohol, and tobacco, which they attributed to participation in tennis. Yvonne said, for example,

> Like a lot of his peer group, going to parties and things, and their mothers have got the worry of drinking and drugs. I've noticed the kids in the tennis scene don't seem to follow that. They have always got their tournaments, they are worrying about getting to bed at a reasonable hour. And there's no smoking.

Beth explained that their move to the city had been to provide her daughter with the opportunities for challenges, so that as a teenager she would not get bored in a small country town. However, Beth had reservations about the restrictive effects on a junior tennis player's social life in the city. She called her daughter's life "very rigid," and explained how she had not had the opportunity to foster peer group friendships by sharing time outside of tennis. This worried Beth. She said,

> They have to give a fair bit of their free time [to tennis]. They don't have the real social freedom that other kids have, going to movies, doing this and that, trying this or that. It has to be fairly structured . . . but it's not normal, to me it's not. It's not the average seventeen-year-old's lifestyle.

Trish, too, recalled that when her older daughters were playing junior tennis they had missed out on a "normal" social life, but there was "plenty of time" for it afterward, she said.

> It's time to catch up when they're tertiary students and they're off the tennis reins and they can do some other things with their lives and I think that's fine.

The "tennis reins" hold children at bay through the more problematic teenage years by restricting their lives to ones that are regulated and contained within narrowly defined and "safe" parameters, making aspects of mothering much easier.

Mixing with "nice" people. The third most frequently cited rationale, by ten of the interviewed mothers, was the rewards couched in descriptions of the social contacts and friendships their children were making through tennis. On this topic, mothers were more likely to describe features more specific to tennis than were generally applicable to other sports. For some, mostly the mothers of younger children, tennis tournaments and training squads provided opportunities for their children to meet others from different districts and schools, to develop new friendships, and to generally "play" together informally. Mothers of young daughters were more likely to speak of this, and Louise suggested a difference between her two children that was gender based. She said, "[Daughter] susses out her partner and she's running around arm in arm with her until they go and play. The boys aren't like that at all." Virginia spoke of friendships as a reward for her young daughter, relating to her family, all of whom played tennis. She said,

> For our family that has probably been the reward, that you meet lots of different people with the same interest as you. We can look back now and people we have known through tennis are still friends.

Peggy and Sonia, whose sons went to male-only high schools, appreciated tennis as an environment where their sons could meet and mix with girls. Both described with approval the "type" of girls their sons had met this way. The controlled nature of this social environment was an important consideration and, according to Sonia, there was an additional regulatory benefit. She said, "and I think because the girls are there it makes him more aware of his appearance."

Jill, Peggy, and Di commented on the quality of the people their children were meeting, commonly using the word "nice." Peggy, for example, said, "He has met such a lovely lot of people. He has got a nice lot of friends." There was an understanding that having their children mix with like-minded, like-valued people was an advantage, giving them a desirable social group in which to associate. Jill was embarrassed to admit this because she recognized its elitist pretensions. Nevertheless, after explaining how her daughters' peer group was "really nice kids who were not into smoking and drinking and abusing their physical state," she said,

> I guess too, because tennis, to a point, is somewhat an elitist sport, an individual sport, it costs money to play it, they are, it sounds elitist to say it but they tend to be mixing with people, children of families whose parents put a lot of time into their children. So they will be socially desirable, you know what I mean? I don't want to sound (trails off), but you know what I mean. It's parents who care about their kids and that reflects in the children.

While this described an impression of the social environment in which the children mixed, mothers of the older children, such as Yvonne, Lyn, Rita, and Kath, tended to refute the notion of meaningful friendships developing among the junior players. I sensed the rivalry amongst a very small, close group of successful junior tennis players who regularly compete against each other and are continually vying for seedings, championships, limited places on State representative teams, and teams to travel abroad. It seemed as the stakes got higher, and the rewards more material, it was not an environment particularly conducive to the development of peer group friendships, even among like-minded people.

Professional playing "is just not on." Generally, these mothers rejected the possibility of financial return from having a child progress to a professional playing career as being a reward. This was an interesting issue as it had been suggested to me at various stages throughout the research, and exclusively by men,[2] that "obviously" financial reward was the mothers' primary motivation for their dedication to their child's tennis as an equally "obvious" trait of investiture characteristic of the middle class. This is perhaps fueled by the high profile of a few international professional tennis players and the publicity of their immense earnings. I am suggesting this may be a particularly androcentric view of middle-class motherhood, that any investments made through the practices of mothering may be far more complex and not necessarily connected to direct material returns.

Although the mothers interviewed were not directly asked, three emphatically eliminated any implication that financial return was or may become a motivation to their labor. Beth, for example, said, "We (sic) have never played for money. Money has never come into it. We have never been professionally minded," and Kath, "We have never sat here and said, in five years time I hope you're winning X amount of dollars. No, I think we can only take it virtually a week at a time." In most cases, the rejection was based in pragmatism. They recognized the limits of their children's abilities and saw professionalism as an exceedingly unlikely, if not impossible, outcome. As Trish said, "Besides that, well, we know she's not that good anyway. Because we know you've got to be a world beater by thirteen." Beth recalled how the likelihood of this as an outcome was deliberately refuted by a tennis official, responding to what was believed to be the ambitions of junior players' parents. She said,

> We had the National Director of Coaching talk to us and he was saying a lot of parents are looking at the dollars signs when they're getting their kids involved in these tennis programs and things like that, but he said, if you are realistic about it all, he said it is only about 1 percent of the whole population in the world that is going to make a lot of money out of tennis. He doesn't think there's anything in it for a lot of people.

Two mothers were emphatic that they did not wish a professional playing career for their children. Rosemary said of her son, "I personally wouldn't like to see him go onto world class tennis. I think that would be an awful life," and Trish said of her daughter's future, "To be a professional tennis player is just not on, in our view anyway." At the time of the interviews, Yvonne's son appeared the closest of all of these children to potentially becoming a professional player. He and his father had gone overseas pursuing this end. Yvonne expressed huge reservations about this, based partly on her reluctance to join them and leave other children in Australia, and partly because of the extreme demands it was making on her son. She said,

> It's so hard. I often think, why doesn't he become a plumber or do an apprenticeship or something. Most kids don't have to start thinking about their careers until . . . but I mean, he's been thinking about it and working towards it for all these years, since he was eleven!

Lyn's daughter started playing tennis later than most and had only become "serious" about it in the last year. As a proficient sports player in many sports, she had deliberately chosen tennis and, Lyn said, intended "to make her life out of it." Lyn's support of this daughter toward her goal was comparable, she said, to that which she gave her other daughter's university studies, but, she continued,

> If I used my head I wouldn't encourage her at all, because I am going to lose her through it, . . . and I will probably end up hating it (laughs), but you can't not do it.

She would "lose" her daughter when by necessity she left Western Australia to compete internationally.

Career prospects facilitated by tennis were discussed, however. Peggy's son, for example, was about to leave for a university in the United States, where he had gained a scholarship through his tennis, and he planned to study engineering. He had chosen the university from several possibilities for what it offered him academically. Peggy explained how her son-in-law, who had been critical of the time and money spent on her son's tennis, had since "been the first to admit it was worth it." Kath could not envisage her daughter in an office job, and concluded,

> [She] will always do something involving tennis, I think she will probably, if she is not a tennis coach, she will have some involvement with tennis because she loves it so much. . . . She

is not an office girl, she hates being confined to barracks. She is an outdoor girl, so be it, as long as she is happy in what she is doing.

Jacqui's aspirations for her son's future in tennis were a reflection of her and her husband's experiences, not as professional players but as owners of a successful retail business that had been based on their tennis knowledge and connections.

Twelve of the mothers spoke of their children's education being a higher priority than their tennis. Rita, for example, expressed the opinion that it would be better if her son paid more attention to his school work and less to tennis, but by making comparisons with her own upbringing, in which she said, "all I knew was study," he was enjoying "the best of two worlds."

A healthy way of life. Five of the mothers spoke of the perceived health benefits of their children's involvement in sport, with two connecting this to it being outdoors, or as Sonia said, "out in the fresh air." Louise felt that perhaps her children were outside too much during the summer, considering the ultraviolet rays of the sunshine, but "it's better than being locked up with the television set, getting too many adult ideas in their heads." Rosemary explained how she and her husband had always encouraged their children in sport because "it's a good, healthy way of life." However, Di made a break from the all-too-simple connection between sport with health by recognizing psychological trauma as being health related. Her ambivalence about the value of her son's participation in tennis, evident throughout the interview, was based on her assessment of how poorly her son had been treated by tennis administrators. She considered that he had received such severe "knocks" that he was now so despondent she worried about his mental state. She said of his tennis, "It was a healthy . . . well, we *thought* it was a healthy way to go."

It was not always possible for the interviewed mothers to be clear about whether the rewards they spoke of could be attributed to tennis specifically or from their children's involvement in sport generally. Along with Jill's explanation of her daughter's increased self-esteem, for example, she said,

Then again, you don't know whether some of those [rewards] would've just been there anyway or whether it is a result of their sport. Not so much tennis but sport.

When asked, the mothers generally believed, sometimes hesitantly, that the rewards they described could have come from any sport if the child was equally as successful. Some offered reasons why they particularly liked tennis, such as Rita, who described it as an "intelligent game. It is 75 percent in the mind," and she added, "I don't like football, so many injuries. I'm glad he's not a football player." Kath and Virginia, both players themselves, valued tennis particularly for its longevity. In other words, they were happy that their child was playing a sport they could continue with for many years, and thus stay within the culture. Kath explained that no matter what the future held for her daughter as a top-class competitor, "The beaut thing about it is she will always play a super game of social tennis."

What's really in it for her? So far the rewards discussed have focused mainly on what the children were perceived to have gained from their sport. Asking those I interviewed to specify the rewards for themselves produced only a partial shift, as these stayed predominantly focused on the child. There were points, nevertheless, where they could be provisionally separated. The most frequently cited reward for the mother herself (by eight mothers) was related to her relationship with and enjoyment of her children. Four mothers spoke of how much they delighted in watching their children play, such as Rita, who said, "Watching him play, that's my reward. I love to watch him play." For Lyn, following her youngest child's tennis was a treasured time she knew would soon end. She said,

> I'm trying to enjoy every minute of it because she will be gone in another four, five months, which I find rather sad. I don't begrudge doing it, I thoroughly enjoy it. Some people say to me, "You are too thin, you don't eat, you race around like a gnat in a fish, you race around after those kids too much," they are very kind because they love you and they want you to look better or not race around. Well I think to myself I wish you would all shut up. I'm enjoying this, why don't you leave me alone, type of thing. I may get nervous at a match, I know I do, terribly nervous but I still wouldn't not want to be there. And as far as taking her while she is hitting up, I mean, when she goes with [coach] for the hour, there is no point going anywhere for an hour, it's only a waste of petrol and energy so I sit there and that's my real good time of the week, because they are entertaining to watch, and you sit back in the sun, it's

lovely. . . . and there is no one there to bug you, you can either drift off or watch what they are doing. [The coach] has got this beautiful English sense of humor, so it's pure entertainment and other people are saying, "That poor girl she, has had to drop everything and rush to that court," and I'm thinking, leave me alone, I'm enjoying this.

For mothers who were themselves tennis players it could provide a special dimension to relationships with their children. Ellen said the best thing about her sons' tennis was the way it had enabled her to become a "friend," not just to her sons but enduringly to their sporting peers as well. For Kath, her daughter's tennis playing had put her in the middle of an extraordinary intergenerational bond. She explained,

> There is no more satisfaction than to be able to play with your daughter. Because I did with my mother for many, many, many years, so I can understand. I had the best of both, playing with my mother and playing with my daughter.

Lyn relished her child's successes.

> Oh you have a heck of a lot of highs. You can imagine standing on the steps of [place name] . . . and they called out the Australian team. . . . Well, to hear her name, that was a tremendous high, because I knew how much effort she had put in, and to hear that. You get highs like that.

Yvonne, however, had said these sorts of "highs" were very short lived. While such moments, and the achievements and individual recognition of their children provided affirmation of the mothers' self-sacrificial labor, without exception they would talk about it in terms of how hard their children, rather than they themselves, had worked for these rewards. The pleasure Di gained from her son's tennis trips was because, she said, *he* had "earned" them. Yvonne explained, "People say isn't he lucky he's been overseas through tennis, been all over the world, and I think, yeah, and all the work he's done." While such rewards may have been an affirmation to them of their own hard work, this was not readily acknowledged.

Four of the mothers spoke of the pleasures related to having transferred aspirations onto their children from what they had not achieved, or opportunities they had not had. Beth, for example, said, "It's just been good because she's given us a challenge, to see someone be able to play a lot better than any of us could." Jacqui had briefly played tennis on the international professional circuit but had not enjoyed it. She said,

> I just chucked it. I just decided it was the pits. It took me six months, in fact it took me less than that, which means that I didn't have the mental capacity to make it. . . . I just adore what I'm doing now, so much more. I love the business world. I suppose I can see [son] doing what I would have loved to have done. I'm not denying that I love his success, I'm very proud of him, I love that. So I'm sort of getting the best of both worlds and seeing my son do what I would've loved to have done, and I think he'll do it a lot better. He does it a lot better already than what I ever did, I think.

There were other, more direct rewards, such as appreciating and enjoying the social contacts they themselves had made through their children's tennis, or the travel they had done in connection with it. Di talked about this in combination when she said,

> Like the time we went to Tasmania, that was wonderful. All the people that you meet, . . . you have a good social time. You have dinner with them and you all sit at tennis together and because they are all Western Australian boys you barrack together.

Although Yvonne initially cited travel associated with her son's tennis as a reward for herself, she qualified it by saying, "I mean, it was alright, but I'm not raving about the travel because you've still got to go through all the tension of watching matches." Contributing to her ambivalence was the fact that travelling to these tennis tournaments had been the only "vacation" she and her husband had taken for approximately the previous six years, during which time they had not had a family vacation involving her other children.

Beth talked about the thrill of being challenged by their move to the city, "starting again in midlife," as she described it. She had been motivated originally by the need she saw to provide her daughter with new challenges, but she took a great deal of personal satisfaction from being able to say that, through her own ability to adapt and cope, it had been a successful venture. For Peggy, the satisfaction came from having led what she described as a busy and an interesting life, extended into later years by the fact that her tennis-playing child was her youngest. She recalled a friend her same age saying how much she envied Peggy for still having this stimulating focus. There was undoubtedly a vast amount of security and satisfaction in having not just one's "purpose," but the day-to-day activities of one's life plotted out so thoroughly.

In keeping with their actions and the dedication of their labor to their children's tennis, the rationales and rewards given by the mothers were similarly focused on their children's needs and joys. To an extent, it would have been hard to break from this within the purpose of the interview. It would not have been easy for any of the mothers interviewed to find the juncture in which to speak about what she wanted for herself within a focus already defined through her being the mother of a junior tennis player. I recall at this point a comment made by Louise, indicating with wonder and pleasure that she viewed my invitation to her as a signifier of how successful her son must obviously be at tennis.

Overall, these mothers were motivated in their labor and support of tennis by what they considered best for their children. This reflected what they valued as being important to the development of their children in the process of becoming adults, and the resources available to provide the conditions which assisted in the developmental process.

Their concern for keeping their children "out of trouble," mixing with the "right" people, and developing personality traits that bode well for success in a capitalist labor market, is all about accumulating what Pierre Bourdieu (1984) would call "cultural capital"—the tastes, habits, values, and demeanors that are the symbols of social class. These children's sporting experiences were valued for the way they were seen to help reproduce middle-class culture. The resource these women could call upon for their children's needs was their time and unpaid domestic labor, free from the necessity of paid labor. They were committed to the institution of sport, specifically tennis, because of what they thought it could give their children, and negotiated their way the best they could within the institution so their children could obtain the desired rewards. These rewards rationalized and affirmed their labor. As a summary of the motivation behind the mothers' dedication to her children's sport, Trish said,

> Well, [husband and I] both unanimously agree that you've only got your children for a short time so that if you don't give them the opportunities and put the effort into them while you've got them for that short time, what did you have them for, and you know later on you'd regret it, ten years down the track. Yet to say that you've given the child the time and the effort and the financial backing and they haven't made it or they have made it, well so what, at least you've tried. I mean it's no good thinking back later, I wish we'd, or if only we'd, you know. That's how we approach it

It is the "doing" of the labor, the "trying," which is important to these women and which excuses the need for rewards for themselves.

Could she resist? While the interviewed mothers had their reasons and could identify rewards for their labor, having committed themselves to a self-sacrificing form of mothering, their choice about whether or not to do this work may in fact have been limited. Apart from any possible agenda setting from their children's fathers, eleven of the sixteen mothers spoke of their tennis-playing children in ways that suggested that the momentum stemmed from the children themselves and could not have been easily resisted. This may have been a child's intense interest in sport, her or his physical abilities, or the compelling mystique of "talent." Di said, for example,

> We couldn't have said to him, no, you're not playing tennis, you're not playing football, you're going to stay at home and make cubbies in the back yard. He was just such a highly motivated person. . . . If I'd said to Matthew I didn't want him to play, well, we just couldn't do that to Matthew. Sport has been his life.

Kath described her daughter's "natural ability, her athleticism. She is an extremely athletic kid. She has always liked a lot of sport." Trish was surprised by what her daughter had achieved in tennis. Because Trish felt she had had enough of the junior tennis routine through her two older children, she said, "So we didn't really foster her that much, we honestly didn't (laugh), but she's done all this!" Yvonne's account of her son's tennis career included an account of the attention paid to his advanced neuromuscular abilities.

When he was one [year old], he didn't like toys. He used to crawl around with a tennis racket tucked under his arm. When he was about eighteen months [old] he could actually stand and hit the ball. . . . He is good at all sports so it's hard, he wants to do them all. That is the trouble when you are good at them all. When he was three [years old] they did a film on him at [the university] and they are still showing it, . . . because he could serve, because of his muscle coordination at that age.

Beth felt as if she was part of "the system," which happened as a result of her and her husband accepting the country scholarship money for her daughter to travel to city tournaments, which had eventually led the family to move to the city. This led her daughter, and therefore herself, into what she felt was no choice. She said,

So being given the money, that was probably the cause of it all. It started the intensity of it all. Up until then it had been a fun thing. When money comes into it, then you think you've got to do more and coaches start looking at you and saying you'd better change this and alter that, and all of a sudden you're in the system, sort of. . . . And the kids become part of a system that adults create. It is a much different world to what we were used to. I had never heard about it before I came [to the city], never really knew what I was getting into, never even thought about it. I've always been free to pick and choose and do what we like without any pressure of *having* to do anything. I didn't have to go into a tournament if I didn't want to, whereas Natalie *has* to.

It would also seem that once the momentum took hold, once the children were fully incorporated into the junior tennis "system" and continued to perform adequately enough to stay there, the mothers had no power to call it to a halt, even if this is what they wished. To do so would have been considered unacceptably selfish, prioritizing their own interests to a level that could not even be verbalized. Jill illustrated this in the following explanation, which shows the insidiousness of her incorporation as well as how she could only speak about its encroachment in terms of "everybody's" lives and not her own:

Yes, it just rolled. And often when we're very tired and exhausted, I would think what is all this for, we've got to stop it. My husband says, well how can you at this stage say suddenly, kerplunk, no more, finished, when the child is still keen and doing well and there is no obvious reason not to do it, except that maybe you feel it is encroaching too much on everybody's lives. I know people who have made conscious decisions to stop children in sport, not necessarily tennis. They put their child into a sport and have suddenly been told the child is talented and should go into this program or that program, or perhaps have even started and realized the disruption to family life or the fact they don't really feel it is worthwhile and they've said to the child, no more, that's it. In the initial stages I never thought of making that decision. Perhaps I'm a slow learner (laughs). It hadn't occurred to me until much later, and by that point the wheels were in motion and there was too much momentum to pull out at that stage, unless the child herself had wanted to.

Jill reminds us that there were some mothers who can and do resist being incorporated into their children's sport to the extent these mothers of squad tennis players portray. The women interviewed were mothers who were still incorporated, not those who, for whatever reason, had said "no more, that's it." It shows clearly that there are conditions and rewards that keep some mothers in the system, providing the labor and thinking they should or could not stop.

Wives: Negotiating Reciprocity

When we move from women's relationships with children to their relationships with adult men, the rhetoric of sacrifice shifts to one of anticipated reciprocity based on the notion of partnership in marriage. It is expected that the labor a wife does for a husband should necessarily have rewards that in some way return to her, more so than from labor done for children, where there is no such expectation. Her work therefore is a means of negotiating rewards for herself. This was very clear for the women tennis players for whom their sport was a reward. For the wife of a tennis player the extent to which she perceived rewards, or could at least identify rationales that helped compensate for the demands his sport made of her, defined the line between being contented or discontented. Generally speaking, the wives interviewed who played tennis alongside their husbands, and the wives who did not, fell on either side of that line.

While the mothers of junior tennis players may have had some degree of choice in providing the necessary labor for this sport, and did so with deliberate consideration of its rewards, for the women married to men who played tennis it came with the territory. The labor a woman contributed to her husband's sport was seemingly an automatic and integral part of being "a wife." Four of the interviewed wives did not fully condone their husbands' tennis playing, and it was vigorously opposed by another two. Such attitudes, however, made little or no difference to whether or not the husbands of these women continued to play, nor to how frequently they did so. Furthermore, being opposed to a husband's participation in sport did not necessarily mean she was excused from doing the domestic labor it demanded. Nor could she control its impact on her life. In fact, her opposition to his sport, or at least her resistance to joining it, usually resulted in these being greater because, for example, it meant she did a good deal more child care. Certainly the interviewed women who were not tennis players were left with greater responsibility for child care than those who played tennis alongside their husbands, where sharing child care was more frequently negotiated. It is therefore quite possible for men to play their chosen sport regardless of their wives' attitudes toward it, and still expect it to be facilitated and serviced. To this extent, women could be in marriages where they have little option but to provide the space and conditions that allowed their husbands' leisure. They provided it by picking up the responsibilities their husbands reneged in pursuing their sport, and the women were therefore tolerant of the situation more than proactive in its creation.

Once again, it should be remembered that the group of wives of tennis-playing men interviewed consisted of women who still fit this definition. In other words, outside the scope of the study were women who, as a result of their opposition to their husbands' tennis, or for any other reason, may have not provided the necessary support to sustain their husbands' playing such that they ceased to play. These results do not suggest the scenario is impossible, only that it might depend more on the will of the husbands than the desire of the wives. Also not included in this study are women who may have left marriages because of the demands and stresses caused by their partners' tennis. Nevertheless, these results clearly show that this is not outside the realms of possibility.

The majority of the wives interviewed, however, did condone their husbands' tennis and had therefore identified rationales for its impact upon their lives, based on the rewards they felt it offered.

Again, these were mainly expressed in response to questions that asked what the women considered "the best thing" about their husbands playing tennis. Similar to the interviewed mothers, several benefits would usually be listed, but overall the tendency to give multiple rationales occurred less frequently from the wives than it had from the mothers, and the rewards were fewer in total. Furthermore, four wives, all nonplayers, struggled to find any answer at all to the question, a situation that had not occurred with any of the mothers. In summary, the rationales given by the interviewed wives involved their husbands' health and fitness, social contacts and travel, wives' assimilated joys, and space for themselves. They were not, however, without contradictions or expressions of ambivalence.

"It keeps him fit." The most frequently cited reward of a husband's tennis, expressed by nine of the fifteen wives, had to do with the husband's being physically active, and the opportunity for exercise. This was based on a concern for his physical fitness and its associations with health. Even the women who struggled to concede anything positive about their husband's participation in tennis found this a possible rationale. For example, Marie's only response to the question was, "Well, it's good for him," and Tania said, "It keeps him fit."

June put the associations of health and sport participation in the context of her children also playing tennis, and said that one of the best things about this was, "I think I've got a fairly active, healthy family. . . . I think basically the family [is] very healthy because they are very sporty minded." For Trudi, the belief in sport as a means to physical fitness and an ideal body for both herself and her husband became increasingly important with age. She stated,

> We think it is a very good thing, to become fit. As you become older, I think it is really important that you play sport, . . . to keep your figure and that you don't become overweight or you don't drink too much alcohol.

While the women called upon a general understanding of connections between their husbands' participation in sport and their health, this was not necessarily the motivation. Karen explained that the exercise her husband "loved" had to be done within a competitive milieu, which for him was limited to tennis. Contrary to a state of physical fitness, his knees were in very poor health and he was having to restrict his play because of this. She said,

So when I say he loves exercise, I don't know what would happen if he couldn't play tennis. He's past football or cricket. It's limited in what exercise it is.

Five of the nine wives who described tennis as making a contribution to their husbands' health and fitness spoke contradictorily of tennis-related injuries suffered by their husbands, which had prevented them playing for various lengths of time. Three others also spoke of their husbands suffering injuries.

The "unhealthy" alternative to tennis, used as both a rationale and a threat, was drinking excessive alcohol. Tania had immediately followed her comment about how tennis kept her husband fit with ". . . and he's not holding up a bar stool." Marie explained how her husband had used this to silence her protests, saying, "He said it was either put up with him playing tennis or he'd go to the pub," even though, she said, he was not a "drinker."

Alcohol is available for purchase at most tennis clubs in Perth, which suggests that the issue of drinking is laden with far more concerns than just those related to physical health, such as social control and keeping men "responsible." There is historical resonance here concerning the measure of success of a "good wife." Rich's description of the "ideal wife," invented to shift women from work to home during the Industrial Revolution, included, "Women were warned . . . that if they failed to create the comforts of the nest, their men would be off to the alehouse" (Rich 1977,49).

More current associations surrounding men's patronage of pubs and bars are of excessive alcohol consumption and drunken, abusive behavior being directed at wives and children. Given this as a threatening possibility, a wife would likely consider a husband's tennis playing a safer alternative, and value tennis culture as an environment where excessive drinking may likely be moderated by fitness and physical performance criteria. In other words, as long as a husband played tennis, he would likely treat his wife more reasonably, not be "squandering" the family's financial resources, and he would be less likely to develop health problems that demanded his wife's care. The sport therefore carried strongly coercive rationales within the rhetoric of health and safety.

If he's happy so am I. The third most frequently cited reward, by five of the interviewed wives, was the assimilation of their husband's pleasures and joys as their own, such as when Kerry said, "I suppose because he gets so much pleasure out of it that gives me pleasure too." Rebecca acknowledged the benefits her husband gained from playing tennis, saying, "I suppose it's good for him to feel good about being good at something." Anthea took this effect more onto herself.

> What is the best thing? He enjoys it. He just really, really enjoys his tennis, and he is getting better, and when he feels good about it I just think that is fantastic.

Sarah felt pride in her husband's skills as a tennis player, saying, "I'm still very proud to see him in the middle-old age he is, still playing so well." Sally, however, felt ambivalent about the pleasures of having a husband who was much in demand for all sorts of tennis-related matters. When asked how she felt about that, she replied, "I suppose you have to be flattered. I mean, there is no point in feeling abused and used, which you probably are."

Pauline turned the notion of reflected happiness around, giving a sinister angle on the dynamics of domestic harmony as they pertain to a husband's tennis. She said,

> The best thing? I suppose it keeps him happy. I think if he didn't have it he'd be quite miserable. He'd be crabby because he didn't have that outside interest. I suppose it makes him a more complete person in himself. And in that way it probably helps all of us, I guess, because if he was unhappy and miserable none of us would benefit from that.

Aside from the double standard here, where an acknowledgment of a husband's need for an "outside interest" to be a "complete person" is in stark contrast with the denial of the same for his wife, the pressure on her to maintain harmony is clearly illustrated. In order to placate him and dissipate the tensions he would otherwise create if "crabby," his interests are entertained and serviced. This is particularly insidious when one considers that all of the "us" in this household were women—his wife and three daughters.

There are several layers to this domestic dynamic in relation to men's tennis. On one level, a man's "need" to play, and the ramifications to his family if he does not, would be highly compelling of a wife's support. June said, for example,

> I often tell him he's addicted to it, it's like a drug, he needs to be playing tennis. He likes to be healthy, he likes to be fit, and he's happy when he is playing well and he's fit, and of course when they're happy you're happy as well.

At the time of the interview, she was experiencing his "withdrawal symptoms" because, as a result of an injury, he had not played for the past three months. She described how her husband being "at a bit of a loose end" was "irritating," and she explained how, "it's funny," but she had "noticed" his tennis more in the last few months when he was not playing than all of the prior years when he did.

On another level, wives might facilitate husbands' tennis if it is seen as a means of transferring tension to somewhere other than the home, releasing it on something other than themselves and their children. Karen, recognized this, explained,

> He [has] a really pressure type job and I think without tennis, tennis is his greatest means of relaxation. He can come home fed up and ready to scream and he can go and have a game of tennis and come back and the whole world is wonderful and life's worth living again. Honestly, it's his greatest relief and form of relaxation.

Tania had hoped for a similar outcome and had provisionally condoned her husband's tennis for this reason. However, she said,

> No matter what he does he seems to be stressed out. He's stressed out from work. I thought the tennis would help ease this but it doesn't. He gets more tired from it and that stresses him further.

She had struggled to find a rationale for her husband's tennis, and even this one had escaped her. Facilitating his tennis as a way of bargaining for his reasonableness, or simply to dissipate the tensions within which she and her children had to live, had not proved rewarding because he did not get the hoped-for cathartic effect from playing tennis.

A further dynamic concerning tension is that which may be produced by a husband's actual play. The joy Sally spoke of was associated with her husband playing well. She said,

The best part is when he comes home and he's won or beaten somebody or done something right that has really appealed to him. He is actually gratified, he's actually achieved what he set out to do, . . . he is very satisfied.

If the atmosphere in which a wife has to live may be created by her husband's response to the outcomes of his participation in a competitive activity, it is perhaps little wonder that she will find joy in his happiness when he wins. June described how their house was full of tangible evidence of her husband's successes.

There are a lot of possessions we have in the house that have been tennis trophies. Glasses to burn (laughs), travelling rugs to burn, and tennis bags. It's been rewarding. I mean, while it doesn't compare with prize money in top golf or something, it's very satisfying to come home from a tennis tournament with a new tennis bag or a new tennis shirt or something.

"It's a marvelous way of mixing." The second most frequently cited reward of a husband's playing tennis was comments made by eight of the interviewed wives concerning the friendships and social contacts their husbands enjoyed through tennis. Sarah said, "He's very well respected in tennis circles, he has some very good friends." Lorelle stated this as being the best aspect of her husband's tennis, detailing how his closest friends were men he had played tennis with since he was a teenager. In five cases, the friendships of which the women spoke in this context were also part of the social rewards associated with their own tennis.

Some wives, however, did not need to be regular tennis players to enjoy their husbands' tennis friends. The "best thing" about Bronwyn's husband's tennis was, "The guys he is with are great, and it is good because they meet up again at the end of each year. I think that is really good for him." Her additional comment, ". . . and that is the best benefit of it for me as well," was in reference to the several social occasions spent with his tennis associates and their female partners. Enjoyment of his friends and the social events he condones meant that as a couple they could socialize together and both find it mutually satisfying.

It seemed too that as well as appreciating their social life as "a couple," some women cared about the quality of their husbands' social life and how well their husbands functioned socially on their own. Kerry appreciated her husband's tennis for the opportunities it gave him to mix with others, particularly other businessmen. She described his tennis club as a site where he socialized at times outside those designated for playing the sport.

> Even though they're business people that he's associated with down at the tennis club, they're very diverse from his type of business and so I suppose they have plenty to talk about. He really does enjoy going down there. He *really* looks forward to going down there on Friday night for the socializing.

Many years before, when Kerry's children were very young and her husband's paid work took him out of town for the entire week, she vehemently resented his spending Friday evenings when he returned "home" at the tennis club rather than with her. Her reappraisal of the situation, seeing the same behavior many years later as one of the best things about his tennis, and talking about how much pleasure it gave her to see him happy, illustrates the temporal and circumstantial specificity of how rewards are assessed.

Kerry's comment about the social advantages of her husband mixing with other businessmen were given a different edge by Bronwyn. She described at some length the valuable contribution her husband's tennis, especially his ability in the sport, made to his professional career and the way it "opened doors" for him. She said,

> Because it is so social I think it has helped him a lot, it has really opened up a lot of doors for him. He's met a lot of influential people, it's allowed him to travel. A lot of people in the profession play tennis and respect him automatically and will talk to him on a social level, about tennis because they have played with him many times before. . . . And he normally always wins or comes runner up in the Law Society [tournament] so he's known for that. It is an introduction. But there are many other people out there in business who, if you are down at the club and you are a good player you are known for that. If you are an ordinary player, people don't remember you.

She was employed in the same profession, and without recognizing how it might therefore place her at a disadvantage, she spoke of the corporate value of being known as a competitive sportsperson and the sporting "boys network" that operated informally to her husband's advantage. She continued,

[. . .] firms are very keen to employ people who have got a strong competitive sport, because it's very good release for them and they won't get so stressed out, and it shows that they have that competitive edge and are able to cope with it. They don't say that, but when you look around, most of the department, the successful [ones] are very competitive in terms of sport or have had a strong sporting background, state grade level somewhere. Sport is more important for guys too, than it is for girls and very much a boys thing. When you go down to the clubs and things like that, they always talk about sport and how you are going and stuff like that.

The advantages that accrued to the men could, however, spill over to their wives. Janet, for example, spoke of her husband's tennis opening doors to social situations that she enjoyed by immediate association. She explained,

It's a marvelous way of mixing, it opens up so many doors, . . . We have done some wonderful things through tennis. Even travelling, like when we go to Wimbledon, because we have been involved locally we are able to get seats, better seats, that sort of thing.

She described many occasions when she had shared and enjoyed the rewards resulting from her husband's high profile in tennis. At the time of the interview, her life was focused almost exclusively on supporting him in his administrative role, and her answer to the "best thing" question was "because he thoroughly loves it, and I love being part of it all."

Space for themselves. Four women spoke of their husbands' tennis as giving them space for themselves. Rebecca explained that the best thing about her husband's tennis was, "It gives me time by myself. It gives me an excuse to do whatever I want. He could never say you can't do that when most of the time he's played tennis." She considered this a negotiated "bargain," providing space for her interests and some individual autonomy within their marriage. It was within a similar "bargaining" context that Kerry, for example, and many of the women tennis players negotiated their participation in sport.

This "space for themselves," however, may not always be within the woman's control. Its timing, duration, and quality may be limited and determined by the husband's tennis schedule, and something that the women claim for themselves only by way of default. Moreover, for three of these four women who had children at home, this "space" was still taken up with responsibilities for child care. For example, Karen explained,

> He plays after work on a Wednesday night and [he and his team members] always go out to tea on a Wednesday night, so that makes it a very easy night for me, because it's a casual night, [the children and I] will have scrambled eggs or something, I don't do a big dinner. . . . I used to get a bit fed up that I was still sitting at home while he was having his [tennis] hit. Although now I don't feel that at all. I love the nights when I have an easy night, midweek, when he goes out to play his tennis. I feel that's great. It gives me a night for myself and I'm not rushing to cook a special tea and it's quite a low key kind of night.

Even though the night "for herself" still involved the care of her children, removing the additional responsibility for her husband's care gave her a sense of extra freedom. Tania said of her husband,

> It's just easier when he's not here. It's not only the tennis washing, things like that, it's meals as well. When it's just me and the kids we can have something simple. But he'll want steak or something like that.

Karen also illustrated the subtle way in which the space to do one's "chosen" activity may also occur by default, in that the activity itself may have been coerced. She said,

> He never ever has said to me don't you think you are playing [tennis] too much. Lots of the girls, their husbands get a bit fed up if they play too many days a week or whatever. He has never done that, but I think only because he felt he has played so much. But he has encouraged me to play, so I suppose from that point of view it is not quite fair to say he's gone out and said you stay at home and look after the kids. He always wanted the kids to come and me to be playing as well.

Karen explained how her real passion was gardening, but her husband did not share this interest, and she had difficulty finding time to garden when she spent most of her weekends at tennis. This example makes problematic the concept of her tennis being space for herself and highlights the ways in which women's "self-space" may be provisionally negotiated and contradictory.

An important distinction between whether or not these wives could easily identify rewards from their husbands' tennis lay in whether or not they were also players. For seven of the wives who were tennis players themselves, the rewards of their husbands' tennis were strongly related to rewards ascribed to their own play, especially those concerning social relationships and friendships. These women expressed significantly fewer feelings of "missing out," being "left behind" to look after the children, or having one's labor abused, which is what strongly characterized the responses of wives who did not share their husbands' interest in tennis. Non-playing wives who experienced no semblance of sharing child care or domestic work, and little reciprocity in opportunities for leisure, found it virtually impossible to identify positive outcomes from their husbands' tennis.

On the other hand, when both wife and husband played, each of their play was "guaranteed" by the participation of the other, reciprocating the opportunity. Although it was still predominantly the wife's labor that facilitated play for both of them, she did this on the basis that it was also "for her," and for which she could identify her own rewards. Her participation was in itself negotiated space and held rewards that were expressions of agency, even though, and often because, it could be integral to the maintenance of family relationships and servicing the interests of family members.

Players: The Negotiated Reward

Clearly illustrated in the accounts by women players in chapter 4 were the joys they experienced from participation in the sport and the extent to which they had negotiated this as a leisure space for themselves. A question asking these women what the best thing was about their tennis required an answer that by necessity focused on them. However, their responses also could be conflated with how the sport was featured in the lives of her family members and its contribution to her identity as a wife and mother. So while attempting to highlight the personal rewards she derived from her play, we should not forget that these were nevertheless negotiated out of her family responsibilities, whether or not those family members were also tennis players.

The rewards of participation in tennis expressed by the women players demonstrated the contestable process of having agency, particularly the complex shifts between "inner" personal and "external" social interests. Being a sportswoman is by definition something that one does with one's own body. Whatever the rewards of servicing the physical activities of one's children and/or one's male partner, having chosen to and being involved in the activity oneself presupposes some highly personal motives and rewards. Those which the women players identified as rewards from their tennis included their own health and fitness, having an "outlet" from the home, enjoying social contacts and friendships, and it being an evident site for recognizing personal achievements.

"I'm healthy because of it." Four of the interviewed women who were veteran tennis players and three of the interviewed wives who were players described as a reward of playing tennis the opportunity it presented for physical exercise and its contribution to their own health and fitness. Dorothy, for example, said, "I like sport and being involved in it. I feel as though I'm healthy because of it. Touch wood, I'm a healthy person and I think that's got a lot to do with it." Linda said quite simply, "It keeps me fit." As Frye succinctly phrased it to explain women's autonomy,

> . . . it will not do that I arrange everything so that *you* get enough exercise; for me to be healthy, I must get enough exercise. My being adequately exercised is logically independent of your being so. (Frye 1983, 70, original emphasis)

A woman's physical fitness depends on exercising her own body, just as she can only feel "leisured" from her own leisure. These women tennis players understood this distinction.

"It gets you out." Six of the fifteen interviewed players spoke of how they valued their participation in tennis as an "outlet." By this, they meant it allowed them to get out of their homes, away from the responsibilities of domestic labor, and to be active in something that was defined as being for themselves. Ruth, who was widowed and lived on her own, said the best thing about her tennis was, "Getting out of the house (laughs)." She continued, "It gets you out, you meet people, it's a day's outing." Linda considered it important for women who were "stuck around the house." She said it provided a social outlet and intellectual challenge that men received through their paid work. For herself, she explained,

It's just wonderful. I think it's a wonderful setup. I mean, you could be sitting around doing housework. How boring! . . . I think it makes it easier to do your housework and the boring things if you know you've got some fun thing to do at the end of it.

Dorothy said,

My word, [tennis] has been a big part [of my life]. I think it's been a crutch quite often, when things have got tense, and you go down there and put it out of your mind. As I say, when the girls had their calisthenics and so on, [tennis] was my outlet, to be able to go down there and put it out of my mind and forget about it and do something for myself, instead of running after them all the time.

Associated with these comments were references to how playing tennis provided these women with a form of relaxation and tension release. Betty talked about the demanding hours of her full-time paid employment, and said,

It was go, go, go all the time, and I don't think that's good for anyone, especially running a home, coming home, cooking a meal, doing the washing, and all that. I think no one should be as busy as that but . . . I couldn't relax much, only on the tennis court, then I'd forget all my troubles. I don't have any troubles on the tennis court.

Dorothy's resistance to playing lawn bowls included the following justification:

You can't go down and release all your frustrations with [a bowl] or it will finish up in the ditch all the time. At least with tennis, you can go and have a good whack and feel a lot better for it afterwards.

Having "an outlet" was, in as true a sense as it was possible, something for themselves.

Friendships, "first and foremost." It was the social rewards of tennis, however, which were most frequently cited and more likely given the first or highest priority. These were described by fourteen of the fifteen veteran players interviewed and also mentioned by all seven of the interviewed wives who played tennis.

There were several nuances to the social benefits accrued through tennis. One was the enjoyment of meeting lots of people, which the structural organization and practices of the sport were seen to especially facilitate. The women's midweek pennant competition was highly valued for this because teams of women traveled to each other's clubs to play other teams. It was this structure that was most frequently referred to as being the essence of where their enjoyment of tennis lay. Overlying this, most of the interviewed players were involved in the Veteran's Club competition where teams were deliberately made up of women from different metropolitan clubs. Connie said,

> This is why it's been so popular, because women found that they were playing with [someone] that maybe they'd played against in the pennants in other years. It's really lovely.

After a similar explanation, Linda said, "So, you get to know a lot of people over the years."

The servicing structures and women's organizational collectives were also considered to have socially beneficial opportunities. Marilyn valued her position with the Women's Auxiliary for the opportunity it gave her to extend her circle of associates. She said, after describing the workload associated with the position,

> But I have loved my involvement in Women's Auxiliary. I have met so many women I would never have met through being a member of [tennis club].

Most "really close" friends, however, were members of the women's own clubs, and had developed through, for example, repeatedly sharing the rituals, joys, and frustrations of tennis competition. Again, membership in a pennant team was an important part of this process. Connie talked about how enjoyable it was when all four members of her team would travel to the other clubs in one car. She said,

> At the end of the match, win or lose, we would collapse in the car and go to one of our places and have a few drinks and mull over the match. What we should have done and what we shouldn't have done, always in good humor, in good fun.

Patricia provided details of after-competition rituals during women's midweek tennis, which were a celebration of the shared culture and provided the fabric of women's close relationships.

> After pennants are finished the other team stays for lunch and the girls all sit with their opposition, and there might be five teams in the clubhouse and five opposing teams, and when the opposing teams have all gone home they zoom over to everyone, 'We won! we beat that lady,' you know, or 'We lost again.' It's hilarious. And then the teams that have been playing away at other clubs drive back and they all have their stories to tell. Oh, I really enjoy it. I suppose to a man walking in the door, he'd think hell this is so bitchy. It's not. It's really fun.

These sorts of specific cultural practices, focused around shared experiences and heightened by the intensity of involvement in physically active competition, provided the basis for easy and close friendships. In addition, there is the understanding of sharing like circumstances, which underpin the support given to one another, such as described in the previous chapter. All of this contributes to the development of friendships, which were intense and lasting. Noelene talked about "the early years" when "we never had anything" and would invite the women she played tennis with back to her house afterward. She said,

> We all had three or four kids, all of us. I've still got those same girlfriends today, and we'd have all these little kids sitting in there and the room would be full and we'd be changing [diapers] and we'd sit there and we'd laugh, have cups of tea and a piece of bread or toasted sandwich or whatever I had made and sit there and laugh about what we'd done that day, how we'd played awful tennis or good tennis or whatever we thought. We thought we were champions in those days. Yet we could hardly hit a ball over the net. We should have done this or we should have done that and didn't we have a ripper of a time.

Jean's reply to being questioned about the rewards of her tennis was,

> Friendship, I would say would come first and foremost, definitely. You make a lot of great friends through tennis and they're friends you have for a long, long time.

She then turned to Frances and asked how long they had been playing tennis together, synonymous to how long they had been
friends.[3] The resulting discussion illustrated the time frames by
which women may come to understand their own and each other's
lives when such things are shared. They pinpointed the specific
tennis court where they first played together and then referred to
Jean's daughter who "was about three or four and she's thirty-two
now, so I suppose [that long]."

While there was a great appreciation of tennis as a means of
meeting and forming strong friendships with other women, there
were some who appreciated the sport for its structural inclusion of
men. Club social tennis was mixed, and Alice said, "The fact it's
social with both sexes is good because I really don't like doing
things with just women."

The structural integration of men and women in some aspects
of tennis opened the possibility of social rewards that included and
usually depended on the involvement of the women's husbands. To
begin with, there was the appreciation of having met one's husband
through tennis, which had been the case for four of the interviewed
players. Carol's reply to the question about "the best thing" was,
"Well I met my husband through tennis. That probably is the best
thing in my life from my sport." This was a surprise to hear in the
context of the rest of her interview, which highlighted her considerable achievements in tennis and its absolute centrality to her life
since childhood. These four, along with Marilyn, valued tennis particularly for the way it had contributed to their marriages through
being an activity that both partners enjoyed, enhanced by the social
opportunities this situation easily afforded. For example, Brenda
said,

> It really has been a lot of fun in my life because we have had
> some wonderful weekends away, as groups. Then with my
> husband, we used to go away just the two of us . . . we'd go to
> country weekends. We've had a lot of enjoyment out of tennis.

Being one of a couple who both played tennis appeared to open
up further possibilities for involvement in the culture that could
correspondingly offer greater social rewards. One of these was travelling to highly sociable tennis events, such as country tournaments, as was mentioned by four of the interviewed players.
Another was the way in which being a tennis-playing couple provided passports into new communities. Those who had relocated as

adults, particularly to country towns, appreciated the sport for how it paved the way to rapid social inclusion. Brenda, for example said,

> It's very important in the country. I mean, country life revolves around sport and if you don't play sport in the country its very difficult to make friends, actually, to get involved in the community.

She explained how when she and her husband moved to a country town there was another married couple who had arrived there six months earlier,

> and they had not met a single soul and we introduced them to people from the tennis club. They hadn't met anyone, but we went straight down to tennis. That's how you meet people, so it's very difficult in the country if you don't play.

Four of the interviewed players spoke of similar experiences. The relative significance of sport in rural communities of Western Australia was further explained by Sarah. She said,

> If you weren't religious or you didn't play tennis you might as well be dead, in the county, in our situation. You know, you move into a town and you're either a churchgoer or you played a sport and that's the only way you'd make it. . . . I think we were very lucky that we played tennis. We had a beaut time in the country, mainly because of our sporting interests I think.

It is not only in rural areas where this process of social inclusion was appreciated. Carol, who had also left Perth following her husband's employment, valued the tennis they both played because,

> We've met so many friends and we've found, when you're away for seven years like we were and you come back, all your friends have gone their own separate ways. But when you've played sport it's so easy to move back into a situation where you move into a club and friendships are made straight away.

Brenda described the social benefits of tennis clubs for "outsiders," "for someone like yourself," she said, "coming from New Zealand." She explained that in her tennis club such people "stuck together," and it was those people "that they do things with, you know, Christmas and that." Tennis club colleagues became the social support that may have otherwise been provided by families. This had certainly been the case for Sally. Having moved to Perth from the other side of Australia in the early years of her marriage, she described the circle of friends she and her husband had made through tennis as their "surrogate family," sharing child care, holidays, crises, and celebrations. She could not overemphasize the closeness of this group, nor how important it had been to all of its members. She said,

> Our very best friends belong to the tennis club, and this is a close-knit group of six couples. This is because several of us didn't have parents in this state, so we all sort of clubbed together and fostered each other's children. They would call you auntie and uncle and things like this and became very attached to each other. And in fact that attachment still remains.

She added,

> [We] need each other and [we] look to each other for strength and it really is an interesting situation. Probably a unique situation. I mean, I wouldn't have found Western Australia anywhere near as appealing if it hadn't been for them.

When both partners in a marriage played tennis, inevitably, it seemed, their children became involved as well. Patricia valued this most about the sport, saying,

> I suppose, broadly, it's made our family very compact as far as our interests are concerned. We all talk the same language, we're all interested in what each other does, so therefore that's probably the happiest aspect of it, most fulfilling aspect of it.

During Anne's interview she reflected back on what she described as "a very happy life," one that had almost entirely pivoted around tennis. She said,

> We were five kids, and we were all very happy together. We didn't have family arguments or anything, ever. And we all did things together, always. Especially because of sport, we were

able to keep together, and the tennis club kept us together really. My sister married a boy from the tennis club, you see, and I married a boy from the tennis club, and my other brother married a girl from the tennis club, but [another] brother's the only one that didn't. . . . [He and his wife] always joined us in everything though, even though they weren't in the tennis club.

The overlap between the women's self-interests and those of others is well illustrated. These women were capable of appreciating a multitude of rationales, reflecting a complexity of benefits and joys, which shift and overlap between definitions of themselves as individuals with independent interests and as social selves whose interests are not divorced from those of others. This, and the juggling to accommodate any conflict, is evident in Betty's struggle to distinguish the importance she placed on her tennis from her attentiveness to others, both within tennis and at home. She said,

But you get into that team, you see, and you can't let the team down. [I play] Tuesday, Wednesday, Saturday, and Sunday if I want to. But I don't make it the . . . if something else turns up [at home], unless I'm involved in a particular thing [at tennis], I wouldn't put it first, but I can't imagine not playing.

Her decisions about when she played and when she did not were made by continually balancing the relative weight of responsibilities to others, along with her own desires.

"It's something I do fairly well." The second most frequently cited rewards, by ten of the interviewed players, are those that can be classified as being related to distinctively individual desires and achievements. Five players spoke of the way in which tennis provided them, through competition, with a personal challenge that they particularly enjoyed. Connie mentioned this as being the second most enjoyable aspect of tennis after friendships, saying "and the competition of course," and she continued by recalling the loss of a significant championship match as being the most difficult time of her long, tennis-playing career.

Being active and skilled was an important source of joy. When Betty was asked what was "the best thing" about tennis, she replied, "The association with other people who like playing tennis and the joy of hitting a good ball over the net." Brenda said, "If you're really playing a good, hard match, I find that's the nicest thing. I really enjoy it. It's the challenge I suppose."

Molly was the only one of the interviewed players who did not especially value the social aspect of tennis culture. She said she had had enough of "the social part" of sport through associations with the sport played by her children and husband (which was not tennis), and, "I went [to tennis] purely and simply for the physical part of it. I was after more of a challenge than anything else." She described at length how this was as much a mental challenge as a physical one, and that for her the fun was "strategy." She explained,

> The best part of tennis is meeting the opposition and seeing who you've got to play and trying to work it all out. Trying to work out your challenge. That's the best part. That's what I like.

Seven players cited personal achievements, recognition, and tributes as rewards from their involvement in tennis. Betty and Patricia spoke of these rewards as having come through their playing, valuing themselves as sportswomen who made recognizable distinctions. Betty spoke of winning medals, cups, and being club champion three years in a row. Her list of "best things" included,

> and also perhaps having won a few prizes. You rather live in the past when you do things like that. You realize you were good once and although you're now not so good you can still hit a ball, probably. You can rest on your laurels. . . . I think it's just something I can do fairly well, which is why I like it so much.

Second to its contribution to her family unity, Patricia spoke of her tennis career.

> I suppose the highlights would have to be, originally getting to a State level as a child. And then succeeding in a coaching capacity and then I'd say, probably, finally, getting selected to represent Australia at a time in my life when I thought that tennis was certainly over, this whole Veterans idea cropped up and I felt very proud to be wearing the Australian Coat of Arms. It was something I never thought I would ever do.

Five others spoke of the recognition and tributes they received for the service work they had done for tennis. Noelene and Anne described being awarded life membership status at their respective clubs as a tribute to long service. Noelene received hers five years earlier than her husband and talked about how she thought his was delayed long past deserving it because "they usually don't like two in the one family because you don't pay [membership] fees." Anne and her husband had been given a "testimonial day" at their club when they retired after seventeen years of coaching and a lifetime of club involvement.

> First of all, they named the new gates they had put up after us, 'The [Surname] Entrance.' We could ask anybody we wanted to for tennis and we had 140 playing tennis and they had a dinner in the night and we had 210 at the dinner and the ladies did all the catering themselves. It was just beautiful. And they gave us a nice big fat check to go back to New Zealand because we'd always been talking about New Zealand and when the chap presented it, he said, "now there you are, you've got enough money for you and [husband] to go to New Zealand." So that was wonderful.

For four of the interviewed players, a highlight of their tennis careers had been their inclusion in a public relations team sponsored by Government House and including the wife of the then Governor General to Western Australia. Connie had captained that team. These women explained how the twenty-four women who comprised it were chosen for having done, as Jean said, "a lot for tennis in different ways," and it was considered a recognition of and reward for dedicated service to their sport. Marilyn said,

> I had such a wonderful time with [Governor General's wife] that it's something I will never forget and I really think that it's only occurred through my involvement at Women's Auxiliary level. . . . My tennis ability could never have got me to those heights, but my organizing ability did.

She listed the best things about her involvement in tennis that were all achieved through service roles and her obvious ability in those areas.

> The friendships I've made through the [Women's] Auxiliary. The people I've got to know at State level, which I would

never have done without Women's Auxiliary because I'm not a State level player. Yeah, Women's Auxiliary has been a highlight of my tennis career. And being the first woman president at [tennis club] gave me a very big thrill. That was very special to me. Perhaps more so than being president of Women's Auxiliary. . . . And being in [Governor's wife's] team would have to be the highlight.

It is nonsense to consider that the rewards women derive from the work done as service to others are somehow "false" for not being somehow defined as independent unto themselves. It would be destructive to women's autonomy, however, if this were the only channel through which they could find rewards, or despite doing the servicing labor, there were no rewards. The involvement of women as players of tennis highlights the difficulties of attempting an understanding of women's involvement in sport as anything but a multidimensional experience. It is neither a purely self-determined and self-indulgent privilege, nor is it blind incorporation into an unresponsive, patriarchal institution. Whatever the joys and pleasures derived from their participation in playing tennis and their involvement in its administration, the fact that the women were there at all showed their own leisure empowerment, even though it was a reward negotiated within social constraints that deemed such involvement an immense privilege. In a global sense, the sporting lives of these women in Western Australia were afforded not only by the economic and political security of the country in which they lived, but also by the geographic, climatic, and historical conditions under which a culture had evolved to present such opportunities. Linda, for example, who had emigrated to Australia, described "a whole new life." She explained,

In America they just don't have the setup they have here. It's a beautiful setup here for tennis, particularly for the women. I don't even know if they have it in the eastern states [of Australia], but any woman here can just go and play on a grass court. I'd never seen a grass court before. We just didn't have them, if [we did] they would be in very expensive country clubs. You just couldn't go and play. So the setup here is just so ideal. It doesn't cost that much, and you can just join a club and be part of it.

The opportunities were, however, disproportionately afforded to white, middle-class married women, who by virtue of their husbands' income, did not need to be employed in paid work under conditions that excluded their participation in tennis at times scheduled for female players. Furthermore, in Boudieu-ian terms, race and class privilege provided the currency by which these women found tennis culture accessible and comfortable, such as their having the necessary physical and social skills. However, the opportunity to do something for oneself, such as play tennis, had been negotiated within women's lives defined as being first and foremost of service to others.

The process of negotiation meant, for one, taking servicing roles with them when they went to tennis, thus providing much of the background labor upon which the organizational practices and structures depended. This labor "bought" women time and space in the sport, "allowing" them to be there. First, however, they had to negotiate their way out of their own homes and away from the expectations of service for its other occupants. Again, this could be achieved by taking some of it with them, such as when their family members also went to tennis. When family members were not included in their own tennis, such as when those family members do not also play, the space for women to do so could only be negotiated by their attending to the quality of service at home. Women's tennis was therefore a negotiated reward.

SUMMARY

The women I interviewed were still within "the system." In other words, all had some compelling reason to stay within the roles and identities by which my research had found them, and they were, for the most part, content with those roles. Some, however, were more happy in their roles than were others, and this happiness depended mainly on the degree to which the role was voluntary and how tennis contributed to what they valued in their lives and their families' lives. Those women who were least happy were the wives of male tennis players, for whom their expectations of reciprocity and partnership in marriage had been severely denied because of their husbands' tennis, and who struggled for control or change. Similarly, mothers of tennis-playing children who had been hurt or disappointed through their experiences in tennis, gave more conditional rationales for their support of the institution. The issue of choice was sometimes debatable in all three interview groups, however, highlighting the constantly contestable ground of agency. There are common background themes in all of these women's lives, and it is these themes that we will next discuss.

SIX

GENDERED INSTITUTIONS
SERVICE GENDERED INSTITUTIONS

If I had been a working Mum . . .

—*Kath*

Everyone's got a partner.

—*Molly*

OVERVIEW

An intention of this study was to "make visible" women's labor by detailing what the interviewed women did and discussing the context in which it was done, illustrating how this labor maintained the sport of tennis. Mothers of junior Squad players were intensely involved in facilitating the participation of their children, and the requirements of providing transport placed huge demands on, and structured the lives of, these women. Their primary responsibility for child care meant they serviced children's sport. The same responsibility, along with the other domestic labor done by wives and partners of adult male tennis players, created space for and serviced men's participation in sport. This occurred regardless of whether or not these women sanctioned their husbands' tennis-playing, but was experienced very differently depending upon whether or not they also were tennis players. Women who played tennis alongside their husbands were the most fully immersed in tennis culture, and their multiple roles created further labor demands. Women tennis players largely facilitated their own participation in the sport out of their domestic responsibilities, and these women detailed the management required to achieve this, showing how, with child care especially, they helped each other. Furthermore, women's work in tennis clubs and organizations makes an immense contribution to the smooth running and continuation of tennis culture. The labor of the interviewed women in all three groups ensured its maintenance and reproduction.

The veteran women players with tennis-playing husbands and the tennis-playing wives of male players were two groups in this study that could have been easily collapsed into one because of their similar experiences. That is, with both partners playing the same sport, the woman became "immersed" in it, and her servicing work was mostly hidden among that which she did for herself. However, the group of women players whose husbands did not play and the group of nonplaying wives of male players offered important contrasts. The major differences were the extent to which the sport made an impact on domestic management and was visible to other family members.

The tennis of women players with nonplaying husbands remained separate from their family relationships and was contained in such a way as to have minimal impact on the lives of family members. The tennis of the men with nonplaying wives was separate from family relationships but was by no means hidden. Imagining reversed situations clarifies this succinctly, because it highlights how impossible, verging on ridiculous, the reversal actually is. It would have been totally inconceivable for Molly, for example, to have behaved toward her family as Marie's husband had toward his, even though strong parallels can be drawn between characteristics of their tennis-playing profiles, and alternatively, for Dorothy to have ignored the care of her three daughters as Pauline's husband had done of his. Even Linda, whose tennis crept out of "hidden" time, did not take that freedom for granted as had Rebecca's husband, whose tennis had arguably the most moderate impact on his family out of all of the husbands of the wives interviewed.

There is an overriding theme to the situation in which mothers facilitate and service junior sport, wives similarly facilitate men's sport, and sportswomen contain theirs within the boundaries of domestic responsibilities while also servicing tennis practices. These women's lives were defined and constructed by the material and ideological relations by which they participated in the public arena and at home. Gendered relations that mediated their motivations and activities have prescribed divisions of labor in which women are disproportionately responsible for domestic labor and child care. This, along with the economic relations that support it, rendered these women in positions of inequality, co-opting their labor but maintaining their marginality.

Sport in society both constitutes and is constituting of these hegemonic relations, which means that sport is both supported by them and instrumental in reproducing them. In other words, sport is maintained by women's labor constituted in predominantly gender-prescribed roles. These roles and associated identities are constructed and affirmed within sport, which perpetuates the conditions from which this labor is motivated. It is a seemingly closed loop.

I propose that the ideological practices that drive this phenomenon are associated with the normative, nuclear family and the construction of women's labor within and for it. I view "the family" not in a Parsonian sense (Parsons and Bales 1955), but look to discussions within feminist analysis that sought and still seek to understand the bases from which women's lived experiences of inequality and oppression can be explained.

Michele Barrett (1988) deliberately linked what she called "familial relations" to her Marxist/feminist analysis of gendered labor relations, describing what this interrelationship meant to women's economic position in the labor market. She explained,

> The family household constitutes the ideological ground on which gender differences and women's oppression are constructed, and the material relations in which men and women are differently engaged in wage labor and the class structure. Women's dependence on men is reproduced ideologically, but also in material relations, and there is a mutual strengthening relationship between them. (Barrett 1988, 211)

Barrett views "the family" as being the ideological "nexus" for themes that characterize our conceptions of gender and sexuality, connected with and mutually affirming material relations (1988, 205). These familial ideologies prop "the family household system." This "system," a phrase that Barrett attributes to Mary McIntosh (1979), is one in which the members are expected to be dependent primarily on the wages of the husband and father, with the unpaid work of domestic maintenance mainly being done by the wife and mother.

In Australia, the potency of this construction of family, the assumption of the "domestic wage," and the normative influence of the nuclear family still prevails (Bittman and Pixley 1997) and is supported by ideologies of motherhood and wifehood. Within this framework, women service the lives of others. In this study of sport, all of the interviewed wives and mothers were, and all of the players were or had been, living in families constituted on this model, organized around heterosexual marriages and the care of the couple's (own) children. The key familial ideologies that surrounded these women's lives, therefore, had to do with heterosexuality, wifehood, and motherhood. While highly interrelated, it is useful to separate these to understand how they are played out in the context of a sport culture such as tennis.

MOTHERHOOD

Feminist studies of motherhood have gone through transitional stages that have sought to differentiate the biological and essentialist connections between women and motherhood from the social and political implications of motherhood as a female experience. Motherhood has been viewed as being central to women's inequalities in that it has placed women in positions of dependency, mostly outside of the labor market and within isolated, patriarchal nuclear families. (Eisenstein 1979; Firestone 1971; Oakley, 1979; O'Brien 1981). Few studies have focused on women's (diverse) experiences of motherhood, partly, according to McMahon (1995), because of the theoretical tensions between conceptualizing motherhood as being negative and oppressive, on the one side, and positive and empowering on the other side.

Mothering remains primary to the way in which most women's lives are structured and shapes their relations to all other institutions. The lives of women I interviewed within the institution of sport were shaped, mediated, and controlled by motherhood, whether in the way they, as players, delayed joining the midweek pennant competition until their children were at school, or how, as wives, they were left to look after the children while their husbands played tennis. Most salient was the ways in which the lives of the mothers of junior tennis players were constructed and regulated by the sport's structures and practices. They illustrated how mothers serviced their children's sport from two highly interrelated foundations, one being their relationship to material resources and waged labor, the other being their commitment to "familial ideologies," specifically the ideology of motherhood.

Material Relations

Considering the first of these foundations, all of the interviewed mothers fit the norm of the household family "system" by being mainly or exclusively dependent on the income of the children's father for financial support for themselves and their children. Even though women may have done paid work, while not dismissing its importance to the women for reasons such as personal autonomy (such as Jill or Rita), or its economic contribution to childrearing costs (such as Monica explained), their income was still additional and subsidiary to that of their male partners. The male partners of all of the women interviewed were employed in, or retired from, full-time paid employment. In a situation where a mother's paid work is defined as being subsidiary, and her labor of child care as being primary, servicing children's activities become part of this labor. Furthermore, it must be attended to before a mother's own leisure can be validated.

Richardson (1993a) noted that, in Britain, motherhood and women's paid employment have been defined as being incompatible by the denial of adequate public child care and a decree that women should choose between staying outside paid labor to raise children or being in paid work and not having children at all, a choice that Oakley (1981b) pointed out as being fundamentally sexist because this is never asked of men. In this context, motherhood is a critical defining factor for women's relationship to paid work, also influencing how mothers who are in paid employment continue to provide most of the care for their children.

Inequalities in the labor market play an important role. For example, women's lower pay, restricted access to secure, skilled positions, harassment, and other forms of alienation structure women's positions in and relationships to paid work, such that women's responsibilities to their families could be considered in reverse, as having stemmed instead from their marginality in the workplace (Cockburn 1983; Barrett 1988). Both Boulton (1983) and Wearing (1984) cited examples from their empirical research of women who considered the unpaid work of caring for children and dependence on men's wages as being preferable to the paid work they engaged in prior to motherhood. Alongside this, men's greater rewards from paid work in the form of higher wages can be both a powerful and pragmatic justification for them not doing child care, as found by Thiele and Grace (1990). It is not the personalities of men as much as the advantages accorded men by male labor power. The structure of the Australian work place assumes that the organization of family responsibilities is not its concern, that this is managed privately and does not impinge on paid work. Women have borne the cost of this denial and the neglect of these "private" responsibilities by labor force structures.

There is now substantial evidence that women's involvement in paid work does not significantly reduce their responsibility for, or level of, engagement in child care and housework (Baxter et al.1990; Bittman and Lovejoy 1991; Bryson 1983a; Hochschild 1989; Martin and Roberts 1984; Piachaud 1984; Russell 1983). Furthermore, it is becoming increasingly recognized that the most intransigent resistance to the breakdown of gendered labor divisions is men's reluctance to take on these tasks (O'Donnell and Hall 1988; Rich 1977; Thiele and Grace 1990).

In Russell's (1983) study, Australian fathers made minimal contributions to the day-to-day activities of child care, and this increased only marginally if the child's mother was in paid employment. Men's contribution was most likely to be in lighter and more pleasurable tasks, such as playing with the child (Wearing 1984). It could be speculated from this suggestion that if Australian men were to be involved at all with their children, it was likely to be in the sporting domain. This would give substance to the popular perception of fathers being equally, if not more, involved in children's sport as mothers. It is where fathers are most likely and most visibly to be engaged in child care, following a supposed male, more than female interest. However, in tennis particularly, the sport is organized on the assumption that one parent is not in (full-time) paid labor and therefore available to facilitate a child's activities. If this parent exists, it is almost invariably the child's mother. Fathers may play with or contribute to a child's tennis during the weekend, but are unavailable to do so during the week for such demands as Squad training or school holiday tournaments.

The assumption on which the organization of junior tennis is predicated, that mothers are available because they are not in paid work and are supported by a male wage, is somewhat at odds with the reality of how most Australian women are now living their lives. For example, Baxter (1992) pointed out, from the Australian Bureau of Statistics figures, that the "traditional" nuclear family consisting of a married couple with dependent children and one "breadwinner" described only 16 percent of Australian households, and a broader definition of such a family, which included two incomes, accounts for only 32 percent. Castles (1993) cited data which showed that sixty per cent of married women with children in Australia are in paid work. Furthermore, that women make up thirty-two percent of the full-time and seventy-five percent of the part-time paid labor force (Castles 1993, 123). The institution of sport, therefore, especially tennis, is founded on practices that rely on gender and capital relations that are quickly becoming anachronistic, confirming Stoddart's argument "that sport is amongst the most conservative of Australian social institutions" (1986, 13).

As a result of these dimensions, tennis as an experience is increasingly likely to become available only to "privileged" Australian children. For Australian women, especially those living in and/or supported by heterosexual relationships, the choice to not be engaged in paid work could be viewed as a privilege and a mark of middle-class affluence, albeit with its own specific set of oppressive practices.[1]

There were obvious connections between the interviewed mothers' "choices" about paid work and the labor dedicated to the service of their children's tennis, which could be considered one of the strongest class inscriptions of the sport. For example, Kath described herself as being "lucky" because she did not "have" to be in paid work, and related this to her daughter's tennis success. She said,

> If I had been a working mum there is no way that she could have been involved with squads and if you are not involved with squads and not prepared to be there you are not looked at, of course. So I've been lucky in that aspect, that I've been able to do it.

Mothers being freed from paid work, even if this was sustained with a degree of financial strain, was considered necessary if a child was to participate in tennis at this level. Beth's tennis-playing daughter, age seventeen, was her youngest child. Beth commented,

> You've got mothers that are forced to go out to work and are still trying to keep their kids in squads and things like that. And they are running ragged, they really are. And you wonder how long they are going to do it for. Because I look at them and think gee, your child is only twelve or something. I often wonder how they are going to do it, I really do. I don't envy them. I think, thank goodness my time's nearly through; in some ways, although I'm not saying I don't enjoy it, but I'm saying I wouldn't like to have had to do it the way they're doing it. I wouldn't like to have to, for instance, be working all morning and then have to leave work and race off to squads and get home and not be organized.

If a mother "had" to be in paid work, in hours that were long and outside the realm of her choice or control, it would be impossible for her to provide the labor required to sustain a child in competitive junior tennis, as women currently are in Western Australia. In other words, if a woman was not financially secure in a middle-class marriage or sustained by the history of one,[2] it is likely that her child(ren) would be unable to aspire to this level of sport participation and reap the rewards described in the previous chapter. The servicing of junior tennis is most afforded by the unpaid work of mothering and the lack of conflict between its demands and those of paid work. Being free from the necessity of paid work allows mothers to provide their services to junior tennis. Those who try to combine it may do so at considerable expense, such as their leisure, health, and attention to other children. They are likely to be, as Beth said, "run ragged." The interviewed mothers whose paid work was least flexible and/or most demanding were also those whose husbands were more involved in sharing the day-to-day servicing of their child's sport.

Women in financially dependent mothering roles on the margins of paid labor are therefore crucial to the maintenance and reproduction of the sport. Conversely, the structures that demand such gendered labor relations mean the sport becomes a repository for associations with traditional and conservative family compositions and privilege. While the interviewed mothers may have talked about the expenses of tennis equipment and petrol, for example, it was their time that was most demanded. It was the availability of mothers' time and service outside of the paid labor market, more than the continual cost of tennis shoes, rackets, club membership, coaching or travel, which defined the political economy and material parameters of junior participation in tennis in Western Australia.

With the intensity of training and continual competition now associated with junior tennis in Western Australia (driven by capital imperatives via corporate sponsorship) and the perceived need for children to embrace this package wholly if they are to achieve any rewards through the sport, the perpetuation of these relations seems assured. Mothers who value their children's participation in tennis or any similarly demanding sport are likely, if they have the choice, to remain in materially dependent relationships in order to provide this service for their children. With organizational practices that rely on this, the sport will be overly represented by children from traditional, well-off, nuclear families that are based on these gendered capital relations and that are increasingly in the minority in Australia. They will be mainly two-parent, white, middle-class families with a male "breadwinner" and a mother whose time and labor is prioritized for child care.

Ideologies

Mothers' acceptance of the junior tennis squad "package" is both constructed and legitimized by the ideology of motherhood. Wearing (1984), from her research involving 150 mothers of pre-school children in eastern Australia, identified several tenets of this ideology that were stated and negotiated by the mothers she interviewed. These included the belief that motherhood has an intrinsic worth, with the role offering nonmaterial rewards, and that a "good" mother puts her children first, and their needs before her own. There were women in Wearing's study who in practice modified the concept of "the ubiquitous availability of the mother" (Wearing 1984, 49), but she identified a core of ideas about "good" mothering that emerged from her sample. While these were recognized as being an unattainable ideal, they still provided a guiding principle about the "rightness" of certain standards of action and underpinned the normative vales associated with mothering. However, Wearing's findings showed that on a daily basis, these actions translated mainly into housework, cleaning for, feeding of, and the physical care of family members: "good" motherhood in pragmatic terms in our society means "good" housekeeping and the daily tasks associated with the care of children" (Wearing 1984, 60).

When ideas about "good" mothering incorporated sport and were translated into the daily tasks of care and housekeeping, it is no surprise that the interviewed mothers were prepared to drive a child to tennis fixtures wherever and whenever it was demanded, and that doing so required the complicated juggling of housework and child care that compounded the demands on them at that time. Nor is it surprising that the mothers interviewed seemed to consider it unnecessary to detail their performance of tasks such as cooking or laundry, except in terms of management, because as mothers, such tasks were taken for granted. The labor that services a child's tennis falls neatly into the category of being a "good" mother, who in Wearing's words "is basically concerned with the needs of her children both physical and emotional and who will make every endeavor to satisfy these needs" (Wearing 1984, 51). It is merely part of the day-to-day process toward this perpetual goal. "Prioritizing" the work represents a particular style of mothering that involves accepting the current ideological tenets of good mothering and incorporating a belief in the value and rewards of children's participation in sport. "Doing" the work is made possible by the material conditions of these mothers' relationship to capital resources.

In 1977, Adrienne Rich made the important distinction between women's experiences of motherhood and motherhood as an institution. Her comments about institutionalized motherhood begin with her assertion that the institution is not identical with bearing and caring for children, just as the institution of heterosexuality is not identical with the specific practices of intimacy and sexual love (I shall return to this latter point). It is significant, in Rich's view, that these two institutions be considered in tandem, as "both create the prescriptions and conditions in which choices are made or blocked" (Rich 1977, 42). She goes on to explain how women's experiences of maternity and sexuality have been channeled to serve male interests, with behavior threatening to the institutions, such as illegitimacy, abortion, and lesbianism, having at times been considered deviant or criminal. Conversely, experiences that support male interests obviously would be sanctioned. Rich concluded that, "Patriarchy would not survive without motherhood and heterosexuality in its institutionalized forms" (43), and she provided historical illustrations of the ways in which institutionalized motherhood revived and renewed all other institutions.

The everyday practices of motherhood, supporting children's participation in tennis, collectively served the "fathers" of the administration and patriarchal interests of sport. Within heterosexual-based families, this also may serve the interests of individual men who are the fathers of these children. For the mothers I interviewed, the rewards they saw from the tennis participation of both sons and daughters provided the rationale for reproducing the institution of sport. They were not, as Arcana phrased it, "antisports" (1983, 132). The labor done in this process of maintaining sport was simply a hegemonic form of "good" mothering, involving their children in a highly valued social institution to ensure their cultural inclusion and success.

WIFEHOOD

In her work *Married to the Job* (1983), Janet Finch makes the useful distinction between being a mother and being a wife when she discusses how the structure of men's jobs affects the lives of the women to whom they are married. She emphasizes marriage, rather than childbearing, as a feature of women's subordination because of the way wives become incorporated into their husbands' work. Finch described the relationship between a wife and her husband's work as being "a two-way one: his work both structures her life and elicits her contribution to it" (Finch 1983, 2). Finch explained that, on the one hand, a husband's work imposed a set of structures that had consequences for the way his wife lived her life, and on the other hand it described the process by which her labor generally contributed to his work and thus his economic credibility. Thus she becomes incorporated into it. Finch's own research was based in the United Kingdom and was principally informed by earlier studies of wives by Papanek (1973) in the United States and Delphy (1977) in France. To Finch, the process of wives' incorporation must necessarily be viewed against larger backdrops, to inform understandings of issues such as

> the relationship between the productive and domestic spheres in a capitalist economy; the significance of forms of organization of paid work; the context and dynamics of contemporary marriage; and above all, the economic, social, and personal significance of being a wife. (Finch 1983,18)

Husbands' sport is intertwined at economic, social, and personal levels—simplistically, if the sport he plays is professional, hence his "work" (for which he may receive substantial reward and recognition), complexly, if it is his leisure.

Material Relations

Finch described how being "married to" a man's paid work makes sense for most women because

> it has its own inherent internal logic. This internal logic has three strands: it makes economic good sense; the organization of social life makes compliance easy and developing alternatives very difficult; it provides a comprehensive way of being a wife. (Finch 1983, 168)

This economic logic relies on the understanding that most wives are unlikely to be able to develop an independent economic base greater or even equal to that of their husbands, so it makes sense for a wife to invest her time and energy into her husband. The assumption that wives do this work means social life is generally organized in such a way that women who attempt to resist being co-opted into it can meet considerable obstacles, are considered deviant, and may jeopardize not just their husbands' work prospects but also the marriage itself. Finch's third strand of logic refers to the public performance of being a wife, particularly a "good" wife, and how being incorporated into a husband's work is both the script and the display of the partnership notion on which marriage is based.

Finch's analysis is highly pertinent and applicable to men's leisure, and it is within this context that the women in my study most readily fit. When women are incorporated into men's work, it follows that they also service men's leisure. For men defined and identified in paid work roles, as "provider," "breadwinner," or simply as "masculine," work and leisure can be inextricably interdependent and oppositional concepts. Just as men's paid work has its own powerful rationale for economic and domestic work relations, so too does men's leisure. The process of reproducing a man "fit to work" requires catering to the "recreation" of him as a worker. The same economic relations apply and are similarly gendered. "Her" domestic labor is necessary for this process and must therefore extend to "his" leisure activities. In this way, a husband's leisure, such as his playing tennis, takes on an economic imperative derived from capital relations that validate it and thus incorporate his wife. For example, despite Marie's feelings about her husband's neglect of his domestic and conjugal responsibilities and her anger at the time he spent at tennis, she followed a statement about his away-from-home activities with the comment, "We always paid our bills."

It was the validation of men's leisure that gave rise to Pauline's situation, whose husband played tennis and squash on Saturdays, Sundays, and three nights a week, while she admitted to having no leisure. It is this validation that had Molly restrict her tennis to weekdays, going with her husband to watch football during the weekend. It helps explain Janet's married life, as time spent with tennis being its central focus, despite her not having played the game herself all that time. It lay behind June's story of suggesting to her husband when their children were young that he join the tennis club because he was "at a loose end" at home, which began the chain of events leading to her saying, "Tennis *is* our life. I've said it so many times."

Following the rationale that servicing a husband's work and his leisure are derived from the same set of capital relations, I believe that Finch's "making sense" analysis is still applicable. It is in the context of leisure as restorative for work that her explanations of why women become incorporated into men's work also apply to wives' incorporation into husbands' sport played as leisure.

To begin with, his tennis has an economic logic. It may be so directly, as in the case of Bronwyn who described her husband's tennis as "opening doors" in his profession, or it may be indirectly, such as the benefit described by Karen of it helping reduce her husband's work-related stress, which was also Tania's hope. Sometimes it is an imperative derived simply from economic dependence. Marie, for example, had little option but to accept the entry of tennis into her life; it came with the marriage package. The only way she could have avoided incorporation would have been to leave the marriage.

Ideologies

A further comprehensive way of being a "good" wife is to be supportive of a husband's activities and uphold the concept of partnership. Finch explained how the ideology of marriage emphasized the concept of partnership as "a cooperative alliance of two individuals, each with distinctive and different things to offer, who engage in joint enterprises as a team" (Finch 1983, 147). The interviewed wives demonstrated a commitment to this ideology: Sally relaying the telephone messages associated with her husband's tennis involvement; Brenda shopping for the tournament trophies when her husband was club captain; Lorelle taking the children to watch her husband's important matches; Bronwyn volunteering to join the tennis club social committee because she promised her husband she would "become involved" in his interest; Janet keeping meals in the freezer in case her husband unexpectedly brought a visiting tennis administrator home for dinner. These are all examples of a woman's incorporation into her husband's tennis through a sense of partnership, displaying and deriving affirmation of that partnership through being a "good" wife.

Despite this logic, and the capital-based connections between a husband's work and his leisure, from my data it is apparent that the incorporation of wives into servicing their husbands' leisure activities is not as seamless as the argument might suggest. Inherent in the notion of partnership is the understanding of some reciprocity, that a "joint enterprise" implies some expectation of equal outcomes. While the ideology of motherhood carries with it an acceptance of self-sacrifice, self-denial, and a lack of extrinsic rewards as a part of the relationship between mothers and their children, marriage is a relationship between adults in a supposedly voluntary, cooperative, and mutually beneficial arrangement. Because of this, a wife's compliance to a situation that prioritizes her husband's leisure is not straightforward. There is room to ignore, complain, and resist. The ideology of wifehood allows more flexibility for women to assert their own needs, and the interviewed wives responded to having a tennis-playing husband in a variety of ways.

Those who accepted and serviced it most willingly and unproblematically were the women who played tennis themselves. Because it assured their own leisure, the rewards of their own participation dissolved any possible tension caused by their husbands and blurred the line between what they did to enable their own play and what they did for their husbands. The old adage "If you can't beat them, join them" seemed to ring true from this study. The wives who shared their husbands' sporting interest were those who appeared most content and were gratified in their marriages. So too were the veteran women players whose husbands also played tennis. It would be accurate to say that they felt this situation had made a considerable contribution to the quality of their marriages, maintaining the ideology of partnership.

Contrasting tennis-playing wives with those wives who did not play tennis (or, such as Kerry, some other sport), there is a considerable difference in their attitudes toward their husbands, their marriages, and their life satisfaction generally. Not all women had been able to join their husbands in playing tennis, even if it had been their wish. It required a certain amount of cooperation from their husbands, which for some had not been forthcoming. Pauline had attempted to become a regular tennis player because, she explained, "I thought it was something we could do together, something that a family could do together." Marie also talked about how she would have liked to have been able to play. Both had been hampered in this by their total responsibility for child care and their husbands' refusal to compromise their tennis to facilitate their wives' participation.

The wives who most resented and resisted servicing their husbands' leisure were those who did not play and for whom their husbands' tennis had meant a breakdown of any semblance of "partnership" in childrearing. When a husband's tennis caused him to become an "absent father," a woman's tolerance of it became stretched.[3] His level of participation in a leisure activity actually created her leisure deficiency and highlighted the extreme contrast between them. This lack of reciprocity that centered on child care as a partnership led to anger, frustration, and despair for Marie (age sixty), simmering resentment in Pauline (age forty-two), and the pending marriage breakdown for Tania (age twenty-seven). The ages of these women are perhaps significant, indicating generational shifts in what women expect from and will tolerate in a marriage. Each of these women could not avoid servicing their husbands' tennis by creating the space for it, free from the responsibilities of child care. The tasks of motherhood itself were not negotiable. However, the women's doing other domestic tasks seemed to depend on the extent to which they felt that the notion of partnership in child care had been abused, and therefore, what they no longer considered they needed to do as a "wife." For example, Pauline still did her husband's tennis laundry with minimal complaint, Marie had expressed her anger through the way in which she did this for her husband but continued to at least wash his tennis clothing, and Tania had entirely ceased to launder her husband's tennis clothes.

Of the three other wives in the study who did not play tennis, two did not have children, hence this aspect of their partnership had not been tested by their husbands' commitment to sport. Nevertheless, they were young partnerships, and the desire to be a "good wife" and service a husband's interest was evident. For example, despite being in full-time paid employment, Anthea, age twenty-seven, did all of her husband's tennis laundry and the majority of all other domestic labor, which she admitted allowed him to play more tennis. They had no children. Her greater responsibility for domestic work was driven neither by economic relations nor by motherhood, but purely by gendered behavior encompassed in wifehood.

Twelve of the wives, at the time of the interview, were in paid employment, half of whom worked full time. Two others had worked part time in earlier years but were now retired. These scenarios began to undermine an easy application of economic rationale for a husband's leisure to take priority over his wife's. Other factors contributed. The contradiction for women's leisure is that women in paid employment, particularly part time, are frequently those who have the least leisure time because they may still be providing all of the domestic support for their husbands and families. On the other hand, a woman's own paid employment still provides a degree of negotiating power, personal space, financial independence, and confidence, which can be translated into leisure. Kerry and Sally described how they had been able to negotiate doing less of the domestic work after moving from being a full-time home-maker into paid work, although for both of them it had been a slow, difficult, and tearful process. June had done the same, but no longer played tennis. Her priority remained the care of her home, her family, and their tennis.

Ellen had a different basis for her perception of marriage partnership and its display as wifely behavior, showing the temporal, transitional, and hence variable ways it is lived. She was married for the second time to a man she met though tennis. She had always, within this marriage, worked full time in paid employment. She had spent some time raising her two children on her own, both of whom now lived elsewhere, and she had played a lot of tennis throughout her life. She replied to the question about what she did for her leisure as though it were a ridiculous one to be asked. She said emphatically, perplexed by the question, "I do whatever I want to do!"

HETEROSEXUALITY

I turn now to consider the institution of heterosexuality. As an organizing principle, heterosexuality underpins the coupling that is instituted in marriage, creating the role of "wife" and the formation of nuclear families. It is a significant feature surrounding the patriarchal construction of sport, which is clearly illustrated by the specific social and sexual dynamics of club tennis in Western Australia.

Wearing's (1984) study concerning motherhood included a group of women who were solo parenting, "single" mothers. This group was useful to her discussion because of how the experiences of living within a heterosexually based partnership were informed by the accounts of those women who did not do so. While Wearing detailed their stories of relative economic deprivation, she also highlighted those women who had become aware of the conditions of living in an oppressive heterosexual relationships after the relationship ceased to exist. While the ideologies of motherhood remained strong in these women, those of wifehood and marriage were considerably modified, largely because the "... designation of 'head of the house' as an exclusive male preserve, legitimated by the breadwinning role, no longer [had] meaning" (Wearing 1984, 152). These women's beliefs were influenced by a wider range of associates than those of the married women, and there was more variability in the way their lives were structured. From this, Wearing concluded that the heterosexual relations of marriage, with the presence of an adult male as husband/breadwinner, helped preserve traditional gendered modes of behavior.

Johnson (1988) argued that it is heterosexuality, not motherhood, that is at the core of women's oppression, because it is the role of "wife" that is subordinate, characterized by economic dependence and accompanying psychological characteristics such as deference. VanEvery (1995) studied heterosexual women attempting different constructions of family by "Refusing to be a 'wife'!" The major hegemonic and institutionalized form of heterosexuality is marriage. Surprisingly though, this has been given little attention theoretically, is rarely acknowledged, and its "normality" less likely problematized (Richardson 1996). Jackson argued that there is a "need to analyze heterosexuality critically, to explore the ways in which it is implicated in the subordination of women, but without conflating heterosexuality as an institution with heterosexual practice, experience, and identity" (Jackson 1996, 21). In other words, we need to develop an understanding of what it means to be living in a social world that is organized on the principle of heterosexual coupling, which is separate from thoughts about "normal" or "natural" sexual practices. Discussions regarding the need to do this theoretical work, the conceptual problems involved, and the implications to knowledge concerning gender relations are well advanced (Katz 1995; MacKinnon 1987; Rich 1980; Richardson 1993b, 1996; VanEvery 1996; Walby 1990).

What is important to the structures and practices that maintain tennis is that they are organized on the basis of heterosexual relations. It is not just that institutionalized motherhood and the capital relations surrounding "at home" mothers mean that children's sport will be serviced. Nor is it enough to say that being a good wife and committed to "partnership" automatically presupposes a woman's joining and/or contributing to her husband's sport. These familial ideologies are based on gendered relations that are specifically organized around heterosexual principles, carrying inequalities of power between women and men that are manifested in how family life is organized. This power differential serves and helps maintain men's interests in tennis and the infrastructure of the sport.

Hegemonic heterosexuality and the institutions of motherhood and marriage intersect and mutually reinforce each other, leading to a comprehensive concept of family that dominates tennis culture. The social milieu of tennis in Western Australia is structured on the principle of heterosexuality, contextualized as universal within the game, and perpetuated by the formal and informal practices within the sport. Women service men's sport because of and in accordance with this principle. Such gendered relations within this context take on meanings that have implications for the ways in which wifehood and motherhood are experienced. The ability and willingness to service a child's tennis as it is currently structured is almost entirely reliant upon these relations, which afford these mothers the time and material resources to provide the necessary labor. The servicing of men's tennis depends equally as much on their having wives to do the domestic labor and child care.

An overwhelming outcome of the interviews, which resulted in a considerable and an unexpected overlap of the three focus groups, was the extent to which several members of one nuclear family were involved in playing tennis. When I interviewed the veteran women players, nine had husbands who were players; when I interviewed the mothers of junior squad players, eight also played tennis and ten of the children's fathers played, and when I interviewed the wives of male players, eight were or had been players themselves. These patterns of family participation were very marked and became a strong feature of the social practices within the tennis culture, as well as the expressed ideological beliefs and values. Comments about the "familiness" of tennis were common and came even from women players who did not have other family members involved. As outlined in the previous chapter, this was a dominant theme in many women's expressions of their rewards and joys in tennis. An extract from a document written to commemorate the twenty-first anniversary of the formation of a tennis club in Perth included the following:

> As with all clubs I guess, a lot of families have married into other members of the club families and these are again the backbone of the club as they have had tennis with them all through their childhood and know what to expect when they hold office, which is pleasing to see as we have many such couples in our club. (Bullock 1981, no page reference)

This "familiness" worked best, in fact it seemed, only worked at all, if both members of a married couple played. Family ideologies were incorporated into tennis and structured by them. The reproduction of tennis was dependent on certain kinds of familial relations, namely those mediated by heterosexual and middle-class values and practices.

Among the forty-six interviews in total, twenty-four heterosexual "tennis couples" were represented. Seven of the interviewed women had met their husbands through tennis. Dorothy explained how two of her daughters had married men they met through playing tennis. One of whom had done so by joining a "singles" tennis club. Most frequently, wives had been coerced into tennis because of their husbands' interest, but for Carol, Marilyn, and Trudi it would be more accurate to describe the coercion as having been the other way around. They had been keen and successful players before marriage.

My asking interviewed players to help me identify nonplaying wives led to a conversation about how rare it was to find only one member of a married couple in tennis and the envisaged marital problems resulting from such a situation. For example, June said,

> [Tennis is] a family situation. It's funny because there were two situations at the tennis club, and we've been there a long, long time, where a marriage broke up and in each case one was very heavily involved in tennis and the other one wasn't.

June herself had been "coerced" into tennis after her husband became a keen player. She explained,

> Had I been in that situation, had [husband] not involved me, maybe that would have been the path our lives would have taken, because tennis to [husband] was almost a full-time job, you know.

Apart from the obvious male agenda setting, there is the comprehension that marriages are better maintained if both partners are part of the tennis culture. Molly, whose husband did not play the sport, spoke of being marginalized because of this. She explained,

> If you've got a husband that's involved in the same club, makes a lot of difference. If they both go down at the same

time. They have twilight meetings, you both go. They have tea after twilight meetings. . . . And in the weekends you can go down there, you can take a bit of a barbecue. The kids go down and play as well and they can make an afternoon of it. That's when the husband's involved as well. But the ones like myself that haven't got a husband involved, it's not much point in me staying down there really, because you find, that when you get in social groups down there, everyone's got a partner.

As an organizing principle, institutionalized heterosexuality helps determine the familial ideologies and how they translate into women's experiences of sport. Furthermore, because this is displayed and upheld so clearly in tennis, its acceptability and accessibility as a sport for women is confirmed, contributing to the reasons why it is played by such large numbers of women in Western Australia. Tennis upholds traditional gender relations.

Further to the issue that Molly identified, of being marginalized for not being "conspicuously" heterosexual by having her husband alongside her and engaging in coupled, family activities, is the marginalization of the invisible "other," that is, those who do not prescribe to or identify with hegemonic heterosexuality. Most obvious of this group would be those who identify as homosexual.

Institutionalized heterosexuality is a pertinent issue in the analysis of sport, largely because both ideologically and in practice, sport has been a significant location for the emphasis on gender differences and for maintaining the dominance of hegemonic heterosexual masculinity (Bryson 1983b, 1987; Curry 1991; Duncan 1990; McKay 1991b, 1992b, 1993b, 1997; Messner and Sabo 1990). This has specific relevance for women, especially those who are sports players.

Women have played sport through a long, well-charted history of male-imposed controls and restrictions throughout many cultures (Blue 1987; Dyer 1982, 1986; Guttman 1991; Hall and Richardson 1982; Hargreaves 1985, 1990; 1994; King 1978; Lenskyj 1984, 1986; McCrone 1988; Mangan & Park 1987; Parratt 1989; Phillips 1990; Stell 1991; Stoddart 1986; Talbot 1988c). There are, of course, cultural, class, and race variations in this history regarding the forms of control women have experienced, their responses to them, and how much of their specific "herstory" has been documented. Lenskyj (1984, 1986) and Vertinsky (1994) traced the medical "panic" about the so-called misuse of women's bodies for physical activity other than bearing and raising children and how, when women persisted in playing sport, the controlling emphasis shifted to those concerning compromised femininity. Griffin (1992) and Cahn (1994) argue it was this climate in which women's sport became associated with "mannish" behavior. Initially this had no sexual connotations but was merely construed as crossing gender boundaries. With later sexological discourse it became associated with lesbianism. Griffin (1992) explains how effective this association, and the homophobia that went with it, has been in controlling women's participation in sport and maintaining male domination.

Griffin (1992) discusses how the power of homophobia maintains sexist and heterosexist society. By this she means a society "in which heterosexuality is reified as the only normal, natural, and acceptable sexual orientation" (Griffin 1992, 252), and outlines how it is specifically manifest in women's sport. She described the first two manifestations as being silence and denial, both of which keep lesbians hidden by "covering up" their existence. Another two she called "apology" and the "promotion of a heterosexy image," which when combined mean an emphasis on heterosexually defined femininity and conspicuous "evidence" of heterosexuality. Festle (1996) provides a comprehensive account of how this has been woven through decades of women's sport, with a particularly detailed treatise of women's tennis and its impact on high-profile players.

There are several ways in which the tennis culture in Western Australia has upheld heteronormality and defined women's experiences of tennis as manifestations of institutionalized heterosexuality. For example, the "correct" clothing for women tennis players includes a short, mainly white, skirt. In Western Australia, this is upheld by formal regulations as well as informal practices, as Ruth's following account illustrates:

> This girl (sic) plays with me, our number one player. She's a Sri Lankan, . . . and it's against her religion to wear a tennis skirt, so she wears pedal pushers, just under her knees. She only wear saris everywhere else she goes. Anyway this girl from [opposing team] came up the other day and she said, "We have a complaint to make with your team" and I said, "Why, what's wrong?" and she said, "I hope you know that girl playing in that outfit is not allowed to play pennants." She said, "WALTA won't allow it." I said, "I played with her last year and this was all confirmed with WALTA and WALTA says she

can play in it if that is her religion, and she said, "All the other teams should have been notified about it." She got real shitty, you know, "She shouldn't be playing in it. It's not right." The regulations are that you wear the proper uniform.

Evident in the aforementioned passage is the popular practice of naming sportswomen by a term of sexual immaturity, *girls*. More noticeable is the historical and cultural specificity of tennis. Despite Australia being statistically, through immigration, one of the most multicultural countries in the world, the ethnocentrism of tennis has become so naturalized that indigenous players and different cultural codes are virtually nonexistent. This resistance to difference, however, focused on the "proper" clothing for tennis, formalized as apparel associated with heterosexy femininity and policed by the women themselves. In Australia, short skirts are associated with women's public performances of sport and physical activity beyond just tennis, including netball, the dominant sporting code for Australian women. Shorts skirts, especially pleated or kilt styles, are the accepted apparel for women's institutionalized physical activity, such that girls and their female teachers wear short, pleated skirts for school physical education classes in Western Australia.

As heterosexualized as they may be, this clothing is nevertheless considered a symbol of women's liberation, simply because of its association with women being physically active, who "get out" and play tennis. Molly, for example, talked about a group of much older women at her club. She said,

Some of them are bent over like this and out like that, but they're still there. Got their little pleated skirts on and little Adidas tops and their little peaked hats. They love it. It's really great.

Later she explained how, in her past, women who played sport

. . . were really talked about because you were supposed to be home, look after children, and do the housework. That was really what you were supposed to do. . . . You just didn't put on a little pleated skirt and take off.

On the tennis calendar in Western Australia was the "Miss Tennis" contest of which Jean had spoken proudly, having initiated it as a fund-raising event. Here, (young) women's physical appearance and energy were used for financial purposes in a way that affirmed the terms of their participation in the sport, having to both look sexy and be of service. These two conditions were conflated and deigned to be mutually exclusive. In 1989, two separate awards were made. The association's official publication reported

> the highlight of the first weekend of the State Closed tournament was the presentation of Miss Tennis and Miss Charity Tennis. [Man's name] did an excellent job as compere of the event, making all entrants proud of their involvement in the quest. (*Westennis* 1989a, 11)

"Miss Charity Tennis" was awarded to the young woman who, representing her tennis club, had raised the most money in the time proceeding the judging. The criteria for awarding the "Miss Tennis" title was not specified, however the lineup of contestants in the accompanying photograph showed that they were all young white women, wearing short white skirts and looking normatively feminine. One of the sponsors, a company manufacturing women's tennis clothing, provided "outfits" for the contestants, which were shown being "modeled" by a young woman, while behind her two men "give a look of approval" (*Westennis* 1989b, 31).

Conspicuous attention to honorifics for women as signifiers of marital status is also evident in tennis. Take for example the renowned tournament held annually at the All-England Croquet and Lawn Tennis Club at Wimbledon. Men are addressed simply by their last names but women are given an honorific, reflecting their marital status, in other words, their heterosexuality. Self-identified "out" lesbian Martina Navratilova, for example, was persistently called "Miss" Navratilova. When Chris Evert was married but still known worldwide by that name, at Wimbledon she was referred to as "Mrs. Lloyd." Subsequent to her divorce, Wimbledon officialdom reverted to calling her "Miss Evert."

In the WALTA administrative offices, "honors" boards are hung around the walls listing past significant administrative office bearers and playing champions. Women's names are relatively few, but where they appear, unlike the men's, they have an honorific of "Miss" or "Mrs."

According to Carol, the need to display sports players as related to men is more firmly structured in golf. In her club, she explained, where women could only be "associate" members and had no voting rights, married women were listed by their husband's first names, even in cases where their husbands were not members of the club. Carol showed me a (1989) club publication where she, as president of the women's section of the club, would have been listed as Mrs. "Peter" [last name], had she not "caused a stir" and insisted her listing was changed to her own name. She explained that she had "tried to do it quietly," but "it was so traditional to have your husband's initial" that to suggest otherwise caused a stir.

Sexism and homophobia are prevalent in tennis as they are in most institutionalized sport, and this combination affects all sportswomen but has an especially destructive impact on lesbians (Griffin 1992; Griffin and Genasci 1990; King 1982; Lenskyj 1990, 1991; Navratilova 1986; Palzkill 1990). They also serve to divide and control women. After Navratilova won the 1990 women's singles championship at Wimbledon for a record-breaking ninth time, the major West Australian newspaper carried a large photograph on its outside back page of Margaret Court, a local woman who had herself won many Wimbledon championship titles, surrounded by her three young daughters. The accompanying article (McGrath 1990b) reported Court denouncing Navratilova as a poor role model in women's tennis because of her "lifestyle off the court." This theme was continued in a further article within the newspaper headlined, "Youngsters Lured By lesbians: Court" and quoted Court as saying, "If I had a daughter on the [tennis] circuit I'd want to be there" (the *West Australian* 1990, 108). The deliberately incited and sensationalized criticism of one woman by another, juxtaposed with the powerful imagery and ideology of motherhood as a normative heterosexual experience, is a controlling mechanism that defines the restrictive boundaries within which all women are expected to live.

The mothers interviewed did not mention homophobic "fears" for their daughters' experiences in tennis, or the need to "protect" them. Lesbianism and lesbians were rendered invisible by the hegemonic heterosexuality of tennis culture and were not mentioned by any of the women interviewed. In contrast, gay men were visible. Two of the interviewed wives spoke of the club to which both of their husbands belonged as being known for having gay male members. Term of derision were frequently used to refer to these men. Institutionalized homophobia was also evident in Marilyn's account of her "worst experience" as her club's president. Referring to a gay member of the club, she said,

> He got into an argument with our club captain who hit him. I
> think it was over being called a name, something to do with
> being a homosexual. Anyway, the homosexual threatened to
> sue the captain for assault. . . . I had to mediate and it was
> awful because it was two men and I was a woman. . . . The
> captain resigned, although the sympathy was with him. No
> one liked the homosexual.

Although in the right, this man's sexual identity made him an outsider within the sexual economy of tennis. The oblique and deroga-
tory references to gays contrast markedly with the public face of
tennis sociability, to the extent that in none of the accounts of
social occasions in tennis clubs was there a sense in which the participation of gay partners was apparent or imaginable.

Social occasions, however, were places where women were
called upon to display conspicuous signs of their wifehood and
domesticity, serving their husbands and the men collectively
through their catering and other supportive labor. It is a site that
Finch (1983) would describe as "making sense" of the social and
personal significance of being a wife, which in its institutionalized
form within tennis clubs means that all women are expected to do
"wifely" tasks. The organization of tennis culture urges compliance. In a leisure setting, such as a sport club, which depends on
voluntary labor and has the overt purpose of facilitating pleasurable
social experiences, it would be courting "social suicide" for a
woman to refuse to participate. For example, it would be necessary
for her to take her turn at making the tea or bringing a salad if that
was the club's expectation of her. If she did not wish to do these
tasks, it is likely that she would eventually leave, such as Bronwyn
had done when the expectations of her from her husband's tennis
cub had become more than she was prepared to do. The coercion of
wives into male-dominated sport structures is an effective means of
incorporating women's labor. In some cases, it may happen formally. For example, Dorothy described how women members of
her husband's lawn bowls club would be fined if they did not take
their turn going to the club on "Men's Day," dressed in their bowling uniforms, to make tea for the men. She had joined the club but
found the only way to avoid doing this labor was to discontinue her
membership. This had disappointed her husband, who wished her
to share his interest. In most cases, however, it is a far more subtle
incorporation, working on women's personal commitments to family members.

CONCLUSION

In her article "Vanishing Acts in Social and Political Thought: Tricks of the Trade," Beverly Thiele (1992, 26) described the various ways in which women have "magically" disappeared in social theory because it has been predominantly written by, for, and about men. Through such "tricks" as pseudo-inclusion, decontextualization, and naturalism, women's lives have been systematically rendered invisible. "Presence, *being there*, is no guarantee of visibility" (Thiele 1992, 32, original emphasis), because of the ways in which that presence is conceptualized.

Ignoring, denying, and undervaluing women and their contributions are yet other forms of rendering women invisible. Such has been the case with social theory about sport, particularly concerning women's relationships to the institution of sport, their domestic lives, and the contributions they make. I am reminded by Hall (1996), who made reference to Stanley and Wise (1993), that issues of women's inequality and subordination remain with us, and feminist theorizing remains relevant. Hall argues that deconstructionalist scholarship may have shifted academic work away from feminist praxis, which is politically about producing knowledge about and for women to bring about real social change. "Making visible" women's labor for sport, and its connections with familial ideologies, provides a way to understand how androcentric sport is maintained, how gender relations are reproduced through sport, and what this means to women.

After interviewing Virginia at her home, we were standing beside my car chatting generally about my research before I departed. Our conversation went like this:

VIRGINIA: I must admit, when I read what you were doing I didn't think it was "up there" enough (gesturing with her hand above her head) for university research.

SHONA: Well, it's an important aspect of sport which has been largely ignored. Mothers make a big contribution.

VIRGINIA: You're right! If we didn't do it, it wouldn't happen. Kids wouldn't get themselves there. Australia would fall apart!

We laughed at this together, both enjoying this notion of "truth," the subversive act of calling it so, and the ridiculousness of an implied alternative.

Imagine an alternative. What would happen in our societies if women did not do this labor for sport. What would sport look like? Who would play? How would this change the ways in which motherhood and wifehood were experienced?

As a way of concluding, I look to the work of Marilyn Waring, who wrote an economic analysis called *Counting for Nothing* (1988). In this book, she analyzed the United Nations System of National Accounts (UNSNA), the method used to measure production and growth throughout the world by placing value on all goods and services that entered the market. Excluded from this measure, of course, are unpaid household activities, the reproductive work of women, because this is not seen to be marketed. Its value and contribution to a country's GNP is therefore denied. Waring argued that "this system acts to sustain . . . the universal enslavement of women" (1988, 44) and serves as propaganda about who is and who is not productive in the world.

Could the denial of women's unpaid labor in the reproduction of sport be similar propaganda, denying the extent to which women are involved and could exercise power? It would seem that sporting codes wishing to remain viable will need to develop in ways that are flexible to changing economic and social pressures. How these impact on women of different cultures, colors, and classes is sure to determine who plays sport in the future. On the other hand, we need to watch carefully the ways in which dominant sporting ideologies and practices develop so that they do not become even more exploitative of women's unpaid labor. It seems to be a very delicate balance between agency and exploitation.

APPENDIX A:
THE METHODS

PROCEDURES

The findings reported here were based on qualitative data obtained primarily through in-depth, focused interviews that took place in Perth, Western Australia, between November 1989, and December 1990. In total, forty-six women were interviewed. These women were identified in three groups, each being defined by a specific relationship to tennis. They were mothers of junior elite tennis players (sixteen), wives/domestic partners of adult male tennis players (fifteen), and women who were tennis players themselves (fifteen).

The focus on these groups of women was based on an assumption that there were specific experiences associated with each of their three relationships to the sport. As it transpired, there was a considerable overlap between the groups. Many women were interviewed because they were members of one particular group, but they also could have been included as members of either or both of the other two groups. For example, Ellen was interviewed because her husband was a veteran A grade player. Her interview revealed that she was a regular, Veteran-aged tennis player and that one of her sons had been a junior State representative player. This sort of overlap was typical and added a further dimension to the discussion concerning the women's relationship to the sport. In total, twenty-nine of the forty-six women interviewed were mothers of tennis players, thirty-four were wives of tennis players, and thirty-one also played the sport.

The first group of women interviewed were those identified because they were tennis players. These women were located through their current membership of the Veterans Tennis Club of Western Australia, which thereby defined them as being over forty years of age and affiliated participants in a regular tennis competition.

The focus upon veteran players was based on the expectation, later justified, that the women had had long careers as tennis players and therefore a wealth of experience to call upon. Their contribution to the research came from their lengthy experience as active participants in the sport and as members of the sport's organizational structures. During the interviews, I asked these women to reflect on their tennis careers and recall different stages of their lives. I thought it best to do this group of interviews first. Through the explanations and observations of these women, my understanding of the tennis culture, its structural details, and the relations of women within it would develop in ways that were helpful in subsequent interviews.

The names and addresses of veteran women tennis players were taken from a possible 224 female members on the Veterans Tennis Club of Western Australia 1989–1990 membership list. In a preliminary attempt to include women from a variety of class backgrounds, residential addresses were identified as being mostly associated with upper-middle, middle-, and working-class suburbs. After this was done, names were randomly selected from each of these groups and letters were sent explaining the research and asking each member if they would agree to be interviewed. Arrangements with fifteen of those who replied "yes" were then made by telephone, and the interviews took place in the women's own homes.

The second group of interviews were with sixteen women identified as mothers of elite junior tennis players. The initial point of contact was the Western Australian Lawn Tennis Association, which provided the names, addresses, and parents' names of junior tennis players who had been selected by the Association for sponsored coaching in age and gender groupings (Squad training). Most of these junior players had at some stage represented Western Australia in age group competitions between teams from other states of the Australian Commonwealth, or internationally. They were generally referred to as the Junior State Squad.

Mothers of an equal number of girls and boys were initially sent letters explaining the research, followed by telephone calls to ask if they would agree to being interviewed. Two of the mothers who received letters were immigrants to Australia and spoke no English. In one of these cases, an older sibling of the child who played tennis offered to translate. However, after several attempts to find a suitable time, and arriving at one of the appointments to discover the mother had been called away for a tennis engagement, this interview did not take place. In the other case, the twelve-year-old tennis-playing son declined on his mother's behalf. Two other mothers declined, saying they did not have time for the interview. The impression I gained, and also from some of the women who were interviewed, was that they saw this request as being yet another demand made upon them by their child's involvement in tennis. In contrast, on three occasions I came off the phone after arranging interviews with mothers who had agreed to it with screeds of notes on things they had wanted to tell me, there and then, about their experiences as a "Tennis Mum"! In these interviews, the women were asked to relate what having a child who played tennis at State level required of them as mothers, focusing particularly on their day-to-day activities, the management of the family and household, and the rationales and values that drove them.

The final set of interviews were with a group of women currently married to or living with an adult male tennis players who played at various levels of the men's metropolitan pennant competition. The majority of these men played at State A Grade level.

Identifying and contacting these women proved problematic in several ways. The Tennis Association could provide the names of men who were members of teams playing in the local tennis competition, but no formal information was available concerning their domestic circumstances, such as their addresses or if they lived with a wife, female, or male partner. Because I wished to communicate directly with the women to be interviewed, rather than attempting to contact them through their male partners, I used two male acquaintances from within tennis as key informants. From a list of names of male State Grade and Veteran A Grade players they were able to tell me those they knew to be married to or living with a female partner, the women's names, and generally where they lived. This process gave me ten "leads." Letters were sent, followed by telephone calls, and seven of these women agreed to be interviewed.

Initially I had wished to focus on the partners of men who were playing in the top ("State Grade") level of competition in Western Australian because of the commitment and intensity of involvement this required in tennis. However, many of the men playing in this grade were young, often in their teens, and not living in partnerships. To extend the list, I included men playing in the top (A) Veteran's grade, who were therefore over age forty.

I began the interviews with less than the target number of fifteen and relied upon a "networking" process to find the rest. I asked women I interviewed if they could tell me of others in circumstances similar to their own. As the interviews progressed, it became apparent that a large proportion of the "wives" being interviewed also played tennis, so a deliberate effort was then made to seek out wives who did not.

These women were not easy to find which, in itself, provided some interesting insights. For example, June and her husband had to search through the large membership list of their tennis club before they could name any male members whose wives did not play. They identified three, of whom I interviewed two. Ellen provided more names of several she knew. Both she and June mentioned that it would be "interesting" to find out what these women thought about their husbands' tennis involvement. Karen told me about a friend of hers, a nonplayer married to a member of Karen's husband's pennant team, but said, "She would shoot me if I gave you her name. It would open up too big a can of worms." Between the lines of these women's comments was the acknowledgment that conflict within a marriage did or might occur in this situation.

The final two contacts were made after an acquaintance who played in a small, low-profile club gave me the names of the wives of his fellow club members. The club did not have representative teams in the top levels of either the men's or the women's pennant competition.

Because of the method used to identify this group, it became more varied in composition than had originally been planned. This turned out fortunate, for it added additional insights that might otherwise have been missed. For example, the men to whom the interviewed women were married played tennis at competition levels that ranged considerably, yet the level of competition appeared to bear little relation to the depth of their devotion to the sport. Interviews with these women focused on their husbands' playing schedules, its impact on them and other family members, and the demands and rewards.

In contrast with the women in the previous two groups, many more of the wives approached refused to be interviewed. Again, reasons were not solicited and were not always volunteered, but there were hints that discussing one's husband with a stranger transgressed the boundaries of privacy more than did discussing one's children or oneself. Refusals were usually curt. One woman declined to come to the phone when I asked to speak to her, but I overheard her say to her husband who had answered it, "Just tell her I'm not interested." Another said to me, "I've been married to my husband for thirty-six years and I feel our life is something private and I don't want to discuss it with someone I don't know." The privacy associated with marriage provides a sanctity for gender relations that can make their analysis difficult.

THE GROUPS

Veteran Women Tennis Players

Table A.1 shows the main characteristics of the group of veteran women tennis players interviewed. As tennis participants, these women could best be described as long-term, committed amateur players. The shortest tennis career in the group was that of the only woman in this group not born in Australia, but who had emigrated from the United States as an adult.

Although my attempts to include women from different class backgrounds were by no means reliable, this group of women included four whom I assessed to be working class, nine middle-class women, and two who were affluent middle class. I made these subjective assessments based on information that included their and their husbands' paid employment and its associated education levels, the estate values associated with the residential area in which they lived, and the material conditions of their homes, including size, decor, and material evidence of "lifestyle."

As can be seen from Table A.1, four women were currently working or had worked in full-time paid employment. For three of them, this work had been interrupted only briefly by the birth of their children or by their husbands' work transfers. The fourth had moved from a homemaker to part-time work, then to full-time paid work as her children became older and more independent. The part-time employment of two women had been intermittent during marriage and motherhood.

TABLE A.1
CHARACTERISTICS OF VETERAN WOMEN TENNIS PLAYERS

Age	Range (years)	42–72
	Mean	56.8
Tennis Career Longevity	Range (years)	13–61
	Mean	41.6
Marital Status	Married	13
	Divorced	1
	Widowed	1
Number of Children	Range	1–5
	Mean	2.8
Paid Work	None (full-time homemaker)	6
	Full Time	2
	Part Time	2
	Retired From Full Time	2
	Retired From Part Time	3
Tennis-Playing Husbands	Yes	9
	No	6

TABLE A.2
CHARACTERISTICS OF MOTHERS OF JUNIOR STATE SQUAD TENNIS PLAYERS

Age	Range (years)		37–52
	Mean		44
Marital Status	Married		15
	Divorced		1
Number of Children	Range		2–4
	Mean		2.8
Paid Work	None (full-time homemaker)		5
	Full Time		2
	Part Time	(fixed hours)	5
		(flexible hours)	4
Tennis Players	Yes		8
	No		8
Tennis-Playing Husbands	Yes		10
	No		6

TABLE A.3
CHARACTERISTICS OF THE MOTHERS' TENNIS-PLAYING CHILDREN

Age	Range (years)	10–18
	Mean	14
Gender	Daughters	8
	Sons	11
Sibling Order of Tennis-Playing Child	Oldest Child	7
	Middle Child	1
	Youngest Child	11

In addition to being members of the Veterans' Tennis Club, the women were also members of a "home" tennis club. Their memberships represented twelve of the possible sixty-one clubs within the Perth metropolitan area, including those located in working-class as well as middle-class and affluent residential areas.

Mothers of Junior State Squad Tennis Players

The mothers interviewed represent a slightly younger group. The characteristics of this group are shown in Table A.2.

Two of these women had been born outside of Australia. The remaining fourteen were Australian-born Caucasians. All were middle class, although there was a range in levels of affluence. I would describe two as being very wealthy.

Table A.3 details the characteristics of the children, who were the focus of their interviews. Three of the mothers had two children who were State Squad players, hence the statistics represent a total of nineteen children.

None of these children was an only child. In the case shown of the one "middle" child, her younger sibling was also a junior State Squad player. There were two families of two children in which both were State Squad players.

The details of whether or not the parents of these children also played tennis are shown in Table A.4, differentiated by the gender of their children.

Among this group of parents, two mothers and two fathers had been Australian National representative tennis players, two of whom were a couple. Three fathers had coached tennis professionally.

TABLE A.4
TENNIS-PLAYING BACKGROUND OF JUNIOR STATE SQUAD PLAYERS' PARENTS

	Mothers Only	Fathers Only	Both Parents	Neither Parent
Daughters	1	0	5	2
Sons	0	3	4	4
Total	1	3	9	6

TABLE A.5
CHARACTERISTICS OF WIVES OF ADULT MALE TENNIS PLAYERS

Age	Range (years)	27–60
	Mean	41.2
Number of Children	Range	0–6
	Mean	2.2
Ages of Children	Range (years)	0.6–38
	Mean	20.1
Paid Work	None (full-time homemaker)	1
	Full-Time Work	7
	Part-Time Work	5
	Retired From Part-Time Work	2
Tennis Players	Yes	8
	No	7

TABLE A.6
CHARACTERISTICS OF ADULT MALE TENNIS PLAYERS

Age	Range (years)	29–61
	Mean	44.4
Paid Work	Full Time	14
	Part Time	0
	Retired	1
Tennis Level	Senior State Grade	7
	Veterans "A" Grade	4
	Other Pennant Competition Grades	4

Wives of Adult Male Tennis Players

Details about the group of women interviewed because they were married to or living with adult male tennis players are shown in Table A.5. For two of these women, this partnership was their second marriage and their husbands were not the biological fathers of their children. All of these women were Caucasian, although three had emigrated to Australia. I defined two as working class. Two had no children. The relevant characteristics concerning their husbands are shown in Table A.6. The man who had retired from paid work was now working voluntarily as an administrator for the Tennis Association which, his wife explained, was more demanding of his time than his paid work had been. Of the four who played tennis in "other" pennant competition grades, one had just joined a pennant team for the first time and, when the interview took place, had played in the competition only once.

ANALYSIS

In this research, I endeavored to adopt a grounded theory strategy systematized by Glaser and Strauss (1967), which describes the close, interdependent relationship between empirical data and the development of theory. The interview texts were paramount, allowing the data to inform both the description of the social world and its analysis. Priority was given to the data as it was voiced and to anchoring it within the context of the interviewed women's lives, following Kirby and McKenna, who suggested,

> Giving priority to intersubjectivity and critical reflection on the social context throughout the analysis ensures that we are able to hear and affirm the words and experiences of the research participants and at the same time be able to critically reflect on the structures that influence the actualities of their lives. (1989, 130)

The analysis, therefore, developed from an attempt to portray the inherent richness of the data as it described its own context, while reflecting upon it from a critical feminist perspective that emphasized the women's experiences and interpretations within an understanding of oppressive gender relations.

All but two of the forty-six interviews were fully recorded on audiotape and later transcribed verbatim. Extensive notes were made during the two that were not recorded, and these were written out in full within the hour immediately following the interview. At this stage, with the help of the notes, most of the women's words could be remembered exactly as they were expressed, therefore I had no reservations about their accuracy when quoting them later. These two interviewees were Marie and Tania. Marie had requested that her interview not be recorded, but facilitated detailed note taking. During Tania's interview, her three-year-old child wished to play music on his tape recorder in the same room. He was unwell, and she had spent a disturbing morning visiting a doctor and did not want to upset him further by not letting him do as he wished. Under the circumstances, and knowing my tape recorder could not compete with his, I turned mine off and took notes.

The qualitative data derived from the interviews was analyzed with the assistance of a computer package designed to help manage large amounts of unstructured, text-based information ("NUD-IST").[1] There has been some debate concerning the use of computer software for the analysis of qualitative sociological research following skepticism about the ability of technology to cope with the complexities and nuances of people's lives (Richards and Richards 1987) and the form of theoretical knowledge generated through this process (Richards and Richards 1991). In my experience, the computer program was merely (and very usefully) a tool that helped manage and organize the data, replacing the stacks of shoeboxes or envelopes thumbtacked to a wall that may have otherwise been employed to hold the collected snippets of text in hard copy. It did not replace the process of coding—the separating, defining, labeling, collecting, sorting, and reviewing of the women's words, nor the cognitive process of thinking, testing, and more thinking, required to present a plausible theoretical analysis.

LIMITATIONS

Although qualitative methodology that involves interviewing people about their lives is recognized for its potential to reflect those lives as they are perceived and experienced, there are limitations, particularly when the interview is a one-off occurrence, as these mostly were.

In effect, the information volunteered by those being interviewed can really only be considered a frozen moment in time in their lives, mediated by their response to me as the interviewer. The interview process itself, the questions posed, and the reflections made in response, irredeemably change, if only in minute ways, the interviewees' understandings of the topic being discussed and how they will perceive it afterward. Even when the interview requires reflecting on one's life, interpretation is an ongoing process, as was clearly demonstrated in Anna Troger's (1986) work with older German women survivors of World War II.

Given such limitations, efforts were made after the interviews took place to ensure that the information gathered was as true to the women's interpretation of their experience as possible, including checking missed or ambiguous details after the interviews with follow-up telephone calls. Five of the women were later contacted to verify aspects of which I was uncertain. One woman phoned me twice after her interview to add further information to a theme in her interview.

In an attempt to authenticate the women's stories, and more important, my interpretation of them, I sent the women reports at several stages after the interviews. These included copies of early analyses written as articles or conference presentations (Thompson 1992a, 1992b) and the report written for the ASCNSRC (Thompson 1995). Each time a letter of explanation was included, as was an invitation to telephone me or write to me if they wished to comment. I had hoped they would, but I received only one call. It was from a veteran woman tennis player who she said that, from her experience, my description of their participation in tennis (Thompson 1992a) was very accurate, and she thanked me for portraying it as such.

This follow-up was important and necessary, but also difficult. I found myself modifying and rewording passages I had originally written for an academic audience, not so much to remove academic jargon but to be more moderate in my analysis. I felt the women were always at my shoulder as my readers, and while this served in the best possible way to keep me "honest," it also inhibited and threatened to create a closed circle of understanding, reducing my analysis to a tendency to give them back, in summary form, exactly what they had already given me. How could I say anything strongly "feminist" when the women themselves might not describe it that way and would most likely be uncomfortable with being represented in those terms? It left no opening for new interpretations, understandings, different consciousnesses. It left little space for my scholarship and the question begged, what, therefore, was the point? At the same time I recalled Meg Luxton's experience of researching working-class women in Canada, who, after reading Luxton's initial, tentative analysis of their lives, asked her to "do it more" (Luxton 1980). So I knew that somehow I had to be able to tell these women's stories of exploited labor without obliterating them as active, vibrant women who were aware, made choices, had their own reasons, lived their lives with a sense of control, and gained identifiable rewards. They had accepted me and trusted me enough to invite me into their homes to tell me expansively and openly about their lives. I had found the interviews pleasurable, and it was a joy to meet and talk to these women. I wanted to thank them for their generous hospitality (for the cups of tea and coffee, the cakes and biscuits, the dinner and glasses of wine, the bag of lemons, the pot plant), I wanted to be "nice," yet it seemed my analysis might not be seen that way. In most situations, feminism is necessarily critical of the status quo, so to be able to proceed with the research, to make the exercise at all worthwhile and not a waste and abuse of their time, I had to pursue an interpretation that was my own but one that I hoped would speak authentically of and to the women whose lives were its focus. These dilemmas are common in feminist research (Oakley 1981a; Woodward and Chisholm 1981; Stanley and Wise 1983).

Researching From Outside or Within?

My position in this research was both limiting and advantageous. I defined myself as an outsider to the tennis culture I studied, and in many respects I was also an "outsider" to the group of women interviewed. I am not Australian, not married, not a competitive tennis player, not living with a tennis player, and I do not have children who are players; I do not have children at all.

Although reviewers of my first application for funding from the ASCNSRC suggested it would be worthwhile for me to join a local tennis club, for various reasons I did not do so. One of these reasons was the qualms I felt about befriending club members with what might later have been seen as ulterior motives, or on the other hand, facing barriers to any useful level of interaction that may have been created by my fully disclosing my research intentions from the outset. In the long run, I concluded that it would be more honest to remain an outsider to Western Australian tennis culture, with the women I interviewed being fully aware of this position.

There were continual examples of how this stance aided the research process, with women explaining details and confiding situations simply because they saw me as an "outsider" to tennis. One woman in particular, the mother of a young player whom she felt was being treated unjustly by the tennis administration at the time of the interview, said to me, "I must tell you this. This is part of your research, the pain as well as the glory that we have to go through." Twice during the following weeks she phoned me unsolicited to provide an updated report about the situation. During another interview, after I had asked a few questions concerning the administration of junior tennis, one woman wanted to know "who had made up" the questions. She was suspicious about answering them until I assured her that they were my questions and I was in no way involved with the tennis administration office. I am convinced that because the women interviewed could not assume my experience and understanding of the situations we were discussing, they were more expansive and meticulous in providing details. Also, for the mothers especially, my nonmembership in tennis was an important criterion for their trust.

However, it is likely that my "insiderness," in terms of being a white, middle-class, middle-aged woman similar to most of these women, provided an identification that eased access and was also important to the process of their disclosure. As much as they did not assume my knowledge of tennis or, sometimes, my understanding of Australian culture, they mainly expressed values with the assumption that I held them similarly, such as those concerning the welfare of children and the rewards of sport. Many wanted to know why I was studying this topic, which lead me to explain my early background in physical education and my work in sociology on sport and leisure. From that point of view, I could look and speak "the part."

Nevertheless, the suggestion from the ASCNSRC that I could legitimately include the fee for membership to a tennis club into the budget of a research grant application was an attractive proposition. There was a tennis club very near where I lived; all of its courts were made of grass and beautifully maintained; I can play tennis reasonably well; it would have been an authentic part of a "West Australian experience"; my partner was keen to join me; why then could I never bring myself to do it?

I stand by what I said about how I believe that remaining "outside" of tennis culture was actually a more honorable and worthwhile position for me to take in this research. However, I have to admit that the more I learned about tennis culture in Western Australia, the more I realized how difficult it would have been for me to become an "insider."

To begin with, I heard stories about how it can take several years before new tennis club members are fully accepted and integrated into the social fabric of the club, unless they are exceptionally good players, in which case it is likely to happen more quickly. I heard how some groups could be "cliquey," especially if the women had been club members and had been playing together for decades, as most of the women I interviewed had. But it was the type of labor demanded of women in tennis clubs, and the way in which the experiences of women players in tennis culture were constructed in a very classed, gendered, and hyper-heterosexual manner that deterred me the most. I could not have passively taken my turn on the roster to pour tea for men, knowing that they were never required to do this. I could not have gone with my partner to the club's fund-raising social activities, performed my expected role of being responsible for "taking a plate,"[2] and comfortably watched my identity be constructed as half of a heterosexual couple. I cringed at the thought of possibly being expected to wear a little white skirt with matching lacy knickers; I wondered how I would be silently assessed, at midweek "Ladies Shield Competition" matches, after explaining that I did not need to dash off to pick up children; and all along knowing these resistances to "normal" women tennis-players' behavior would have further added to the length of time it would have taken me to be accepted enough for the exercise to have achieved its purpose.

In an early draft of this discussion about the limitations of being an "outsider" to tennis culture, I had included a note about joining a tennis club but did not elaborate. Lynne Star, who proofread the draft for me, wrote in the margin, "Wimp![3] Go on, say it, They would have thought you were weird." Could a "weird" newcomer from another country have successfully initiated changes within the culture, or would she have been labeled a "stirrer" and sidelined? I then realized how much courage would have been needed to do this as a participant observer, and I have the utmost respect for Maree Boyle, who joined a lawn bowls club in Queensland, Australia, for her research on the exploitation of women's labor in that sport setting (see Boyle and McKay 1995).

Another more significant issue in any debate concerning "insider or outsider" standpoints pertains to the feminist commitment to change in social relations that disadvantage women. Considering the participant-driven, quasi-democratic characteristics of community-based sport clubs, change could arguably be best brought about from within, hence my position of researching from the outside provided little or no scope for associated feminist praxis. It would not surprise me to find, years after the research took place, that few of the exploitative practices highlighted by this analysis had changed for the women within tennis in Western Australia. Certainly I was not there to assist in it happening. To exacerbate the situation, following a career opportunity I have moved from Australia back to New Zealand. Since then I have tried to have three lay articles from my research published in the West Australian Tennis Association's official magazine. This was a further attempt to return the information to the informants and change the dynamics of its ownership. Successive editorial staff of that magazine have repeatedly avoided doing so.

The fact that I am not Australian and had not long been in Australia before undertaking the research is another important consideration that raises further issues of integrity and social responsibility. While it has been argued that a researcher from another cultural background has the advantage of "surprise" at seeing differences,[4] feminist theorists in particular have argued that all epistemology must develop from within the experiences of those to whom it refers and should belong (Kirby and McKenna, 1989; Mies 1983; Stanley and Wise 1983). While I know that the very same gender relations surround sport in my country, it somehow seemed easier to critique a culture that is not my own, by allowing me to distance myself from the context of the interviewed women's lives. At the very least, this signifies a cultural bias that must be acknowledged.

DELIMITATIONS

The focus of this research is limited to one sport, tennis. It was neither designed to produce comparative data between sporting codes nor to provide "grand" theoretical conclusions able to be generalized to all women and all sport. A focus on one sport within one social context allowed for an in-depth investigation and facilitated a better understanding of the complexities and interconnections of the multiple relationships women may have to sport. The reasons tennis particularly suited this purpose are explained more fully in Appendix B. One of these reasons, its high participation rate and significance within a particular culture, helps our appreciation of the impact of this sport on social life. However, the sport itself could be considered merely a vehicle to illustrate how a particular set of structures and ideologies is manifest in sport and experienced by women.

Importantly, the research is further limited to women who are still "within the system," that is, the research focused on women who were still involved in tennis through any of the identified relationships. It did not involve women who were no longer involved in the sport, nor did it consider why this was so. For example, mothers of children who have "dropped out" of playing tennis were not interviewed to discover what may have influenced this decision. Nor were the wives of men who had ceased playing surveyed. This meant that the views were not examined of women who may have, for one reason or another, resisted or halted the demands made upon them through tennis, either by being able to influence ceased participation of their family members or by ceasing to play the sport themselves.

In an analysis of women servicing the sport of others, one important dimension is the ways in which women are used to glamorize and sexualize male sporting events, such as through cheerleading, presenting the victors with garlands and kisses, or being otherwise associated with sportsmen for sexual kudos, behavior referred to as "groupie-ism." While this behavior is considered "legendary" around men's sport (Barnes 1973; Bouton and Marshall 1983; Edmonds 1987; Lasson 1989; McKay 1993a), which in itself rings alarms as being an important issue for analysis, it is nevertheless outside the scope of this study and just may have to be the subject of another book!

APPENDIX B:
BACKGROUND TO TENNIS CULTURE
IN WESTERN AUSTRALIA

WHY TENNIS?

Tennis was chosen as the focus for this research for two main reasons. The major one was because, unlike most other institutionalized sports in Australia, it is played in large numbers by women, men, and children. There are few sports that have participation opportunities for large numbers from all three of these groups, thus making it easily possible to maintain a long and continuous playing career. The players represented in this study ranged in age from ten to seventy-two years. This allowed the analysis of a range of women's relationships to sport within the context of one sporting structure, making it possible to understand the interconnections and the ways in which the relationships enhanced, complemented, and contradicted each other.

The other reason relates to the historical and cultural significance of the sport in Australian society. While the history of tennis is undoubtedly connected to its current class characteristics, its early introduction to colonial Australia and the wide extent to which it was adopted give it the status of being a key Australian sport.

HISTORY AND STRUCTURE

Tennis was one of the earliest introduced sports to colonial Australia, "transferred from its middle-class English origins during the 1870s" (Stoddart 1986, 139). At that stage, organized tennis was associated with men's cricket, being the sport the men played during the winter when they were not playing cricket. Women were also playing at that time, although the first known "pennant" competition for women was not recorded until 1903 (Phillips 1995). Stoddart points out that it was a game considered "perfect" for women because it was "social rather than sporting," and he explained how women's involvement in the sport was trivialized in comparison with the men's "serious" competition (Stoddart 1986, 140).

It was a sport that could be adapted well to colonial social life in Australia, being suited to the climate and the abundance of colonized land. According to Stoddart, by the end of the century, it had become *the* social game. He quoted a circular sent to the "gentility" in Perth in 1895, which said,

> The cooperation of the leading citizens has been invited to form a club, such as exists in England and other colonies, not only to provide healthful and desirable exercise for both ladies and gentlemen, but also to furnish that which is absolutely lacking in Perth—a place of general resort where members can readily meet their friends. (Stoddart 1986, 140)

An association that was the forerunner to the current, main administrative body of tennis in Perth, the Western Australian Lawn Tennis Association (WALTA), was established in 1903. During the period 1934 to 1967, women were excluded from what was known as the tennis "council," which meant that they could not be members of the association's executive committee, thus the sport was administered entirely by males (Phillips 1995.) It was during that period, in 1963, that the Women's Auxiliary to WALTA was formed as a service organization to the all-male establishment. This was considered an appropriate and adequate forum for women's involvement in the administration of the sport.

Participation Statistics

In 1990, the year in which most of the interviews for this study took place, the Western Australian Ministry of Sport and Recreation Sports Census figures (Quay 1990) recorded 32,593 registered tennis players in the state, of which 77 percent were in the metropolitan area of Perth (population 1 million). This made tennis the fourth largest sport in terms of affiliated participants. Approximately 45 percent of these players were female, for whom the sport also had the fourth highest participation numbers. It was the fifth highest sport most participated in by men. Of all of the junior, coed sports, tennis ranked highest in the number of registered players.

The same census (Quay 1990) showed that in 1990 there were sixty-one affiliated tennis clubs in the Perth metropolitan area. I was also aware of five suburban clubs that were not affiliated with WALTA, and there are numerous others based in tertiary education institutions, work sites, or church associations, for example.

All tennis clubs with courts and clubroom facilities were sited on public land, owned and operated by local government authorities called "Shires." The clubs are run by their membership bodies on a voluntary basis, who lease the land usage for a very nominal fee (such as one dollar per annum) and cooperate with the Shire over the provision and maintenance of facilities. Usually the Shire assists with the maintenance expenses until the club is sufficiently established to become financially independent. A committee, elected by the membership, undertakes the club's management.

They are all public clubs and, because of the public land provision, cannot be exclusive. However, there are membership fees, and some clubs are more expensive to join than others. Those with a high proportion of grass courts are generally more expensive than those with hard courts because of the higher maintenance costs of the grass surface. Not all clubs remain in operation throughout the year, and those that do not usually have cheaper membership fees.

In most clubs there is a nomination system for new memberships, meaning that a prospective member's application to join the club must be endorsed by at least one existing member. This is a condition required under the Liquor Licensing Act, to allow clubs to obtain a liquor license and to operate a bar. While it undoubtedly helps perpetuate a homogeneity among the group of members, from the tennis clubs' point of view is not invoked to exclude or limit membership. Many clubs need to deliberately seek new members for their continued survival.

As an example, membership fees from one tennis club in Perth are given below (in Australian dollars). This particular club had twenty-six courts (sixteen grass, ten hard) and a membership of approximately 400. It was a slightly larger club than most, but its 1990 membership fees were considered average.

Membership Category	Fee Per Annum (Australian $)
Senior (Adult Full Membership)	$150
Midweek (Adult, Midweek Play Only)	90
Couple (Two Cohabiting Adults)	280
Family (Two Adults, Two Children Under Age Eighteen)	295
Social (Adult, Nonplaying Member)	20
Junior (Age Fifteen to Eighteen)	55
Sub-Junior (Age Fourteen and Under)	15

Competition Structures

The major, ongoing tennis competition is commonly known as "pennants." Teams, usually representing a club, enter into a graded division with five to seven other teams that they play in rotation, usually once per week. Although there are many of these competitions operating throughout the city, there are two main ones. One is administered by WALTA. It is divided into women's, men's, veteran's, and junior competition, and divided again depending on what day the competition is scheduled. For example, both the women's and men's have a Saturday and Sunday pennant competition, which are separate competitions.

The WALTA-administered pennants are the main regular competition for junior tennis players and are divided into a girl's and boy's competition. This is scheduled on Sunday mornings commencing at 9 A.M. On the 1989–1990 WALTA Tennis Calendar, this competition was held in two six-week blocks between early November and mid March, suspended over Christmas and New Year.

The major competition for men is also the WALTA-administered pennants scheduled on both days of the weekend. During the 1989–1990 summer season there were eighteen and nineteen divisions, respectively, entered in the Saturday and Sunday competitions. There were mainly six teams in each division (although eight in State grade) and seven to ten men registered in each team. The highest division of this competition is called "State Grade," which is played on Saturdays. Occasionally in the higher grades, the teams can be drawn to play what are known as "doubleheaders," which means they play on Sunday as well as Saturday. The competition for those in divisions of "Over 35" and "Over 40" years of age is played on Sundays. All of these matches commence at 1 P.M.

The women's pennant competition administered by WALTA is not as large a competition as the one for men. In the 1989–1990 summer season, there were seven divisions entered for Saturday playing and eight for Sunday. Like the men's, the top State grade plays on Saturday afternoon and the "Over 40" division plays on Sunday. There was no "Over 35" division. Fewer players (five to seven) were registered in each team than in the men's teams. Both women's and men's weekend pennants run in two seasons. The summer season runs from early November to mid March, and the winter season runs from late May to mid August. This totals twelve weekends.

The largest women's pennants competition, however, is not run by WALTA directly and does not take place during the weekends. It is the "Midweek Ladies Shield" competition, which is administered independently by the Women's Auxiliary to WALTA and is scheduled on Wednesday mornings. There were twenty-one divisions in this competition during the 1989–1990 summer season. Like the weekend pennants, this competition runs in two seasons, but it ceases during children's school holidays. The women in this competition only play doubles matches, unlike the weekend pennants, when both singles and doubles are played.

In addition to pennant competitions, there are tournaments. Each club will usually have its own championship tournament every year, but there are other tournaments that are regular fixtures on the West Australian tennis calendar. For the 1989–1990 season there were forty-two of these listed.

For older players, men and women, the Veterans Club of Western Australia is an organization that arranges competition for its members age forty and over, separate from that which WALTA administers. These competitions occur on Fridays and Sundays. The 1989 membership list for this club showed 588 members listed, and it was from this list that the fifteen women players I interviewed were drawn. The club is affiliated with a vast national and international network of veteran tennis organizations that provide immense possibilities for tennis globe-trotting and the opportunity to revitalize the intensity of competition.

Social Tennis

The heart of tennis club culture is "club day," when members gather at the club on a Saturday and/or Sunday afternoon for social play. The actual organization of play is usually very complex, with an elaborate system of having players graded and mixing them in various combinations to achieve satisfactorily matched games for the largest number of people. Many clubs have recently computerized this procedure of "putting on the sets." These are mainly doubles matches and one of the few times when women and men will play together in "mixed" doubles.

Club social days also occur during the week, and a player can become a midweek club member, at a lower fee, and play only at this time. This is usually on a Tuesday or a Wednesday, during the morning. Until very recently these memberships were available to women only, and the structure was known as "Midweek Ladies." In most clubs now, men may also play at this time.

This does not exhaust the opportunities to play tennis in Perth, but it outlines the major organizational structures that are important to the discussions in the preceding chapters. The information also is included in an attempt to give an indication of how it is possible to play a great deal of tennis in Perth. The women interviewed, therefore, were not talking about a sport that happens for two forty-minute halves, once a week for three months of the year, such as a seasonal team sport might. They were instead describing an elaborate culture with an immense and compelling range of participation opportunities. As Muir (1991) found in his case study in California, even as a leisure activity, tennis may be taken very seriously.

Junior Tennis Squads

All that is left to describe is the pertinent aspects of junior sport, particularly Squads. The main organizational aspect specific to junior tennis of relevance to this thesis is that associated with the "State Squad." This Squad is a group of approximately forty children, some of whom have been, or potentially will be, selected for teams to represent Western Australia in national or international competition. Their inclusion in the Squad occurs when they are invited by WALTA to take part in sponsored group training sessions, referred to throughout the study as "Squads," or "Squad training." This sponsorship came from the fast food chain McDonald's. Similar squads occur in other Australian states, and overall the program was known as "McDonald's Junior Tennis Australia." During the year the mothers of junior State Squad players were interviewed, the McDonald's sponsorship for Western Australia totaled Australian $86,000.

What this meant for the junior players and their parents was ongoing tennis coaching at a reduced cost. The Squad training sessions were organized into four terms throughout the year. For each of these terms, the total cost to the child was $50, and McDonald's would contribute a further $250. Over the year, this would amount to $200 and $1,000, respectively, per child. In return, the child would receive group coaching two to four times a week and be expected to compete in tennis competition. This was a significant feature in junior tennis in Western Australia, and its impact on the mothers of tennis-playing children was explored in the preceding chapters.

Appendix C:
The ASCNSRC Survey of Parental Support

Method

The purpose of this project was to survey the mothers and fathers of twenty junior tennis players living in the Perth metropolitan area of Western Australia. Twenty-eight households were contacted to achieve this number. Both parents in a household were not always willing to partake in the survey, with mothers tending to be more willing than fathers. Two mothers were solo parents. Overall, nineteen mothers and sixteen fathers of twenty-three junior tennis players were surveyed.

The children had been selected by the State Tennis Association for sponsored coaching. They ranged in age from eleven to sixteen years. Ten were girls and eleven were boys. These children were from a different group than those whose mothers were interviewed.

The mothers surveyed ranged in age from thirty-six to forty-nine years. Of them, ten were Australian born, while the remaining nine had immigrated from elsewhere, mostly from the United Kingdom and Europe. Only two of these women were not in paid employment outside of the home; ten worked part time and seven worked full time in paid jobs.

The fathers surveyed ranged in age from thirty-five to sixty-five years old, although most were around forty-four years old. One was retired, but the remaining fifteen were in full-time paid employment. Nine had been born in Australia, with the larger proportion of those born elsewhere being from the United Kingdom.

Of all the parents, only one individual was not white Caucasian. Most were also tennis players themselves: only two mothers and one father described themselves as not playing any tennis. Six mothers and four fathers played in local pennant competition, and four mothers and four fathers said they played as frequently as three to four times a week.

There were two parts to the survey. First, each parent was to complete a Time Usage Form. This required them to record their major activities during each hour of the day they were awake for an entire week. Although a relatively crude measure, its purpose was to determine the proportion of time each parent allocated to various activities, including servicing their child's tennis away from home. Approximately half of the parents completed this during a week in which their child was playing in a tennis tournament and half during what would be considered a more "usual" week. Complete forms were returned from seventeen mothers and fourteen fathers.

The second part of the survey involved a list of twenty-one tasks that had been identified as being the major demands of servicing a child's tennis. Designed as a series of "tick lists," each parent was asked to indicate which support task they personally had done for their child during the past year, who most often did the task, how frequently each was done, and whose responsibility it was to organize and ensure that the task was done when necessary.

There also was the opportunity given for respondents to write in other tasks they had done for their child's tennis but which did not appear on the prepared list. Eleven mothers and six fathers used this provision. Finally, there were several open-ended questions asking each parent to express the greatest demands and rewards of their child's tennis. The survey took place between April 1991 and September 1991.

RESULTS

Time Spent Involved in Away-From-Home Activities Related to Children's Tennis

The activities recorded on the Time Budget Forms were grouped into the broad categories of paid employment, at home/domestic activities, own time/relaxation, and involvement away from home in children's tennis. The total number of hours engaged in each category during the week was counted for each person. On average, those surveyed spent 111.6 hours awake over the seven days of the diary record. Results are shown as follows:

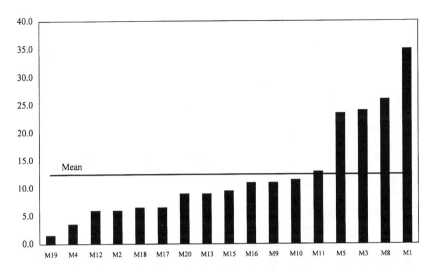

FIGURE C.1
TOTAL NUMBER OF HOURS PER WEEK EACH MOTHER SPENT
AWAY FROM HOME INVOLVED IN HER CHILD'S TENNIS

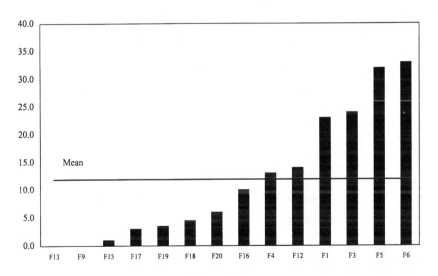

FIGURE C.2
TOTAL NUMBER OF HOURS PER WEEK EACH FATHER SPENT
AWAY FROM HOME INVOLVED IN HIS CHILD'S TENNIS

Support Tasks Done for Children's Tennis

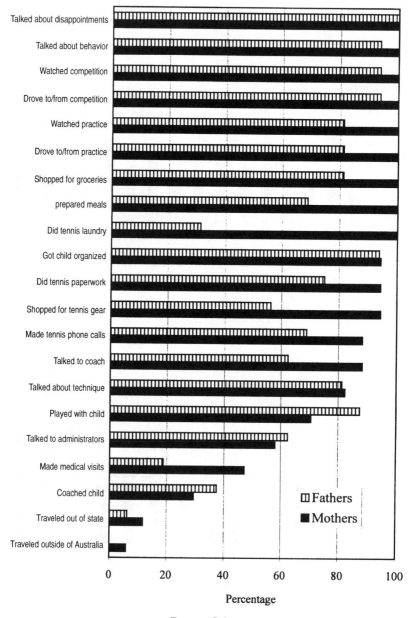

FIGURE C.3
PERCENTAGE OF MOTHERS AND FATHERS
WHO HAD DONE THE LISTED TASKS IN THE PAST YEAR

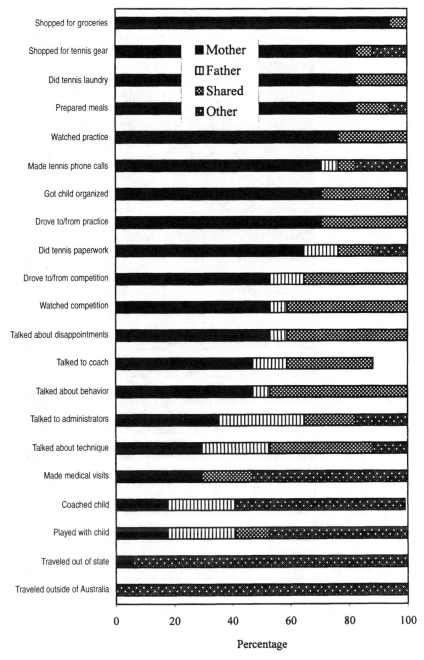

Legend:
- ■ Mother
- ▥ Father
- ▨ Shared
- ▦ Other

FIGURE C.4
PERCENTAGE OF THOSE WHO USUALLY DID
EACH TASK AS REPORTED BY THE MOTHERS

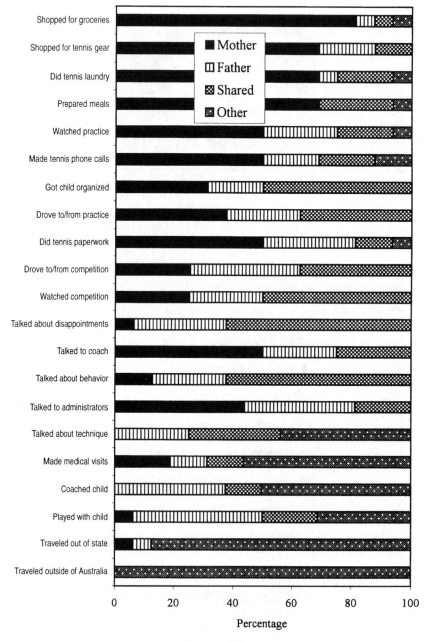

FIGURE C.5
PERCENTAGE OF THOSE WHO USUALLY DID
EACH TASK AS REPORTED BY THE FATHERS

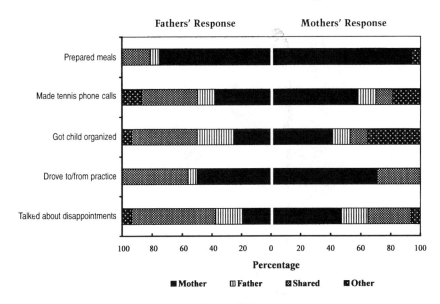

FIGURE C.6
COMPARISON BETWEEN THE RESPONSES OF MOTHERS AND FATHERS
ON WHO WAS RESPONSIBLE FOR SELECTED TASKS

Other tasks parents listed as having done included the following:

Listed by mothers:
  Help them keep to a stable diet
  Diet related to tennis, for example, pre-tournament diet
  Make tennis clothing
  Sew on emblems
  Coordinate the pennant team—child is captain
  Spend lots of money
  Do aerobics together
  Go to sports store(s) to find out child's tennis draw
  Organize younger members of the family to come to tournaments or to be at home with friends
  Travel with child—his ball boy involvement
  Have [child's] friends sleep over before/during tennis tournaments
  Drive other children to tennis

Listed by fathers:
  Assist in hit-up before match
  Raise money—find new sponsors

Give to funding of tennis lessons, tournament fees, spend money
at tournaments
Encourage them that it is a sport for enjoyment
Organize junior pennants
Drive other children to and from tennis

APPENDIX D:
DETAILS OF THE WOMEN INTERVIEWED

MOTHERS OF JUNIOR TENNIS PLAYERS

Di. Age 46; 3 children, ages 16–23; tennis-playing child—son age 16; married (first); part-time paid work; does not play tennis herself; husband in full-time paid work; husband does not play tennis.

Beth. Age 52; 4 children, ages 17+; tennis-playing child—daughter age 17; married (first); no paid work; plays tennis herself; husband in full-time paid work; husband plays tennis.

Jacqui. Age 37; 3 children, ages 6—13; tennis-playing child—son age 13; married (first); full-time paid work in own business (flexible hours); played tennis herself; husband in full-time paid work (same business); husband played tennis, coached tennis professionally.

Jill. Age 47; 4 children, ages 14–19; tennis-playing children—daughters ages 14 and 16; married (first); part-time paid work; plays tennis herself; husband in full-time paid work; husband plays tennis; two other children played tennis.

Kath. Age 43; 2 children, ages 14–16; tennis-playing child—daughter age 16; married (first); no paid work; plays tennis herself; husband in full-time paid work; husband plays tennis.

Liz. Age 40; 2 children, ages 12–15; tennis-playing children—daughter age 12 and son age 16; married (first); part-time paid work; does not play tennis herself; husband in full-time paid work; husband does not play tennis.

Louise. Age 39; 3 children, ages 6–11; tennis-playing children—daughter age 9 and son age 11; married (first); casual work in family business; plays tennis herself; husband in full-time paid work; husband plays tennis.

Lyn. Age 45; 2 children, ages 16–19; tennis-playing child—daughter age 16; married (first); no paid work; does not play tennis herself; husband in full-time paid work; husband does not play tennis.

Monica. Age 44; 2 children, ages 10–12; tennis-playing children—sons ages 10 and 12; married (first); full-time paid work; plays tennis herself; husband in full-time paid work; husband plays tennis.

Peggy. Age 52; 4 children, ages 18–34; tennis-playing child—son age 18; married (first); casual work for daughter; does not play tennis herself; husband in full-time paid work; husband does not play tennis.

Rita. Age 44; 2 children, ages 7–15; tennis-playing child—son age 15; married (first); half-time paid work; does not play tennis herself; husband in full-time paid work; husband plays tennis; emigrants to Australia.

Rosemary. Age 47; 3 children, ages 16–22; tennis-playing child—son age 16; married (first); no paid work; does not play tennis herself; husband in full-time paid work; husband plays tennis; other children played tennis.

Sonia. Age 39; 2 children, ages 9–14; tennis-playing child—son age 14; divorced; no paid work; does not play tennis herself; ex-husband in full-time paid work; ex-husband does not play tennis.

Trish. Age 43; 3 children, ages 12–21; tennis-playing child—daughter age 12; married (first); casual work in family business; plays tennis herself; coaches tennis professionally; husband in full-time paid work; husband does not play tennis; other children play tennis.

Virginia. Age 43; 3 children, ages 10–17; tennis-playing child—daughter age 10; married (first); casual paid work in family business; plays tennis herself; husband in full-time paid work; husband plays tennis; other children play tennis.

Yvonne. Age 47; 3 children, ages 17–22; tennis-playing child—son age 17; married (first); part-time paid work; does not play tennis herself; husband in full-time paid work; husband plays tennis; husband coaches tennis professionally.

WIVES OF ADULT MALE TENNIS PLAYERS

Anthea. Age 27; no children; first marriage; full-time paid work; does not play tennis herself; husband in full-time paid work; husband plays State grade tennis.

Bronwyn. Age 27; no children; first marriage; full-time paid work; plays tennis socially; husband in full-time paid work; husband plays State grade tennis.

Ellen. Age 43; 2 children, ages 24–27; second marriage; full-time paid work; plays tennis herself; husband in full-time paid work; husband plays Veterans A grade tennis; both children play tennis.

Janet. Age 57; 2 children, ages 31–33; first marriage; used to work part time; does not play tennis herself; husband retired from full-time paid work; husband ex-State grade player; both children play tennis.

June. Age 43; 3 children, ages 16–21; first marriage; full-time paid work; plays tennis herself; husband in full-time paid work; husband plays State grade tennis; all 3 children play tennis.

Karen. Age 41; 2 children, ages 11–13; first marriage; part-time paid work; plays tennis herself; husband in full-time paid work; husband plays Veterans A grade tennis; both children play tennis.

Kerry. Age 49; 2 children, ages 25–27; first marriage; full-time paid work; does not play tennis herself; husband in full-time paid work; husband plays lower-grade pennant tennis; 1 child plays tennis.

Lorelle. Age 41; 3 children, ages 14–20; first marriage; part-time paid work; plays tennis herself; husband in full-time paid work; husband plays State grade tennis; no children play tennis.

Marie. Age 60; 6 children, ages 28–38; first marriage; part-time paid work; does not play tennis herself; husband in full-time paid work; husband plays lower-grade pennant tennis; no children play tennis.

Pauline. Age 42; 3 children, ages 14–19; first marriage; full-time paid work; plays some tennis herself (socially); husband in full-time paid work; husband plays Veterans A grade tennis; no children play tennis.

Rebecca. Age 33; 1 child, age 6; second marriage; full-time paid work; does not play tennis herself; husband in full-time paid work; husband plays lower-grade pennant tennis; no children play tennis.

Sally. Age 43; 2 children, ages 16–18; first marriage; part-time paid work; plays tennis herself; husband in full-time paid work; husband plays State grade tennis; both children play tennis.

Sarah. Age 49; 3 children, ages 16–24; first marriage; part-time paid work; plays tennis herself; husband in full-time paid work; husband ex-State grade tennis player; no children play tennis.

Tania. Age 27; 2 children, ages 7 months–3 years; first marriage; part-time paid work; does not play tennis herself; husband in full-time paid work; husband plays A grade pennant tennis; no children play tennis.

Trudi. Age 36; 2 children, ages 5–8; first marriage; no paid work; plays tennis herself; husband works flexible hours; husband plays Veterans A grade tennis; children beginning to play tennis.

Veteran Women Tennis Players

Alice. Age 60; played tennis for 52 years; 3 children, ages 31–39; married (first); has been employed in full-time paid work; husband in full-time work; husband plays tennis; 3 children play tennis.

Anne. Age 72; played tennis for 61 years; 1 child (adult); married (first); has been employed in part-time paid work; husband was in full-time paid work; husband played tennis; both coached tennis; 1 child plays tennis.

Betty. Age 66; played tennis for 54 years; 1 child (adult); married (second); has been employed in full-time paid work; husband in full-time work; husband does not play tennis; child does not play tennis.

Brenda. Age 45; played tennis for 34 years; 2 children, ages 24 and 25; married (first); employed in full-time paid work; husband in full-time work; husband plays tennis; 1 child plays tennis.

Carol. Age 45; played tennis for 40 years; 2 children, ages 21 and 24; married (first); some casual paid work, including tennis coaching; husband in full-time work; husband plays tennis; 1 child plays tennis.

Connie. Age 68; played tennis for 54 years; 5 children (adults); married (first); no paid work; husband in full-time work; husband plays tennis; 4 children played tennis, 1 internationally.

Dorothy. Age 48; played tennis for 27 years; 3 children, ages 23–28; married (first); in no paid work; husband in full-time work; husband does not play tennis; 2 children play tennis.

Frances. Age 60; played tennis for 48 years; 3 children, ages 33–40; divorced; no paid work; ex-husband in full-time work; ex-husband does not play tennis; 1 child plays tennis.

Jean. Age 64; played tennis for 55 years; 3 children, ages 31–36; married (first); no paid work; husband in full-time work; husband plays tennis; 1 child plays tennis (professional tennis coach).

Linda. Age 52; played tennis for 12 years; 2 children, ages 15 and 25; married (first); no paid work; husband in full-time work; husband does not play tennis; no children play tennis; emigrated to Australia as an adult.

Marilyn. Age 42; played tennis for 32 years; 3 children, ages 17+; married (first); has been employed in part-time paid work; husband in full-time work; husband plays tennis; 3 children play tennis.

Molly. Age 49; played tennis for 19 years; 4 children, ages 21–27; married (first); some casual paid work (family business); husband in full-time work; husband does not play tennis; no children play tennis.

Noelene. Age 55; played tennis for 30 years; 4 children, ages 28–35; married (first); has been employed on/off in family business; husband in full-time work; husband plays tennis; 1 child plays tennis.

Patricia. Age 56; played tennis for 47 years; 5 children, ages 15–31; married (first); has been employed in full-time paid work; husband in full-time work, joint professional coaching business; husband plays tennis; 5 children play tennis (one professional player, one professional coach).

Ruth. Age 70; played tennis for 60 years; 2 children, ages 42–48; widowed; no paid work; husband was in full-time work; husband did not play tennis; no children play tennis.

NOTES

1. INTRODUCTION

1. The names of all interviewed women and the members of their families have been changed for this publication.

2. This directly contravened the 1977 Gleneagles Declaration on Apartheid and Sport, which was an agreement drawn up by Commonwealth Heads of Governments to discourage continued sporting relations with South Africa, particularly to avert further boycotts of Olympic and Commonwealth Games. For a thorough discussion of these international relations. see Nauright and Black (1995).

3. Since colonization, the history of the Aboriginal people of Australia has been marked by genocide and dispossession, a situation not conducive to self-disclosure of one's racial identity, even today. None of the women interviewed self-identified as Aboriginal, and none were obviously so from visual appearance. Despite the successes and high international profile of Yvonne Goolagong, Australia's Aboriginal people, especially women, are well underrepresented in tennis and sport generally.

2. BEING THE MOTHER OF A SPORTS PLAYER

1. In 1992, the name of the association was changed to "TennisWest," but the women interviewed referred to it as WALTA and that name has been retained throughout the book.

2. "Tea" is a word commonly used in Australia to name the evening meal.

3. For example, in the *Third Report of the National Sports Research Program* (Draper 1990), reporting fifteen research projects funded by the ASCNSRC from the period July 1988 to June 1990, there were seven reported that made no reference whatsoever to the gender of the subjects. Two more refer to "batsmen" and another to a male sports league but do not acknowledge that the research focused only on men. Of the remaining five, one specified male subjects only, two specified female subjects, and two specified both male and female subjects.

4. She had suggested that the ASCNSRC would be wise to insist that the research be extended to include more than one sport, thus helping ensure that the resulting final report made available to them would perhaps have broader relevance and be of greater use to the ASC in the long term. Although this recommendation was relayed to me, there was no suggestion that it should be incorporated in the research, and it was not made a condition of the funding.

5. This seminar was held jointly by the Federal House of Representatives Standing Committee on Legal and Constitutional Affairs and the ASC as part of the committee's "Inquiry Into Equal Status and Equal Opportunity for Australian Women." The resulting report is entitled *Halfway to Equal* (House of Representatives Standing Committee on Legal and Constitutional Affairs 1992).

6. My report, "The Gendered Servicing of Children's Tennis: An Investigation of Parental Support" (Thompson 1995), was sent to the ASCNSRC in August 1992. Its receipt was not acknowledged until I made inquiries about it in 1995, after which it was quickly produced as a Scientific Report. In the initial document, the tables showing the time surveyed mothers and fathers had spent involved in away-from-home, junior tennis-related activities had been labeled in reverse. The revised document was released in October 1995.

7. See, for example, Greendorfer 1983; Greendorfer and Lewko 1978; Kelly 1974; Lewko and Ewing 1980; Snyder and Spreitzer 1973; Spreitzer and Snyder 1976; Watson 1977. Lewko and Greendorfer's (1988) review of the literature pertaining to sport socialization of children concluded, in agreement with Theberge (1984), that the theory of sport socialization itself is not adequate for explaining the sports participation of children.

8. The section on athletics is based on data from twenty-one swimmers and eighteen tennis players in the United States, both males and females. The athletes and both their parents were interviewed, the analysis focused on family background and the child's years of early development.

3. Being the Wife of a Sports Player

1. This is an interesting issue. There were many times during the interviews when, because the women took for granted the labor they did

and the conditions under which it was done, they had difficulty under-standing why I had asked a question and therefore how they should answer it. At various times, I had to give examples to "prompt" them into recog-nizing and verbalizing what to them seemed "normal" so as to not need explaining. While at times this could have been viewed as "leading" the interviewee, in my experience it often was the only way to get the women interviewed to recognize and detail experiences that were so accepted that they appeared to not need explaining.

2. Here we talked about what support she would have if she was to leave the marriage, how she would manage, and where she could go for assistance. It was a situation similar to that described by Oakley (1981a), who discussed the questions her women interviewees "asked back" and how, because of the nature of those questions, it was impossible to retain "textbook" interviewing techniques and not provide the information sought. Tania's situation, however, raises further ethical concerns that I had not fully anticipated. Brackenridge (1997,139), from her research interviewing women who had experienced sexual abuse in sport, talks of the ethical problem that "lifting stones" can cause and the need in these circumstances to work alongside a social worker or therapist. I did not do this but contacted Tania several times during the month immediately following the interview. Her circumstances did not change during that time.

4. BEING A SPORTS PLAYER

1. Lamingtons are small, square, icing- and coconut-covered cakes. A "lamington drive" describes the effort of making many of these and selling them—to friends, neighbors, work colleagues, and strangers in the street. It is a traditional and common form of community fund-raising in Aus-tralia.

2. The Sex Discrimination Act (1984) is federal legislation based on the United Nations Convention on Elimination of All Forms of Discrimi-nation Against Women, which Australia ratified in 1983. In 1992, a federal inquiry into Equal Opportunity and Equal Status for Women in Australia concluded that Australian women were still only "half way to equal" (House of Representatives Standing Committee on Legal and Constitu-tional Affairs, 1992: xv).

3. References to this debate include: Browne (1992); Scraton (1992); Summerfield and White (1989); Thompson and Finnigan (1990); Turvey and Laws (1988).

4. McKay's study of women executives in Australian sport, entitled *Why So Few?*, showed that only 22.9 percent of administrative positions in national and state sporting organizations were held by women, and that most perceived "that women administrators were systematically disad-vantaged" by an extensive list of external barriers, which included having

to balance work and family responsibilities, informal male networks, gender stereotyping, and the particular masculine ambience of sport (McKay 1992a, 5).

5. REWARDS AND RATIONALES

1. "Cocky" is a term used to describe being self-assured, pushy, cheeky, or aggressive. It is used more readily to refer to males rather than females.

2. For example, the questions and ensuing discussion following my presentation of a paper entitled "Mum's Taxi: Gendered Servicing of Sport" at the conference of the Australian Sociological Association (Thompson 1991), and also from several male colleagues and on two occasions from men I spoke with at the WALTA office.

3.These two women were close friends and requested to be interviewed together.

6. GENDERED INSTITUTIONS
SERVICE GENDERED INSTITUTIONS

1. For examples of some of these practices, see Wearing (1984, 145–47).

2. By this I mean being financially supported by an ex-husband after the marriage no longer exists, such as was the case for Sonia. Delphy (1984) made the point that divorce is merely a transformation of the economic relations of marriage, because the responsibility for children is still assumed by mothers.

3. Many of the interviewed women, Karen especially, illustrated how a husband's way around this problem was to encourage his wife to also come to tennis and to bring the children.

APPENDIX A. THE METHODS

1. An acronym for "Non-numerical, Unstructured Data Indexing, Searching, and Theorizing," copyright Replee P/L (Richards and Richards 1990).

2. It is a tradition at social occasions in both Australia and New Zealand for the women to be asked to bring a plate of food to share. A formal expression signifying this protocol is "Ladies a Plate." See, for example, Julie Park's book (1991) *Ladies a Plate*, or Thompson (1990).

3. Wimp: a colloquial term for someone who, through timidity, opts out.

4. This idea about the benefits to social research of "elements of surprise" was presented by Lawrence Challip in a panel seminar discussing

cross-cultural research at the Olympic Scientific Congress (Malaga, Spain, July 1992). He gave an example that particularly resonated, of meeting young women in New Zealand who had never watched their boyfriends play sport because at the same time they would be playing it themselves. My response was, "Of course," understanding, as a New Zealander who had lived six years in North America, exactly why this was such a good example of being surprised by differing cultural norms. However, I did not think his was the best standpoint from which to *explain* such differences, which highlighted the tensions in the discussion. Seeing and explaining are different positions.

Bibliography

Aitken, Judith, and Ros Noonan. 1981. "Rugby, Racism and Riot Gear." *Broadsheet* 94:16–19.

Andrews, David. 1997. "Imaging America's Suburban Utopias: Soccer and the Cultural Politics of Promotional Representations." Paper presented at ISSA Symposium, Oslo, Norway, June 28–July1.

Arcana, Judith. 1979. *Our Mother's Daughters.* London: The Women's Press.

———. 1983. *Every Mother's Son.* London: The Women's Press.

Baldock, Cora V. 1983. "Volunteer Work as Work." In C.V. Baldock and B. Cass, eds., *Women, Social Welfare, and the State.* Sydney: Allen & Unwin.

Barnes, Laverne. 1973. *The Plastic Orgasm.* Richmond Hill, Ontario: Pocket Books.

Barrell, Gerry, Audrey Chamberlain, John Evans, Tim Holt, and Jill Mackean. 1989. "Ideology and Commitment in Family Life: A case study of runners." *Leisure Studies* 8(3): 249–62.

Barrett, Michele. 1988. *Women's Oppression Today. The Marxist/Feminist Encounter.* (Revised Edition). London: Verso.

Barrington, Rosemary, and Alison Gray. 1981. *The Smith Women: 100 New Zealand Women Talk About Their Lives.* Wellington: Reed.

Barrowman, Rachel. 1981. *A Report on the Molesworth Street-Incident: The Police and the 1981 Tour.* Wellington: Victoria University.

Baxter, Janeen. 1992. "Families and Households." In G. Lupton, P. Short, and R. Whip, *Society and Gender.* Melbourne: Macmillan.

Baxter, Janeen, Diane Gibson, and Mark Lynch-Blosse. 1990. *Double Take: The Links Between Paid and Unpaid Work.* Canberra: Australia Government Publishing Service.

Berger, Peter L., and T. Luckman. 1967. *The Social Construction of Reality*. London: Penguin Press.

Birrell, Susan, and Cheryl Cole, eds. 1994. *Women, Sport and Culture*. Champaign,Ill.: Human Kinetics.

Bittman, Michael, and Frances Lovejoy. 1991. "Domestic Power: Negotiating an Unequal Division of Labor Within a Framework of Equality." Paper presented at The Australian Sociological Association Conference, Murdoch University, December 10–14.

Bittman, Michael, and Jocelyn Pixley. 1997. *The Double Life of the Family*. St Leonards, NSW: Allen & Unwin.

Bloom, Benjamin S., ed. 1985. *Developing Talent in Young People*. New York: Ballantine Books.

Blue, Adrienne. 1987. *Faster, Higher, Further*. London: Virago Press.

Botham, Kathy. 1988. *Living with a Legend*. London: Grafton Books.

Boulton, Mary. 1983. *On Being a Mother*. London: Tavistock Publications.

Bourdieu, Pierre. 1984. *Distinction: A Social Critique of the Judgement of Taste*. London: Routledge & Kegan Paul.

Bouton, Bobbie, and Nancy Marshall. 1983. *Home Games: Two Baseball Wives Speak Out*. New York: St. Martin's/Marek.

Boyle, Maree, and Jim McKay. 1995. "You Leave Your Troubles at the Gate." *Gender & Society* 9(5): 556–675.

Brackenridge, Celia. 1997. "Sexual Harassment and Sexual Abuse in Sport." In Jill Clarke and Barbara Humberstone, eds., *Researching Women and Sport*. London: Macmillan.

Browne, Jennifer. 1992. "Coed or not Coed? That is the Question." *The ACHPER National Journal* 36: 20–23.

Bryson, Lois. 1983a. "Thirty Years of Research on the Division of Labour in Australian Families." *Australian Journal of Sex, Marriage and Family* 4(3):125–32.

———. 1983b. "Sport, Ritual, and the Oppression of Women," *Australia and New Zealand Journal of Sociology* 19(3): 413–26.

———. 1987. "Sport and the Maintenance of Masculine Hegemony." *Women's Studies International Forum*, 10(4): 349–60.

Bullock, Marlene. 1981. *21 Years: 1960–1981*. Perth: Nollamara Tennis Club Inc.

Burns, Anne. 1992. "Malthouse Team Takes Heart from Nanette." *The West Australian*, September 26.

Cahn, Susan. 1994. *Coming on Strong: Gender and Sexuality in Twentieth Century Women's Sport*. New York: Free Press.

Cameron, Jan. 1996. *Trail Blazers: Women Who Manage New Zealand Sport*. Christchurch: Sports Inclined.

Cameron, Kirsty. 1989. "Cricket Widow Jane Hits Her Home Run: Rising from the Ashes." *Sunday Times*, August 13: 3.

Campbell, Gordon. 1985. "Is Rugby Dying?" *New Zealand Listener*. June 29: 22–23.

Castles, Ian. 1993. *Women in Australia*. Canberra: Australian Bureau of Statistics.

Chafetz, Janet Saltzman, and Joseph Kotarba. 1995. "Son Worshippers: The Role of Little League Mothers in Recreating Gender." *Studies in Symbolic Interaction* 18: 219–43.

Chapple, Geoff. 1984. *1981: The Tour*. Wellington: A.H. & A.W. Reed Ltd.

Cockburn, Cynthia. 1983. *Brothers: Male Dominance and Technological Change*. London: Pluto Press.

Crawford, Scott A.G.M. 1995. "Rugby and the Forging of a National Identity." In J. Nauright, ed., *Sport, Power and Society in New Zealand: Historical and Contemporary Perspectives*. Sydney: ASSH Inc.

Curry, Timothy. 1991. "Fraternal Bonding in the Locker Room: A Profeminist Analysis of Talk about Competition and Women." *Sociology of Sport Journal* 8(2): 119–35.

Dann, Christine. 1982. "The Game is Over." *Broadsheet* 97: 26–28.

Delphy, Christine. 1977. "The Main Enemy: A Materialist Analysis of Women's Oppression." *Explorations in Feminism* 3. London: Women's Research and Resources Centre.

———. 1980. "A Materialist Feminism is Possible." *Feminist Review* 4: 79–105.

———. 1984. *Close to Home: A Material Analysis of Women's Oppression*. London: Hutchinson.

Dixon, Miriam. 1976. *The Real Matilda: Women and Identity in Australia, 1788–1975*. Ringwood, Victoria: Penguin Books.

Draper, Julie, ed. 1990. *Third Report on the National Sports Research Programme*. Canberra: Australian Sports Commission.

Duncan, Margaret Carlisle. 1990. "Sports Photographs and Sexual Difference: Images of Women and Men in the 1984 and 1988 Olympic Games." *Sociology of Sport Journal* 7: 22–43.

Dyer, Ken. 1982. *Challenging the Men: The Social Biology of Female Sporting Achievement*. St. Lucia: University of Queensland.

———, ed. 1986. *Sportswomen Toward 2000*. Adelaide: University of Adelaide.

Edmonds, Frances. 1986. *Another Bloody Tour*. London: Kingswood Press.

———. 1987. *Cricket XXXX Cricket*. London: Kingswood Press.

Edwards, Kathleen. 1988. "Glimpses of Coaches' Wives: Betty and Pat Poe." *Texas Coach* 33(3): 52–53.

Ehret, Scott. 1988. "I'm Glad You Asked That!" Wives of Officials View Refereeing Differently from Their Husbands." *Referee* 13(12): 52–54.

Eichler, Margrit. 1983. *Sexism in Research and Its Policy Implications*. (CRIAW Papers/Les Documents de L'ICRAF) Ottawa: The Canadian Research Institute for the Advancement of Women.

Eisenstein, Zillah R., ed. 1979. *Capitalist Patriarchy and the Case for Socialist Feminism*. New York: Monthly Review Press.

Festle, Mary Jo. 1996. *Playing Nice: Politics and Apologies in Women's Sport*. New York: Columbia University Press.

Finch, Janet. 1983. *Married to the Job: Wives' Incorporation in Men's Work*. London: George Allen & Unwin.

Firestone, S. 1971. *The Dialectic of Sex*. New York: Bantam Books.

Fougere, Geoff. 1981. "Shattered Mirror." *Comment* 14:12–14.

Freh, Lynne-Marie. 1990. "Margaret Earp: Married to the Game." *Woman Golfer* (April):75–76.

Frye, Marilyn. 1983. *The Politics of Reality*. New York: The Crossing Press.

Ganahl, Jane. 1979. "Coaches' Wives: Survival Tips." *Swimming World* 20(5): 84–85.

Glaser, B.G., and A.L. Strauss. 1967. *The Discovery of Grounded Theory: Strategies for Qualitative Research*. Chicago: Aldine.

Grbich, Carolyn. 1992. "Societal Response to Familial Role Change in Australia: Marginalization of Social Change?" *Journal of Comparative Family Studies* 23(1): 79–94.

Greendorfer, Susan. 1983. "Shaping the Female Athlete: the Impact of the Family." In M.A. Boutilier and L. San Giovanni, eds., *The Sporting Woman*. Champaign, Ill.: Human Kinetics.

Greendorfer, Susan, and John Lewko. 1978. "The Role of Family Members in Sport Socialization of Children." *Research Quarterly* 49: 146–52.

Griffin, Pat. 1992. "Changing the Game: Homophobia, Sexism, and Lesbians in Sport." *Quest* 44(2): 251–65.

Griffin, Pat, and James Genasci. 1990. "Addressing Homophobia in Physical Education: Responsibilities for Teachers and Researchers." In M. Messner and D. Sabo, eds., *Sport, Men, and the Gender Order*. Champaign, Ill.: Human Kinetics.

Guttman, A. 1991. *Women's Sport: A History*. New York: Columbia University Press.

Hall, M. Ann. 1976. "Sport and Physical Activity in the Lives of Canadian Women." In R. Gruneau and J. G. Albinson, eds., *Canadian Sport: Sociological Perspectives*. Toronto: Addison-Wesley.

———, ed. 1987. "The Gendering of Sport, Leisure, and Physical Education." *Women's Studies International Forum*, 10(4).

———. 1996. *Feminism and Sporting Bodies*. Champaign, Ill.: Human Kinetics.

Hall, M. Ann, and Dorothy A. Richardson. 1982. *Fair Ball: Towards Sex Equality in Canadian Sport*. Ottawa: The Canadian Advisory Council on the Status of Women.

Hall, M. Ann, Dallas Cullen, and Trevor Slack. 1989. "Organizational Elites Recreating Themselves: The Gender Structure of National Sport Organizations." *Quest* 41(1): 28–45.

Hall, Sandi. 1981. "Dykes Against the Tour." *Broadsheet* 92:10.

Hargreaves, Jennifer. 1985. "Playing Like Gentlemen While Behaving Like Ladies: Contradictory Features of the Formative Years of Women's Sport." *British Journal of Sport History* 2: 40–52.

————. 1990. "Changing Images of the Sporting Female." *Sport and Leisure* 31(5): 39–40.

————. 1994. *Sporting Females.* London: Routledge.

Herd, Juliet. 1989. "Mrs Edmonds Delivers a Bouncer." *Sunday Times,* Australia, May 28.

Heyman, Ronni. 1987. "The Double Lives of Hockey Wives." *Goal* 14: 22–25.

Hochschild, Arlie. 1983. *The Managed Heart.* Berkeley: University of California Press.

————. 1989. *The Second Shift.* New York: Viking.

House of Representatives Standing Committee on Legal and Constitutional Affairs. 1992. *Halfway to Equal.* Canberra: Australian Government Publishing Service.

Howard, Dennis R., and Robert Madrigal. 1990. "Who Makes the Decision: The Parent or the Child?" *Journal of Leisure Research* 22(3): 244–58.

Jackson, Steven. 1995. "New Zealand's Big Game in Crisis: Mediated Images of the Transformation, Reinvention and Reassertion of Rugby." Paper presented at the NASSS Conference, Sacramento, November 1–4.

Jackson, Stevi. 1996. "Heterosexuality and Social Theory." In D. Richardson, ed., *Theorizing Heterosexuality: Telling It Straight.* Buckingham: Open University Press.

Johnson, Miriam.1988. *Strong Mothers, Weak Wives.* Berkeley: University of California Press.

Jones, Dean. 1989. "United We Stand." The *West Australian,* September 14:122.

Katz, Jonathan. 1995. *The Invention of Heterosexuality.* New York: Dutton.

Kelly, John R. 1974. "Socialization Towards Leisure: A Developmental Approach." *Journal of Leisure Research* 6:181–93.

Kidd, Bruce. 1987. "Sport and Masculinity." In M. Kaufman, ed., *Beyond Patriarchy: Essays by Men on Pleasure, Power, and Change.* New York: Oxford University Press.

King, Billie Jean, with Frank Deford. 1982. *The Autobiography of Billie Jean King.* London: Granada.

King, Helen. 1978. "Sexual Politics of Sport: An Australian Perspective." In R. Cashman and M. McKernan, eds., *Sport in History: The Making of Modern Sporting History.* St. Lucia: Queensland University Press.

Kirby, Sandi, and Kate McKenna. 1989. *Experience, Research, Change. Research from the Margins.* Toronto: Garamond Press.

Koopman-Boyden, P., and M. Abbott. 1985. "Expectations for Household Task Allocation and Actual Task Allocation: A New Zealand Study." *Journal of Marriage and the Family* 47: 211–19.

Lasson, Sally Ann. 1989. "Sexy Voices from the Edge of the Polo Lawn." *Sunday Times Magazine,* September 17: 62–67.

Lenskyj, Helen. 1984. "A Kind of Precipitate Waddle": Early Opposition to Women Running." In N. Theberge and P. Donnelly, eds., *Sport and the Sociological Imagination*. Ft Worth: Texas Christian University Press.

———. 1986. *Out of Bounds: Women, Sport, and Sexuality*. Toronto: Women's Press.

———. 1990. "Power and Play: Gender and Sexuality Issues in Sport and Physical Activity." *International Review for the Sociology of Sport* 25(3): 235–43.

———. 1991. "Combating Homophobia in Sport and Physical Education." *Sociology of Sport Journal* 8(1): 61–69.

Lewko, John H., and M.E. Ewing 1980. "Sex Differences and Parental Influence in Sport Involvement of Children," *Journal of Sport Psychology* 2: 62–68.

Lewko, John H., and Susan L. Greendorfer. 1988. "Family Influences in Sport Socialization of Children and Adolescents." In F. Small, R. Magill, and M. Ash, eds., *Children in Sport* (3d ed.) Champaign, Ill.: Human Kinetics.

Luxton, Meg. 1980. *More than a Labor of Love: Three Generations of Women's Work in the Home*. Toronto: The Women's Press.

MacKinnon, Catherine. 1987. *Feminism Unmodified: Discourses on Life and Law*. Cambridge, Mass.: Harvard University Press.

Maddaford, Terry. 1996. "Lipscombe's Mother Keen to be Good Parent." *New Zealand Herald*, March 25, 2/4.

Mangan, J.A., and Roberta J. Parks, eds. 1987. *From Fair Sex to Feminism: Sport and the Socialization of Women in the Industrial and Post Industrial Eras*. London: Frank Cass.

Martin, J., and C. Roberts. 1984. *Women and Employment*. Department of Employment/OPCS, HMSO.

McCrone, Kathleen E. 1988. *Playing the Game: Sport and the Physical Emancipation of English Women, 1870–1914*. Lexington: The University Press of Kentucky.

McFadden, Suzanne. 1995a. "Mack Tacks Into World." *New Zealand Herald*, June 23: 2/1.

———. 1995b. "Conner Team Urges New Dad Brad to Take Time Out." *New Zealand Herald*, May 10: 1/1.

McFadden, Suzanne, and Michael Reid. 1994. "Medal Mothers on Top of World." *New Zealand Herald*, August 25: 2/1.

McGrath, John. 1990a. "Sacrifices and Pleasures of Our Sporting Mums." *The West Australian*, May 12: 92.

———. 1990b. "Grand Slam. Martina Cops Court Serve." *The West Australian*, July 11: 144.

McIntosh, Fiona. 1990. "PE Teacher Jackie Keeps Hot Hicks on His Toes." *Sunday Times*, October 21: 107.

McIntosh, Mary. 1979. "The Welfare State and the Needs of the Dependent Family." In Sandra Bruman, ed., *Fit Work for Women*. London: Croom Helm.

McKay, Jim. 1986. "Leisure and Social Inequality in Australia." *Australia and New Zealand Journal of Sociology* 22(3): 343–67.

———. 1991a. *No Pain, No Gain? Sport and Australian Culture.* Sydney: Prentice Hall.

———. 1991b. "Sporting Women and Hysterical Men." *Australian Society*, September: 49–50.

———. 1992a. *Why So Few? Women Executives in Australian Sport.* Report to the National Sports Research Program of the Australian Sports Commission, Canberra.

———. 1992b. "Sport and the Social Construction of Gender." In G. Lupton, P.M. Short, and R. Whip, eds., *Society and Gender: An Introduction to Sociology.* Sydney: Macmillan.

———. 1993a. "Marked Men" and "Wanton Women": The Politics of Naming Sexual "Deviance" in Sport." *The Journal of Men's Studies* 2(1): 69–87.

———. 1993b. "Masculine Hegemony, the State, and the Politics of Gender Equity Policy Research." *Culture and Policy* 5: 223–40.

———. 1994. "Masculine Hegemony, the State and the Incorporation of Gender Equity Discourse: The Case of Australian Sport." *Australian Journal of Political Science* 29: 82–95.

———. 1997. *Managing Gender.* Albany, N.Y.: State University of New York Press.

McMahon, Martha. 1995. *Engendering Motherhood.* New York: The Guildford Press.

McMahon, Peg. 1990. "Suitcase Blues." *The Woman Golfer* (January): 78–81.

Mercer, David. 1985. "Australian's Time Use in Work, Housework and Leisure: Changing Profiles." *Australian and New Zealand Journal of Sociology* 23(3): 371–94.

Messner, Michael, and Donald Sabo. 1990. *Sport, Men, and the Gender Order.* Champaign, Ill.: Human Kinetics.

Mies, Maria. 1983. "Towards a Methodology for Feminist Research." In G. Bowles and R. Duelli Klein, eds., *Theories of Women's Studies.* London: Routledge & Kegan Paul.

Muir, Donald E. 1991. "Club Tennis: A Case Study in Taking Leisure Very Seriously." *Sociology of Sport Journal* 8(1): 70–78.

National Junior Sports Working Party. 1992. *Draft National Junior Sport Policy for Australia.* Canberra: Australian Sport Commission.

Nauright, John, and David Black. 1995. "New Zealand and International Sport: The Case of All Black-Springbok Rugby, Sanctions and Protests Against Apartheid 1959–1992." In J. Nauright, ed., *Sport, Power, and Society in New Zealand: Historical and Contemporary Perspectives.* Sydney: ASSH Inc.

Navratilova, Martina, with George Versey. 1986. *Being Myself.* London: Grafton Books.

Nelson, M.B. 1991. *Are We Winning Yet?* New York: Random House.

Newnham, Tom. 1981. *By Batons and Barbed Wire*. Auckland: Real Pictures Ltd.

Nix, Glenda. 1978. "A Coach's Wife and A Coach's Life." *Texas Coach* 21(7): 21.

Oakley, Ann. 1979. *From Here to Maternity: Becoming a Mother*. Harmonsworth, UK: Penguin Books.

———. 1981a. "Interviewing Women: A Contradiction in Terms." In H. Roberts, ed., *Doing Feminist Research*. London: Routledge and Kegan Paul.

———. 1981b. *Subject Women*. Oxford: Martin Robertson.

O'Brien, Mary. 1981. *The Politics of Reproduction*. London: Routledge and Kegan Paul.

O'Donnell, Carol, and Philippa Hall. 1988. *Getting Equal: Labour Market Regulations and Women's Work*. Sydney: Allen & Unwin.

Palzkill, Birgit. 1990. "Between Gym Shoes and High Heels—the Development of a Lesbian Identity and Existence in Top Class Sport." *International Review for the Sociology of Sport* 25(3): 221–33.

Papanek, H. 1973. "Men, Women, and Work: Reflections on the Two-Person Career." *American Journal of Sociology* 78(4): 852–72.

Parker, Selwyn. 1994. "What a Racket: Brett Steven's Big Year." *North and South* (April): 92–97.

Parks, Julie, ed. 1991. *Ladies a Plate: Change and Continuity in the Lives of New Zealand Women*. Auckland: Auckland University Press.

Parratt, Catriona. 1989. "Athletic 'Womanhood.' Exploring Sources for Female Sport in Victorian and Edwardian England." *Journal of Sport History* 16(2):140–57.

Parsons, T., and R. Bales. 1955. *Family, Socialization, and Interaction Process*. Glencoe, Ill.: Free Press.

Paviour, Andiee. 1992. "Batting On." *Who Weekly* (August 24):58–59.

Phillips, Dennis. 1990. "Australian Women at the Olympics: Achievement and Alienation." *Sporting Traditions* 6(2):181–200.

Phillips, Harry. 1995. *TennisWest: A History of the Lawn Tennis Association in Western Australia from the 1890s to the 1990s*. Caringbah, NSW: Playright Publishing.

Phillips, Jock. 1987. *A Man's Country? The Image of the Pakeha Male*. Auckland: Penguin.

Piachaud, David. 1984. *Round about Fifty Hours a Week*. London: Child Poverty Action Group.

Quay, Susan. (compiled). 1990. *1990 Sports Census*. Perth: Western Australia Government Ministry of Sport and Recreation.

Rich, Adrienne. 1977. *Of Woman Born*. London: Virago.

———. 1980. "Compulsory Heterosexuality and Lesbian Existence." *Signs: Journal of Women in Culture and Society* 5(4): 631–60.

Richards, Lyn, and Tom Richards. 1987. "Qualitative Data Analysis: Can Computers Do It?" *Australian and New Zealand Journal of Sociology* 23(1): 23–35.

———. 1991. "The Transformation of Qualitative Method: Computational Paradigms and Research Processes." In N. Fielding and R. Lee, eds., *Using Computers in Qualitative Research.* London: Sage.

Richards, Tom, and Lyn Richards. 1990. *Manual For Mainframe NUDIST.* Melbourne: Replee P/L.

Richardson, Diane. 1993a. *Women, Motherhood, and Childrearing.* Hampshire: Macmillan.

———. 1993b. "Sexuality and Male Dominance." In D. Richardson and V. Robinson, eds., *Introducing Women's Studies.* London: Macmillan.

———. 1996. "Heterosexuality and Social Theory." In D. Richardson, ed., *Theorizing Heterosexuality.* Buckingham: Open University Press.

Russell, Graeme. 1983. *The Changing Role of Fathers.* St Lucia: University of Queensland Press.

Scott, Joan. 1992. "Experience." In J. Butler and J. Scott, eds., *Feminists Theorize the Political.* London: Routledge and Kegan Paul.

Scraton, Sheila. 1992. *Shaping Up to Womanhood: Gender and Girls' Physical Education.* Buckingham: Open University Press.

Shears, Richard, and Isobelle Gidley. 1981. *Storm Out of Africa: The 1981 Springbok Tour of New Zealand.* Auckland: Macmillan.

Snyder, E.E., and E.A. Sprietzer. 1973. "Family Influence and Involvement in Sport." *Research Quarterly* 44: 249–55.

Sprietzer, E.A., and E.E. Snyder. 1976. "Socialization into Sport: An Exploratory Path Analysis." *Research Quarterly* 47: 238–45.

Stanley, Liz, and Sue Wise. 1983. *Breaking Out: Feminist Consciousness and Feminist Research.* London: Routledge & Kegan Paul.

———. 1993. *Breaking Out Again: Feminist Ontology and Epistemology.* London: Routledge.

Star, Lynne. 1989. "Telerugby—Tele90—Tell it Rightly." *Race Gender Class* 10: 127–38.

Stell, Marion K. 1991. *Half the Race: A History of Australian Women in Sport.* Sydney: Angus & Robertson.

Stoddart, Brian. 1986. *Saturday Afternoon Fever. Sport in the Australian Culture.* London: Angus & Robertson.

Summerfield, Karen, and Anita White. 1989. "Korfball: A Model of Egalitarianism?" *Sociology of Sport Journal* 6(2):144–51.

Summers, Ann. 1976. *Damned Whores and God's Police. The Colonization of Women in Australia.* Melbourne: Penguin.

The Sunday Times (N.Z.). 1993. "Favourite Dalton Takes Nothing for Granted." (September 26): 41.

Talbot, Margaret. 1988a. "Understanding the Relationship Between Women and Sport: The Contribution of British Feminist Approaches in Leisure and Cultural Studies." *International Review for the Sociology of Sport* 23 (1): 31–41.

———. 1988b. "Beating Them at Our Own Game? Women's Sport Involvement." In E. Wimbush and M. Talbot, eds., *Relative Freedoms. Women and Leisure.* Milton Keyes: Open University Press.

————. 1988c. "Women and the Olympic Games." *The British Journal of Physical Education* 19(1):10–12.

Theberge, Nancy. 1984. "On the Need for a more Adequate Theory of Sport Participation." *Sociology of Sport Journal* 1: 26–35.

Thiele, Beverly. 1992. "Vanishing Acts in Social and Political Thought: Tricks of the Trade." In L. McDowell and R. Pringle, eds., *Defining Women*. London: Polity Press.

Thiele, Beverly, and Jocelyn Grace. 1990. "Negotiating the Domestic Division of Labor." *National Women's Conference 1990 Proceeaings*. Canberra: Write People.

Thompson, Shona. 1988. "Challenging the Hegemony: New Zealand Women's Opposition to Rugby and the Reproduction of a Capitalist Patriarchy." *International Review for the Sociology of Sport* 23(3): 205–12.

————. 1990. "Thank the Ladies for the Plates: The Incorporation of Women into Sport." *Leisure Studies* 9:135–43.

————. 1991. "Mum's Taxi: Gendered Servicing of Sport." Paper presented at the Australian Sociological Association Conference, Murdoch University, Perth, December 10–14.

————. 1992a. "Mum's Tennis Day: The Gendered Definition of Older Women's Leisure." *Loisir et Société/Society and Leisure* 15(1): 273–91.

————. 1992b. "Sport for Others, Work for Women, Quality of Life for Whom?" Paper presented at the Olympic Scientific Congress, Malaga, Spain, July, 15–19.

————. 1995. *The Gendered Servicing of Children's Sport: An Investigation of Parental Support*. Canberra: Australian Sports Commission.

Thompson, Shona, and Jan Finnigan. 1990. "Egalitarianism in Korfball is a Myth." *New Zealand Journal of Health, Physical Education, and Recreation* 23(4): 7–11.

Troger, Anna. 1986. "The Contextualization of the Subject in Oral History and Feminist Research. Paper presented at Conference on Feminist Enquiry as a Transdisciplinary Enterprise." Research Centre for Women's Studies, University of Adelaide, August 21–24.

Turvey, Julie, and Chris Laws. 1988. "Are Girls Losing Out? The Effects of Mixed-Sex Grouping on Girls Performance in Physical Education." *The British Journal of Physical Education* 19(6): 253–55.

VanEvery, Jo. 1995. *Heterosexual Women Changing the Family: Refusing to be a Wife!* London: Taylor & Francis.

————. 1996. "Heterosexuality and Domestic Life." In D. Richardson, ed., *Theorizing Heterosexuality*. Buckingham: Open University Press.

Vertinsky, P.A. 1994. "Gender Relations, Women's History, and Sport History: A Decade of Changing Enquiry, 1983–1993." *Journal of Sport History* 21:1–25.

Walby, Sylvia. 1990. *Theorizing Patriarchy*. Oxford: Blackwell.

Waring, Marilyn. 1985. *Women, Politics and Power*. Wellington: Allen & Unwin.

———. 1988. *Counting For Nothing: What Men Value and What Women Are Worth.* Wellington: Allen & Unwin.

Watson, Geoff. 1977. "Games, Socialization, and Parental Values." *International Review for the Sociology of Sport* 121:17–48.

Wearing, Betsy. 1984. *The Ideology of Motherhood.* Sydney: Allen & Unwin.

———. 1990. "Beyond the Ideology of Motherhood: Leisure As Resistance." *Australian and New Zealand Journal of Sociology* 26(1): 36–58.

The West Australian. 1990. "Youngsters Lured By Lesbians: Court." (July 12): 108.

Westennis. 1989a. "Crowning Glory." 13(5): 11.

———. 1989b. "Miss Tennis Quest Nears the Finale." 13(4): 31.

White, Anita. 1989. "Family Influences on the Sports Participation of Young Women in Britain." Paper presented at the XIth IAPESGW Congress, Bali, Indonesia, July 22–29.

Wilkison, Vicky. 1986. "Circuit Mama." *World Tennis* 33(11): 37–39.

Wilson, Noela, David Russell, and Louise Paulin. 1990. *Life in New Zealand Survey: Summary Report.* Wellington: Hillary Commission for Sport, Fitness, and Leisure.

Wolff, Nerida. 1989. "Football Widows." Unpublished paper presented in Women's Studies, Murdoch University, Perth.

Woodward, Diana, and Lynne Chisholm. 1981. "The Expert's View? The Sociological Analysis of Graduates' Occupational and Domestic Roles." In H. Roberts, ed., *Doing Feminist Research.* London: Routledge & Kegan Paul.

Woodward, Diana, and Eileen Green. 1988. "'Not Tonight, Dear!' The Social Control of Women's Leisure." In E. Wimbush & M. Talbot, eds., *Relative Freedoms. Women and Leisure.* Milton Keyes: Open University Press.

Subject Index

Name Index